THUC

BOOK VII

WITH AN INTRODUCTION
AND COMMENTARY BY

K. J. DOVER

President of Corpus
Christi College, Oxford

CLARENDON PRESS . OXFORD

This book has been printed digitally and produced in a standard specification in order to ensure its continuing availability

OXFORD
UNIVERSITY PRESS

Great Clarendon Street, Oxford OX2 6DP

Oxford University Press is a department of the University of Oxford.
It furthers the University⊙ objective of excellence in research, scholarship,
and education by publishing worldwide in

Oxford New York

Auckland Bangkok Buenos Aires Cape Town Chennai
Dar es Salaam Delhi Hong Kong Istanbul Karachi Kolkata
Kuala Lumpur Madrid Melbourne Mexico City Mumbai Nairobi
São Paulo Shanghai Taipei Tokyo Toronto

Oxford is a registered trade mark of Oxford University Press
in the UK and in certain other countries

Published in the United States
by Oxford University Press Inc., New York

ISBN 0-19-872098-x

Printed in Great Britain by

Antony Rowe Ltd., Eastbourne

PREFACE

THE purpose of this book is to help senior pupils in schools and students in universities to read, understand, and enjoy Book VII of Thucydides.

The Greek text and apparatus criticus are the Oxford Classical Text reproduced without change. In the Commentary I have discussed textual problems only where I believe this text to be questionable or demonstrably wrong.

The Introduction offers the reader, as concisely as possible, the information which he should have before he embarks on Book VII.

The Commentary is designed (i) to help the reader to translate the text fully and correctly, with the assistance of standard lexica and grammars; (ii) to draw his attention to those features of language, style, and technique which are characteristic of Thucydides; (iii) to make explicit what Thucydides takes for granted; (iv) to offer grounds on which we may decide whether his historical statements are true or false; and (v) to comment on historically interesting aspects of the events which he describes.

References to other Greek texts have been reduced to a minimum, reference to modern books, articles, and editions is wholly excluded, views which I believe wrong are passed over in silence, and I seldom indicate that more than one answer to a question has been offered unless I feel some doubt about the rightness of the answer which I have adopted. For discussion of the arguments on both sides of the questions treated summarily and dogmatically in this volume the reader may refer to the commentary on Book VII which I am contributing to the completion of the *Historical Commentary on Thucydides* which the late Professor A. W. Gomme left unfinished.

I have tried to put into practice two beliefs about the study and teaching of Greek. First, although I have no sympathy or respect for the currently fashionable view that Classical scholars should spend more time in entertaining the public and less in trying to discover what the Greek authors actually said, I do not believe that the learner should be asked to pass judgement on variant or suspect readings except where the difference of reading really matters; there, he should. Secondly, although I do not believe that any worth-while contribution to Greek studies is ever likely to be made by anyone who does not know the Greek language well, I also do not believe that the learner, however young and inexperienced, should be compelled to confine his attention to matters of grammar and forbidden to dabble in such intrinsically interesting problems as the stratification of Thucydides' work or the sources of the material in his digressions.

Anyone who believes that Thucydides was omniscient, dispassionate, and infinitely wise, and that there is nothing to be said on the other side of any question on which Thucydides has made a pronouncement, may find some of my comments irreverent and cynical. I offer no apology.

I am glad to acknowledge a great debt to two friends, neither of whom should be blamed for the consequences of my occasional refusal to take their advice. Professor Andrewes, my collaborator in the completion of Gomme's *Commentary*, patiently rescued me from superficiality on many occasions and taught me that I did not know half as well as I thought I did what kind of questions one should ask in the study of Thucydides. Mr. J. A. L. Hamilton scrutinized every word of the first draft of this volume; from his experience as a teacher he made me see what a young student of Thucydides needs to be told, and his criticisms on points of substance made me change much with which I had been satisfied too soon.

K. J. D.

University of St. Andrews
May 1964

CONTENTS

ABBREVIATIONS

(i) In the apparatus criticus:

See Introduction III (A) for the *sigla codicum*.

Π^{16}	Oxyrynchus Papyrus 1246 (s. ii/iii p.C.).
Π^{18}	Oxyrynchus Papyrus 1376 (s. ii/iii p.C.).
Π^{30}	Michigan Papyrus III 141 (s. ii p.C.).
A^I, B^I, etc.	Correction by the first hand.
a, b, etc.	Correction by a later hand.
[A], [B], etc.	Reading illegible.
⟨G⟩	Reading of G illegible but inferred from descendants.
codd.	Consensus of the manuscripts ABCEFGM. (See Introduction III on the presence of G in this group and absence of H from it.)
recc.	One or more of the manuscripts descended from one or other of ABCEFGM.
m. 1	First hand.
γρ.	Variant prefaced by γρ(άφεται).

(ii) In the Introduction and Commentary:

GHI	M. N. Tod, *Greek Historical Inscriptions*, vol. i (Oxford, ed. 2, 1946).
IG	*Inscriptiones Graecae.*
LSJ	Liddell and Scott, *A Greek–English Lexicon*, revised by Sir Henry Stuart Jones and R. McKenzie (Oxford, 1940).
SEG	*Supplementum Epigraphicum Graecum.*
Σ^M	The scholia in the manuscript M.

Names of Greek authors and their works are abbreviated as in LSJ, except:

Diod.	('D.S.' in LSJ)	Diodoros.
Dion. Hal.	('D.H.' in LSJ)	Dionysios of Halikarnassos.

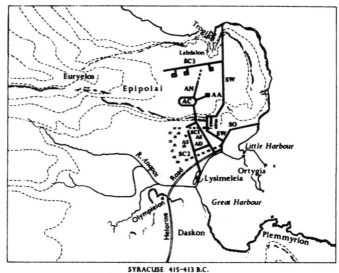

SYRACUSE 415–413 B.C.

------ Contours at intervals of 25 metres   ·····—·— Precipitous ground   ▲ ▲ ▲ Marsh

Note:- The lower reaches of the river were probably not as straight as shown above.

AA Athenian advanced fortification (vi 102)

AC Athenian Circle (vi 98)

AD Athenian Crosswall (vii 60)

AN Athenian Northern Wall (vi 99)

AS Athenian Southern Walls (vi 103, vii 2)

SC1 First Syracusan Counterwall (vi 99)

SC2 Second Syracusan Counterwall (vi 101)

SC3 Third Syracusan Counterwall (vii 4,6)

SO City Wall of Syracuse

SW Syracusan Wall, winter 415/4 (vi 75)

INTRODUCTION

I. THUCYDIDES

1. *Life*

NEARLY all that we know about the life of Thucydides he
tells us himself. He was an Athenian (i. 1. 1) and the son of
a certain Oloros (iv. 104. 4); he owned the working rights of
some gold mines on the Aegean coast of Thrace, and he was
influential with the Thracians in that area (iv. 105. 1). He
began work on a history of the Peloponnesian War when it
broke out in 431 (i. 1. 1). He was elected one of the ten
Athenian generals for 424/3, and during that winter commanded a small force of ships at Thasos (iv. 104. 4), at a time
when the quick and energetic Spartan commander Brasidas
was operating with a Peloponnesian force on the mainland.
Thucydides failed to save Amphipolis for Athens, though
he was just in time to occupy the neighbouring town of
Eion and hold it against Brasidas (iv. 105. 1, 106. 3 f.).
Because of his failure at Amphipolis, he became an exile (v.
26. 5); that is to say, like other Athenian generals in similar
circumstances, he went into exile to avoid what he believed
would be a worse fate if he returned to Athens, and was
condemned to death in his absence. He was in exile for
twenty years (v. 26. 5); he returned, therefore, in 404, after
the war had been lost and all the exiles were recalled in
accordance with the terms of peace imposed by Sparta.
Some part, at least, of his twenty years of exile was spent
on the Peloponnesian side (v. 26. 5); we do not know where,
or whether he also spent some time in regions which were
not involved in the war. Although he makes some passing
references to the end of the war and its total duration (ii.
65. 2, v. 26. 1), he did not complete his history; Book VIII

breaks off abruptly in the middle of the events of the autumn of 411, and the story of the war was completed by later historians.

The *Life of Thucydides* which precedes the text of Thucydides in some manuscripts is the work of a commentator of late Roman times, but incorporates the observations of earlier scholars. It adds a little factual information to what has been stated above : that Thucydides' mother was named Hegesipyle (§ 2), that his grave existed at Athens (§§ 16, 31), and that the inscription on the grave showed that he belonged to the deme Halimous (§ 16). The rest is speculation, but much of it is intelligent and probably correct. Given his parents' names, it is certainly likely that he was related to Kimon (§§ 2–17), the great rival of Perikles in the 460's, for Kimon's father Miltiades had married the daughter, Hegesipyle by name, of a Thracian prince called Oloros (Hdt. vi. 40) ; moreover, when Kimon was dead the opposition to Perikles in the 440's was led by a kinsman of Kimon who bore the name Thucydides (son of Melesias). Again, the *Life* (§ 46) is probably right in saying that it was Kleon who brought the charge against Thucydides for his failure at Amphipolis. In 424/3 Kleon was at the height of his influence, and there are reasons for thinking that he personally prosecuted another general whose achievements had fallen short of expectations ; and Thucydides shows a pronounced malice against Kleon (iii. 36. 6, iv. 27 f.).

The notion, still to be found in works of reference, that Thucydides was born in 471 originated in the first century A.D. and was based on the common 'working hypothesis' that a man is born forty years before the decisive action or the most important event of his life—in Thucydides' case, the outbreak of the war and his decision to write a history of it. When he died, we do not know. It is arguable that what he says of Archelaos of Macedon in ii. 100. 2—'Archelaos did more to equip Macedon for war than all the eight kings before him'—was written after the death of Archelaos in

399; and it is obvious that Lysias in §§ 48–52 of his *Epitaphios*, composed in 392, is using Book I of Thucydides; but there is no further evidence. The *Life* (§§ 31–33) tells us that some scholars believed that Thucydides died in Thrace and that his grave at Athens was a cenotaph.

Note. The second, and briefer, *Life* found in some manuscripts adds nothing of importance about the historian and confuses him with Perikles' adversary, Thucydides the son of Melesias.

2. *Character of Thucydides' Work*

Book I is devoted to the causes and antecedents of the war; the narrative of the war itself begins with Book II. Thucydides organizes his material annalistically, taking each year of the war in turn; his year runs from spring to spring, and is divided into two halves, 'summer' (θέρος) and 'winter' (χειμών). He deals with all the events of each half-year, whether or not they were related to one another, before passing on to the next half-year.

In discussing the difficulty of his task (i. 22. 1 f.) he makes a distinction between what was said (ὅσα μὲν λόγῳ εἶπον ἕκαστοι) and what was done (τὰ δ' ἔργα τῶν πραχθέντων), and he clearly attaches great importance to the former. It is natural that he should, since in the Greek world, and especially in democratic states, final decisions were taken by assemblies under the immediate impact of persuasive oratory, and the speeches made to troops before a battle had an effect for good or ill on their morale and therefore on the outcome of the battle. Thucydides thus presents us with the speeches delivered by politicians, generals, or ambassadors on various critical occasions. The language and style of these speeches are uniform and idiosyncratic, and therefore his own; and there are a few occasions on which we wonder whether the speaker was so casually, yet accurately, far-sighted as he is represented as being. Yet the hypothesis that the Thucydidean speeches are pure fiction, bearing no relation, except by accident, to what was actually said is irreconcilable with the principle which he enunciates in i. 22. 1: 'It was difficult for me to recall precisely what was said in the speeches which I heard myself, and difficult for my informants from elsewhere; but I have represented each speaker as presenting, on a given issue, the case which I thought him most likely to have presented, while keeping as close as I could to the argument, as a whole, of what was actually said.' There is no reason to suppose that Thucydides was equally well informed about all the occasions on which important speeches were made; and it is not safe to assume that he was equally tenacious of the principle of i. 22. 1 at all stages of his work. What is quite certain is that a Thucydidean speech is a skilful and psychologically realistic representation of a man trying to persuade his hearers and, when necessary, to deceive them; statements which occur in the course of speeches should not be accepted as true unless they are supported by other-evidence.

One of the most striking features of the speeches is the excessive use of argument from generalizations to particular cases. This type of argument is conspicuous also in the forensic speeches of Thucydides' older contemporary, the orator Antiphon, and it was no doubt characteristic of late-fifth-century Athens. It is fully in accord with what Thucydides says (i. 22. 4) of the purpose of history: that it should be 'useful to those who want to know exactly what happened and what is likely, given human nature, to happen in the future in identical or similar form'. Thucydides' fulfilment of this purpose is fortunately not obtrusive, for he possessed a capacity for being interested in his material for its own sake and a talent for powerful and vivid writing. He rarely speculates or criticizes, and his own generalizations, even though sometimes exaggerated or one-sided, are never banal and always reflect a determination to penetrate beyond the surface of things. Throughout his narrative he cultivates an objectivity which perhaps did not come easily to him; it makes his occasional moral judgements and expressions of strong emotion all the more impressive. Like all historians, he was necessarily selective, and it is here that the influence of his own standpoint and his conception of the purpose of history is clearest. The thoughts, feelings, and motives which he regarded as deciding the issue of a debate or a battle were important to him; topography, military technique, logistics, finance, and administration were less important, and when we put to him the questions which historical imagination and curiosity prompt in the modern reader we often find him vague, inadequate, or simply silent. Sometimes this is because he was writing for Greeks, and did not tell them what they knew already—how a trireme was organized, for example—but this excuse cannot be made to cover all the obscurities and inadequacies in his account of the sequence of events at Syracuse in 415–413.

Neither Thucydides nor any other historian gives us, or can give us, directly and immediately, 'the facts' of what the Greeks did and thought and felt in the Peloponnesian War. He gives us his picture of the facts, and our business as students of the Greek world is not to treat him as the Recording Angel but to get to know him, as intimately as possible, as the painter of a picture. We are not wholly deprived of independent lines of approach to the reality beyond the painter.

3. *Language and Style*

The characteristics of Thucydides' language and style, by contrast with the norms of Attic prose of the fifth and fourth centuries, are:

1. He uses -$\rho\sigma$-, -$\sigma\sigma$-, and $\ddot{\eta}\nu < \epsilon i + \ddot{\alpha}\nu$, not -$\rho\rho$-, -$\tau\tau$-, and $\dot{\epsilon}\dot{\alpha}\nu$. These features he shares with Ionic, Xenophon, and some early Attic prose, but they never appear in Attic inscriptions.

2. He always uses $\xi\dot{\nu}\nu$, not $\sigma\dot{\nu}\nu$, both as an independent word and in compounds. Both forms are found in fifth-century Attic inscriptions.

3. A profusion of abstract nouns (the formative -σις is especially favoured). This may owe something to the influence of the Presocratic philosophers, e.g. 36. 6 ἐχόντων τὴν ἐπίπλευσιν ἀπὸ τοῦ πελάγους τε καὶ ἀνάκρουσιν; 75. 5 κατήφειά τέ τις ἅμα καὶ κατάμεμψις σφῶν αὐτῶν πολλὴ ἦν.

4. Considerable use of adjectives in -τος, e.g. 13. 2 ἀναγκαστοὶ ἐσβάντες, 'embarked under compulsion'; 48. 1 οὐκ ἐβούλετο . . . σφᾶς ψηφιζομένους . . . καταγγέλτους γίγνεσθαι, 'he did not wish information of their voting to be given'.

5. Prepositional compound verbs are formed very readily, and many of them recur seldom or never in extant Classical prose, e.g. 19. 5 ἀνθώρμουν, 21. 3 ἀντιτολμῶντας.

6. Many other compound verbs, e.g. 48. 5 ξενοτροφοῦντας, 69. 2 ἀρχαιολογεῖν.

7. Qualification of nouns by adverbs or phrases, e.g. 69. 2 τῆς ἐν αὐτῇ ἀνεπιτάκτου πᾶσιν ἐς τὴν δίαιταν ἐξουσίας, 'the possibility which everyone in it' (i.e. their native land) 'had, of living a life free from regulations'; 77. 1 ταῖς παρὰ τὴν ἀξίαν νῦν κακοπαθίαις, 'your present unmerited sufferings'.

8. Substantives formed with the neuter article and an adjective or participle may be qualified, e.g. 71. 3 τὸ ἀκρίτως ξυνεχὲς τῆς ἁμίλλης.

9. Substantives formed with the neuter article often require for adequate translation an English abstract noun, e.g. 4. 4 τὰ ἐκ τῆς γῆς, 'the situation on land'; 61. 3 τὸ τῆς τύχης, 'the role of chance'.

10. The reference of demonstratives is often obscure unless attention is paid to the argument, e.g. 44. 5 τὸ δ' ἐκείνων οὐχ ὁμοίως ἠπίσταντο διὰ τὸ κρατοῦντας αὐτούς . . . ἧσσον ἀγνοεῖσθαι, 'but they did not learn the Syracusan password in the same way, because the Syracusans, having the upper hand, failed to recognize each other less often'.

11. The unemphatic anaphoric pronoun αὐτόν often comes close after the first word of the clause (cf. καί μιν, ὁ δέ σφι, &c. in Herodotos), e.g. 43. 1 ὡς δὲ αὐτῷ . . . κατεκαύθησαν; 43. 5 καὶ αὐτοῖς . . . ἐντυχόντες . . . ἔτρεψαν.

12. The pronoun σφεῖς is normally used in subordinate clauses or word-groups to refer to the subject of the main clause, e.g. 3. 1 οἱ δὲ Ἀθηναῖοι . . . τῶν Συρακοσίων σφίσιν ἐπιόντων ἐθορυβήθησαν. The reflexive σφᾶς αὐτούς = ἑαυτούς.

13. The possessive adjective σφέτερος may refer either to the subject of the clause in which it stands or, when it is in a subordinate clause, to the subject of the main clause. Like ἡμέτερος and ὑμέτερος, it may be reinforced in the former case by αὐτῶν.

14. The infinitive alone is sometimes used in cases where a fourth-century author would use an infinitive with ὥστε or even a final or final relative clause, e.g. 20. 3 τοῦ στρατεύματός τε εἴ τι ὑπελέλειπτο περιέμενε καὶ τὸν Χαρικλέα τοὺς Ἀργείους παραλαβεῖν, '. . . and for Charikles to pick up the Argives'.

15. In the co-ordination of clauses:

(a) The co-ordinating particle in the first clause is often placed later than we would logically expect, e.g. 2. 1 οἱ δ' . . . Κορίνθιοι ταῖς τε ἄλλαις ναυσίν . . . ἐβοήθουν καὶ Γογγύλος . . . ἀφικνεῖται. Many such examples have been emended by editors, wrongly.

(b) The element introduced by the second co-ordinating particle sometimes passes into a fresh finite clause, e.g. 47. 2 ἐπιέζοντο κατ' ἀμφότερα, τῆς τε ὥρας . . . ταύτης οὔσης ἐν ᾗ ἀσθενοῦσιν ἄνθρωποι μάλιστα, καὶ τὸ χωρίον . . . ἑλῶδες καὶ χαλεπὸν ἦν.

16. Thucydides dislikes uniformity of vocabulary or structure, and his avoidance of it is sometimes a little artificial, e.g. 48. 5 ἐπικουρικὰ μᾶλλον ἢ δι' ἀνάγκης.

17. Economy of expression sometimes requires us to understand one part of a verb from another, e.g. 34. 7 νομίσαντες αὐτοὶ οὐχ ἡσσᾶσθαι δι' ὅπερ οὐδ' οἱ ἕτεροι νικᾶν, 'in the belief that they themselves had not been worsted, for the reason for which the other side did not ⟨think⟩ it was victorious'; 69. 1 ἀντεπλήρουν τὰς ναῦς εὐθὺς ἐπειδὴ καὶ τοὺς Ἀθηναίους ᾐσθάνοντο, 'they in turn manned their ships at once when they saw the Athenians ⟨manning theirs⟩'.

18. The nominative case is sometimes used in conformity with the sense but in defiance of grammatical structure, e.g.
3. I κήρυκα προσπέμπει... λέγοντα... ἑτοῖμος εἶναι σπένδεσθαι;
70. 7 πολλὴ γὰρ δὴ ἡ παρακέλευσις ... τοῖς κελευσταῖς ... ἐγίγνετο, τοῖς μὲν Ἀθηναίοις ... ἐπιβοῶντες κτλ.

Where Thucydides differs linguistically from Plato and the fourth-century orators his affinities are sometimes with Ionic prose, especially with the fragments of the fifth-century philosophers, and with the orator Antiphon (who died in 411). In some respects, however, he stands alone, and it is reasonable to suppose that he made syntactical experiments, in the interests of economy of expression and variety of form, which did not commend themselves to later authors; Dionysios of Halikarnassos, to whom all the prose literature now lost was available, regarded him as idiosyncratic and sometimes perversely obscure.

The inadequacy of our evidence for Thucydides' contemporaries leaves us uncertain how far words which we find in him and in poetry, but not in fourth-century prose, really were at the time recognizably 'poetic', how far he coined words, or how far he differed from his contemporaries in doing so. One point which we can make, however, is that he was largely immune to the very great influence which the rhetorician Gorgias exercised on prose literature in the last quarter of the fifth century and the beginning of the fourth. Gorgias made great use of assonance, and the symmetry of his sentences was simple and obvious; Thucydides' assonances are conspicuous and memorable precisely because they are rare, and his love of variation ensures an asymmetry of form which actually conceals an underlying symmetrical and antithetical sequence of thought. It must have been easy to listen to Gorgias as to an incantation, a kind of verbal music; Thucydides, on the other hand, gives us the impression that he does not want us to be distracted by the form of what he says from attending to its content. Since he often tries to say too much in too few words, the reading of him demands an unusual degree of concentration.

4. *Books VI and VII*

The division of Thucydides' work into eight books is one of two (possibly three) alternative divisions which were current in the ancient world, and there is no reason to believe that it corresponds to any division which Thucydides himself envisaged. It is unlikely that he intended any kind of break between Book VI and Book VII, still less between Book VII and the first chapter of Book VIII. Between Book V and Book VI a natural break is imposed by the subject-matter itself, but the opening words of Book VI, 'during the same winter . . .', presuppose our acquaintance with the last part of Book V.

Since Thucydides began to work on a history of the war when it broke out, and yet wrote some of this history in its present form (cf. § 1 *supra*) after the end of the war and left the work incomplete, we cannot help wondering whether he wrote it as we have it, from the first chapter of Book I straight through to the last chapter of Book VIII, after the whole war was over, or linked together portions written at widely different dates and revised them with varying degrees of completeness. Curiosity on this score is increased by the fact that Book VIII differs so markedly from the remainder in the treatment and presentation of its material that it is commonly agreed to be 'unrevised', and by the presence in the earlier books of statements which were falsified later in the war, e.g. the mention in ii. 23. 3 of a territory 'which is inhabited by the Oropians, subjects of Athens', although the Oropians ceased to be subjects of Athens early in 411. The solutions offered to problems of this kind are seldom cogent and always disputed, but that does not mean that the difficulties which they are intended to solve are imaginary. The realistic hypothesis is that Thucydides did compose accounts of some portions of the war before its end and that

831829

he revised these accounts in many particulars; if we could ask his ghost which parts of his work had received their final revision, he would answer, I suspect, that no part of it would ever have received a *final* revision, no matter how long he had lived.

No view of the date of composition of Books VI and VII commands universal assent, but the most important considerations are:

(i) vi. 15. 3 f. refer plainly (in the present editor's view) to the end of the war. The favourable judgement which Thucydides there passes on Alkibiades as strategist accords exactly with the judgement implied in ii. 65. 6 f.—a passage in which he surveys the entire course of the war from the death of Perikles down to the final defeat of Athens—but is out of keeping with the narrative of Books VI and VII as a whole, where many readers feel that Alkibiades does not come up to the expectations which the high praise of him in vi. 15. 4 has engendered. Assessment of this discrepancy, however, is not simple.

(ii) The digression in vii. 27–28 on the effect of the Spartan occupation of Dekeleia is ill suited to its immediate context, obscure in argument, and repetitious in expression. Here at least we can feel some confidence in saying that further revision would have changed the whole passage for the better and probably moved it to Book VIII.

(iii) Nothing is said in Book VII about the worsening relations between Athens and Persia, which take us by surprise in viii. 5. 4 f.—a striking omission in an author who in the earlier books adheres to the principle of 'tidying up' all the events of one half-year before going on to the next.

(iv) The words 'the only large-scale night battle in this war' in vii. 44. 1 could possibly be held to imply 'so far' but more naturally imply that the war was over when they were written; cf. 'the greatest achievement in this war' (vii. 87. 5).

(v) Certain references (vi. 62. 2 and vii. 58. 2) to Himera, which was totally destroyed in 409, and to the temporary

Athenian occupation of Aigina (vii. 57. 2) and Pylos (vii. 57.
8), admit of more than one interpretation and cannot be
treated as decisive.

It is a reasonable hypothesis that the first draft of Books
VI and VII was composed fairly soon after 413, perhaps as
early as 411, and was continuously, but never systematically,
revised and augmented during the following eight or nine
years.

II. ATHENS AND SYRACUSE

1. *Down to 431*

The Peloponnesian War was the climax of an antagonism
between the two states which emerged from the Persian
War with the highest prestige and the greatest power:
Sparta, which had headed the whole alliance of the Greek
states against Xerxes and retained the leadership of an
alliance including the greater part of the Peloponnese, and
Athens, which had become the leader of the insular and
coastal states of the Aegean immediately after the Persian
War and turned these states from allies into subjects.

In the West, the Greeks of Sicily defeated a Carthaginian
invasion in the same year as the Greeks of Greece defeated
Xerxes. In Sicily, however, there was only one pre-eminent
state: Syracuse, which under the tyrant Gelon earned the
credit for the defeat of the Carthaginians and under his
brother and successor Hieron won a resounding naval victory over the Etruscans. The tyranny ended in 466/5, and
Syracuse became a democracy; which it still was fifty years
later, at the time of the Athenian attack.

During the thirty years before the outbreak of the
Peloponnesian War Athens was not indifferent to the West.
We know that she made an alliance with Segesta in 458/7,
with Halikyai in the 430's, and renewed alliances with
Leontinoi and Rhegion in 433/2 (when these last two al-
liances were first made, we do not know); she founded

Thurioi, in South Italy, in 446/5, and we have a few other disconnected items of information, of varying reliability, on minor Athenian interventions in the West. What is obscure is the extent to which the alliance represented a serious and consistent policy and the end towards which they were directed. When Thucydides describes (ii. 7) the preparations for war made by Sparta and Athens in the spring of 431, he does not suggest that Athens troubled to communicate in any way with any state in the West. The Spartans, on the other hand, asked 'their supporters' in Italy and Sicily for money and ships; but it does not appear from his narrative of subsequent years that these supporters—they included Syracuse, Gela and Selinus, as is clear from iii. 86. 2—responded to the request. Racial sympathies and antipathies, to which we find frequent reference in Thucydides, played a part in determining the alignment of states in East and West alike. Most of the states over which Sparta exercised the strongest control were, like Sparta herself, Dorian, while the majority of the states in the Athenian empire were, like Athens, Ionian. Similarly, Syracuse and her closest friends, Selinus and Gela, were Dorian, while Leontinoi and her most consistent friends were Ionian.

2. 427–422

Leontinoi invoked her alliance with Athens in 427; she was now at war with Syracuse; Naxos, Katane, Kamarina, and Rhegion were on her side, Selinus, Gela, and Lokroi on the side of Syracuse. The Athenians responded by sending twenty ships, which they reinforced with another forty at the beginning of 425. These reinforcements did not arrive in the West until the autumn, and they took part in no major operations, for the effect of their arrival was to make the Sicilian states compose their differences. Envoys from all the states met at Gela in the spring of 424; Thucydides represents Hermokrates of Syracuse, of whom we hear so much in Books VI and VII, as the forceful proponent of Sicilian unity in the face of Athenian interference. The Athenians' disappointment was reflected in their punishment of their generals.

The unity achieved at Gela did not last long. Internal conflict broke out in Leontinoi, and the upper class (Thucydides v. 4. 3 calls them οἱ δυνατοί) invoked the help of Syracuse; in consequence, the lower class was expelled and dispersed, and the upper class became citizens of Syracuse. Some of them, however, soon left Syracuse and made common cause with the remnant of the lower class, continuing in a state of war against Syracuse from a base in what had been the territory of Leontinoi. In this situation, Athens in the summer of 422 sent a roving embassy, which included the persuasive Phaiax, to enlist help in the West for Leontinoi against Syracuse. This embassy met with a favourable response in Kamarina and Akragas, but not elsewhere.

3. 415

Thucydides mentions no dealings of any kind between Athens and any state in the West in the period 421–417. Then, in the winter of 416–15, Segesta sought Athenian help against Selinus and at the same time revived the claims of the survivors of Leontinoi. Thucydides clearly implies (1. 1 ∼ 6. 1 f.) that this plea did not create, but merely reinforced, an Athenian ambition to secure control of Sicily. There were good reasons why such an ambition should emerge in 416. The first phase of the Peloponnesian War, ending with the Peace of Nikias in 421, had demonstrated that the damage which Sparta and Athens could inflict on each other was limited and indecisive; Sparta could not detach from Athens a significant portion of the Empire, which was controlled by Athenian sea-power, and Athens could not gain control of continental Greece by a significant defeat of the Peloponnesian land forces. Maritime operations, however, were expensive, and by 421 the financial reserves with which Athens began the war had run perilously low. In the years after 421 Athens built up her reserves, and tried to organize an alliance of anti-Spartan states in the Peloponnese. In the former she was successful, but in the latter her hopes collapsed with the Spartan victory at Mantinea in 418. It was therefore natural that she should now contemplate making full use of her maritime power to extend her Empire, which would bring about a great increase in tribute and consequently an increase in her reserve of money. She could then build more ships, man them with more sailors recruited from the Greek world, and use them to transport more mercenaries recruited from the non-Greek world; and with these forces she could, if necessary, renew the war against Sparta, establish more fortified bases in the Peloponnese, and knock out Sparta's allies by more sustained and destructive seaborne raids against their territories. This was the prospect entertained by Alkibiades; the argument against it propounded by Nikias was that it was strategically and economically sounder to recover those parts of the Aegean which had been in revolt from Athenian rule for many years than to grasp at a more spectacular prize which could possibly be won but would be very hard to keep.

It has been fashionable from time to time to argue that Athens' real motive for attacking Sicily in 415 was to benefit Athenian trade by acquiring a market from which competitors could be excluded. This hypothesis necessarily implies that Thucydides is guilty either of fundamental error or of thoroughgoing distortion or inadequacy in presenting the arguments and motives of Alkibiades and the Athenians generally. It is not, however, an hypothesis recommended by any positive evidence; it seems to rest on a misunderstanding of the relation between the state, the trader, and the manufacturer in the ancient world, and to ignore the strategic situation and the close interrelation between tribute, financial reserves, and naval operations. Moreover, it must be remembered that no expedition could be

sent out from Athens until it had been debated and decided
on by the Assembly; and a reason which seemed adequate
to the Assembly is, by that very fact, an adequate reason.

4. *The Sicilian Expedition*

The response of states in the West which were believed to
be friendly to Athens was disappointing, and before the end
of the summer of 415 the three generals in command of the
expedition were reduced to two by the recall of Alkibiades
to face a charge of parodying the mysteries; he escaped at
Thurioi on his way back to Athens, and made his way
eventually to Sparta.

In order to understand the fighting described in Book VII
it is necessary to recapitulate the events described in the
latter part of Book VI, after the departure of Alkibiades.

The natural features of the neighbourhood of Syracuse
are shown on the map. It is probable (but not confirmed
archaeologically) that the city wall of Syracuse ran from the
northern end of the Great Harbour to a point on the coast
a few hundred yards north of the Little Harbour. In the
winter of 415/14 the Syracusans, in the hope of making an
enemy circumvallation impossible, built an additional wall
which ran north-westwards to take in the Temenites sanctuary, then north-eastwards close to the quarries, and then
northwards across the plateau and along the eastern side of
the big gully which emerges at the place now called Santa
Panagia. The magnitude of the area thus enclosed did not,
however, deter the Athenians from attempting a circumvallation. When they had established themselves on the
plateau in the spring of 414 they built their main fortified
position (what Thucydides calls the κύκλος) in the southern
part of the plateau, not far from the Temenites area, and
then began to build northwards from this position a wall
which would eventually run down to the sea along the
western side of the Santa Panagia gully. While they
were engaged on this, the Syracusans attempted to build

a counterwall westwards below the southern edge of the plateau, so that even if the Athenians completed the siege-wall from their fortified base to the north coast they would not be able to build a similar wall from the base to the Great Harbour. The Athenians, however, captured and destroyed this counterwall, and thereupon, breaking off work on their northern wall, started to build southward from their base. The Syracusans now began a second counterwall, nearer to the harbour than to the plateau, across ground which was protected from the north, as they thought, by tracts of marsh. This counterwall too was captured by the Athenians in a surprise attack. The Athenians then continued to build, towards the Great Harbour, a pair of walls which, with the base on the plateau at one end and the beach at the other, would enclose a substantial area.

At this time, just before the arrival of Gylippos, the Athenians controlled the Great Harbour and its beaches as a whole, and were meeting no serious opposition from the Syracusan fleet.

5. *Other Sources*

Our principal sources, other than Thucydides, for the events of 415–413 are:

(i) Diodoros ('Diodorus Siculus'), xii. 82–xiii. 33. Diodoros was a contemporary of Augustus; his value for us lies in the fact that he drew on two much earlier historians whose works, now lost and known to us only from citations and references in other authors, were widely read and influential in the ancient world: Ephoros of Kyme (c. 405–340) and Timaios of Tauromenion (c. 350–260). Timaios, in turn, utilized another lost historian, Philistos of Syracuse (c. 430–355), who, as a boy, had been in Syracuse during the Athenian siege.

(ii) Plutarch's *Nicias* (especially chapters 12–30) and *Alcibiades* (especially chapters 17–23). Plutarch was a contemporary of the Flavians and Trajan; he too utilized (and sometimes mentions explicitly) Philistos and Timaios.

Thus whenever we find in Diodoros or Plutarch incidents in the siege of Syracuse which are not mentioned by Thucydides we cannot dismiss them without more ado as later embroidery; they may be derived ultimately from Philistos.

(iii) Relevant anecdotes and scraps of information are offered by a variety of later writers, and should never be dismissed without investigation. It is important to remember that most of the work of the numerous historians of the fourth century B.C., and much of the oratory of that period, is now lost but was available to writers of Hellenistic and Roman times.

(iv) The Athenian Andokides was implicated, as a young man, in the mutilation of the herms, and, indirectly, in the profanation of the mysteries. A substantial part (§§ 11–69) of his speech *De Mysteriis* (delivered in 399) is devoted to the events of the summer of 415.

(v) Some valuable information can be gleaned from the fragmentary Athenian official inscriptions of the period, notably: (*a*) the decrees which authorized the Sicilian expedition and made detailed provision for it (*GHI* 77, very fragmentary); (*b*) the record of payments made to generals and officials by the Treasurers of Athena (ibid. 75); (*c*) records of the sale of the property confiscated from the men condemned for mutilation of the herms or profanation of the mysteries (*SEG* xiii. 12–22, cf. *GHI* 79).

III. HISTORY OF THE TEXT

The text of Book VII of Thucydides is constituted from the following sources:

(A) *Direct Tradition*, i.e. manuscripts which purport to be copies of copies of copies . . . and so on . . . of what Thucydides himself wrote.

(i) Papyri, i.e. fragments of copies made in the Hellenistic and Roman periods. Four papyri give us portions of the text of Book VII, but only one of them (*Oxyrynchus Papyrus* 1376, of *c.* 200 A.D.) is of substantial extent.

(ii) Medieval manuscripts, of which there are over seventy. The great majority ('recc.', i.e. *recentiores*, in the apparatus criticus) are either known or reasonably believed to be descendants of the seven 'primary' manuscripts ('codd.', i.e. *codices*, in the apparatus). The primary manuscripts are:

10th century:	'C' = Laurentianus LXIX 2 (Florence)
11th century:	'M' = Britannicus Add. 11727 (London)
	'E' = Palatinus 252 (Heidelberg)
	'F' = Monacensis 430 (Munich)
	'B' = Vaticanus graecus 126 (Vatican)
11th or 12th century:	'A' = Parisinus suppl. gr. 255 (Paris)
14th century:	'H' = Parisinus graecus 1734 (Paris)

(B) *Indirect Tradition.* (i) Citations from Thucydides by other authors, especially (*a*) Dionysios of Halikarnassos, a literary critic, contemporary with Augustus, and (*b*) lexicographers of late antiquity or the early Middle Ages; it is sometimes clear that the text available to such an author was different from what we have in the extant manuscripts.

(ii) Scholia, i.e. the explanatory comments which are found in the margins of manuscripts. These scholia are ultimately descended from ancient commentaries on Thucydides, but medieval scholars added much of their own and omitted or abbreviated some of the ancient material. The scholia sometimes mention readings which were in manuscripts known to them but lost to us; sometimes, again, a scholion is clearly inapplicable to the reading of the manuscript in which it is found and we can reconstruct the reading to which it was meant to apply.

(iii) Translations. Lorenzo Valla's translation of Thucydides into Latin (1452) seems to have been based chiefly on the manuscript H. Since H is now mutilated and ceases at vii. 50, Valla is of peculiar interest and value from that point onwards; and it is evident that he used at least one lost manuscript apart from H.

(C) *Conjectural Emendation.* In cases where neither the direct nor the indirect tradition provides us with a reading which makes satisfactory sense, we have to use reason and knowledge in order to conjecture what Thucydides wrote. Conjectural emendation is not a purely modern phenomenon; ancient and medieval scholars were willing to correct what they believed (often rightly) to be nonsense.

The interrelation of the primary manuscripts in Book VII is as follows:

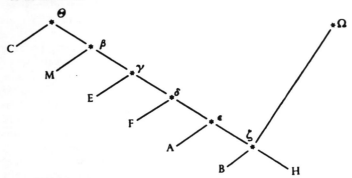

The asterisks and Greek letters represent the minimum number of hypothetical manuscripts the existence of which has to be assumed in order to account for the essentials of the relationship between the seven texts concerned. ζ was a composite manuscript—i.e. included both the readings which it inherited from ε and those which it obtained from Ω—from vi. 92. 5 onwards. Θ is by definition the 'archetype', i.e. the latest common ancestor of all the extant manuscripts, wherever and whenever that existed.

Stemmata (i.e. manuscript family trees) of this kind look too simple to be the whole truth, and it is necessary to introduce into this stemma the following complications:

(i) A source (Φ) independent of Θ was used by the copyist of an intermediate stage between β and M; he drew from it a few variant readings which are to be found in M, and, more important, a mass of scholia which are quite different from those which were in Θ and often relate to readings different from Θ's. This material was added to C and F by fourteenth-century copyists.

(ii) E occasionally has a reading which makes sense in a passage where all the other manuscripts agree in error; this and other peculiarities of E are most easily accounted for by the hypothesis that the copyist of a stage between γ and E drew on another manuscript which was closely related to C but contained material from a source (Ψ) independent of Θ.

The *recentiores* cannot all be dismissed as having nothing to contribute to the text, since we sometimes find in one or more of them an excellent reading which does not seem to be a medieval conjecture and is probably derived from Ω. It seems strange that Ω should have left us no direct descendants; the natural explanation is that it was a very old and badly mutilated manuscript, unsuitable for complete transcription but valued as a source of variant readings.

(*Note*: In the present edition the text and apparatus criticus are printed exactly as in the Oxford Classical Text of 1942. Since then, the study of the history of the text of Thucydides has continued; the account given above summarizes the results obtained by 1964, but it will be seen that in the apparatus criticus H is not mentioned—it is classed among 'recc.'—and G, a thirteenth-century manuscript of composite origin, is treated as a primary manuscript.)

Ὁ δὲ Γύλιππος καὶ ὁ Πυθὴν ἐκ τοῦ Τάραντος, ἐπεὶ 1
ἐπεσκεύασαν τὰς ναῦς, παρέπλευσαν ἐς Λοκροὺς τοὺς Ἐπι-
ζεφυρίους· καὶ πυνθανόμενοι σαφέστερον ἤδη ὅτι οὐ παντελῶς
πω ἀποτετειχισμέναι αἱ Συράκουσαί εἰσιν, ἀλλ' ἔτι οἷόν τε
5 κατὰ τὰς Ἐπιπολὰς στρατιᾷ ἀφικομένους ἐσελθεῖν, ἐβουλεύοντο εἴτ' ἐν δεξιᾷ λαβόντες τὴν Σικελίαν διακινδυνεύσωσιν
ἐσπλεῦσαι, εἴτ' ἐν ἀριστερᾷ ἐς Ἱμέραν πρῶτον πλεύσαντες
καὶ αὐτούς τε ἐκείνους καὶ στρατιὰν ἄλλην προσλαβόντες,
οὓς ἂν πείθωσι, κατὰ γῆν ἔλθωσιν. καὶ ἔδοξεν αὐτοῖς ἐπὶ 2
10 τῆς Ἱμέρας πλεῖν, ἄλλως τε καὶ τῶν Ἀττικῶν τεσσάρων
νεῶν οὔπω παρουσῶν ἐν τῷ Ῥηγίῳ, ἃς ὁ Νικίας ὅμως πυνθανόμενος αὐτοὺς ἐν Λοκροῖς εἶναι ἀπέστειλεν. φθάσαντες
δὲ τὴν φυλακὴν ταύτην περαιοῦνται διὰ τοῦ πορθμοῦ, καὶ
σχόντες Ῥηγίῳ καὶ Μεσσήνῃ ἀφικνοῦνται ἐς Ἱμέραν. ἐκεῖ 3
15 δὲ ὄντες τούς τε Ἱμεραίους ἔπεισαν ξυμπολεμεῖν καὶ αὐτούς
τε ἔπεσθαι καὶ τοῖς ἐκ τῶν νεῶν τῶν σφετέρων ναύταις ὅσοι μὴ
εἶχον ὅπλα παρασχεῖν (τὰς γὰρ ναῦς ἀνείλκυσαν ἐν Ἱμέρᾳ),
καὶ τοὺς Σελινουντίους πέμψαντες ἐκέλευον ἀπαντᾶν πανστρατιᾷ ἔς τι χωρίον. πέμψειν δέ τινα αὐτοῖς ὑπέσχοντο 4
20 στρατιὰν οὐ πολλὴν καὶ οἱ Γελῷοι καὶ τῶν Σικελῶν τινές,
οἳ πολὺ προθυμότερον προσχωρεῖν ἕτοιμοι ἦσαν τοῦ τε
Ἀρχωνίδου νεωστὶ τεθνηκότος, ὃς τῶν ταύτῃ Σικελῶν βασι-
λεύων τινῶν καὶ ὢν οὐκ ἀδύνατος τοῖς Ἀθηναίοις φίλος ἦν,

---

5 πανστρατιᾷ Μ   6 διακινδυνεύσουσιν G   11 πυνθανόμενος
αὐτοὺς ὅμως B   16 ὅσα B   17 γὰρ B : μὲν cett.   18 πανστρατιᾷ B : στρατιᾷ cett.   21 τε B : om. cett.

καὶ τοῦ Γυλίππου ἐκ Λακεδαίμονος προθύμως δοκοῦντος ἥκειν.

5 καὶ ὁ μὲν Γύλιππος ἀναλαβὼν τῶν τε σφετέρων ναυτῶν καὶ
ἐπιβατῶν τοὺς ὡπλισμένους ἑπτακοσίους μάλιστα, Ἱμεραίους
δὲ ὁπλίτας καὶ ψιλοὺς ξυναμφοτέρους χιλίους καὶ ἱππέας
ἑκατὸν καὶ Σελινουντίων τέ τινας ψιλοὺς καὶ ἱππέας καὶ 5
Γελῴων ὀλίγους, Σικελῶν τε ἐς χιλίους τοὺς πάντας, ἐχώρει

2 πρὸς τὰς Συρακούσας· οἱ δ' ἐκ τῆς Λευκάδος Κορίνθιοι ταῖς
τε ἄλλαις ναυσὶν ὡς εἶχον τάχους ἐβοήθουν καὶ Γογγύλος,
εἷς τῶν Κορινθίων ἀρχόντων, μιᾷ νηὶ τελευταῖος ὁρμηθεὶς
πρῶτος μὲν ἀφικνεῖται ἐς τὰς Συρακούσας, ὀλίγον δὲ πρὸ 10
Γυλίππου, καὶ καταλαβὼν αὐτοὺς περὶ ἀπαλλαγῆς τοῦ πολέμου
μέλλοντας ἐκκλησιάσειν διεκώλυσέ τε καὶ παρεθάρσυνε,
λέγων ὅτι νῆές τε ἄλλαι ἔτι προσπλέουσι καὶ Γύλιππος ὁ

2 Κλεανδρίδου Λακεδαιμονίων ἀποστειλάντων ἄρχων. καὶ οἱ
μὲν Συρακόσιοι ἐπερρώσθησάν τε καὶ τῷ Γυλίππῳ εὐθὺς 15
πανστρατιᾷ ὡς ἀπαντησόμενοι ἐξῆλθον· ἤδη γὰρ καὶ ἐγγὺς

3 ὄντα ᾐσθάνοντο αὐτόν. ὁ δὲ Ἰέτας τότε τι τεῖχος ἐν τῇ
παρόδῳ τῶν Σικελῶν ἑλὼν καὶ ξυνταξάμενος ὡς ἐς μάχην
ἀφικνεῖται ἐς τὰς Ἐπιπολάς· καὶ ἀναβὰς κατὰ τὸν Εὐρύηλον,
ᾗπερ καὶ οἱ Ἀθηναῖοι τὸ πρῶτον, ἐχώρει μετὰ τῶν Συρακο- 20

4 σίων ἐπὶ τὸ τείχισμα τῶν Ἀθηναίων. ἔτυχε δὲ κατὰ τοῦτο
τοῦ καιροῦ ἐλθὼν ἐν ᾧ ἑπτὰ μὲν ἢ ὀκτὼ σταδίων ἤδη ἀπετετέλεστο τοῖς Ἀθηναίοις ἐς τὸν μέγαν λιμένα διπλοῦν τεῖχος,
πλὴν κατὰ βραχύ τι τὸ πρὸς τὴν θάλασσαν (τοῦτο δ' ἔτι
ᾠκοδόμουν), τῷ δὲ ἄλλῳ τοῦ κύκλου πρὸς τὸν Τρωγίλον ἐπὶ 25
τὴν ἑτέραν θάλασσαν λίθοι τε παραβεβλημένοι τῷ πλέονι ἤδη
ἦσαν, καὶ ἔστιν ἃ καὶ ἡμίεργα, τὰ δὲ καὶ ἐξειργασμένα κατελέλειπτο. παρὰ τοσοῦτον μὲν αἱ Συράκουσαι ἦλθον κινδύνου.

1 δοκοῦντος προθύμως B   2 τε om. B   4 prius καὶ B : om. cett.
5 τέ B : om. cett.   17 Ἰέτας Steph. Byz. : νετὰς C E F? : γε τὰ
A B : γε G M   τότε τι B : τότε τὸ M : τι F? : τότε cett.   19 ἐς]
πρὸς B   21 ἐτύγχανε B   22 τοῦ B : om. cett.   ἀπετετέλεστο
B : ἐπετετέλεστο cett.   24 κατὰ] παρὰ B   25 post ἄλλῳ add.
ἄνω Marchant, ἀπὸ Wölfflin   28 κατελέλειπτο Cobet : κατελείπετο
B G : κατελίπετο cett.   αἱ B : om. cett.

Οἱ δὲ Ἀθηναῖοι αἰφνιδίως τοῦ τε Γυλίππου καὶ τῶν 3
Συρακοσίων σφίσιν ἐπιόντων ἐθορυβήθησαν μὲν τὸ πρῶτον,
παρετάξαντο δέ. ὁ δὲ θέμενος τὰ ὅπλα ἐγγὺς κήρυκα προσπέμπει αὐτοῖς λέγοντα, εἰ βούλονται ἐξιέναι ἐκ τῆς Σικελίας
5 πέντε ἡμερῶν λαβόντες τὰ σφέτερα αὐτῶν, ἑτοῖμος εἶναι
σπένδεσθαι. οἱ δ' ἐν ὀλιγωρίᾳ τε ἐποιοῦντο καὶ οὐδὲν 2
ἀποκρινάμενοι ἀπέπεμψαν. καὶ μετὰ τοῦτο ἀντιπαρεσκευά-
ζοντο ἀλλήλοις ὡς ἐς μάχην. καὶ ὁ Γύλιππος ὁρῶν τοὺς 3
Συρακοσίους ταρασσομένους καὶ οὐ ῥᾳδίως ξυντασσομένους,
10 ἐπανῆγε τὸ στρατόπεδον ἐς τὴν εὐρυχωρίαν μᾶλλον. καὶ ὁ
Νικίας οὐκ ἐπῆγε τοὺς Ἀθηναίους, ἀλλ' ἡσύχαζε πρὸς τῷ
ἑαυτῶν τείχει. ὡς δ' ἔγνω ὁ Γύλιππος οὐ προσιόντας αὐτούς,
ἀπήγαγε τὴν στρατιὰν ἐπὶ τὴν ἄκραν τὴν Τεμενῖτιν καλουμένην, καὶ αὐτοῦ ηὐλίσαντο. τῇ δ' ὑστεραίᾳ ἄγων τὴν μὲν 4
15 πλείστην τῆς στρατιᾶς παρέταξε πρὸς τὰ τείχη τῶν Ἀθηναίων, ὅπως μὴ ἐπιβοηθοῖεν ἄλλοσε, μέρος δέ τι πέμψας
πρὸς τὸ φρούριον τὸ Λάβδαλον αἱρεῖ, καὶ ὅσους ἔλαβεν ἐν
αὐτῷ πάντας ἀπέκτεινεν· ἦν δὲ οὐκ ἐπιφανὲς τοῖς Ἀθηναίοις
τὸ χωρίον. καὶ τριήρης τῇ αὐτῇ ἡμέρᾳ ἁλίσκεται τῶν Ἀθη- 5
20 ναίων ὑπὸ τῶν Συρακοσίων ἐφορμοῦσα τῷ λιμένι.

Καὶ μετὰ ταῦτα ἐτείχιζον οἱ Συρακόσιοι καὶ οἱ ξύμμαχοι 4
διὰ τῶν Ἐπιπολῶν ἀπὸ τῆς πόλεως ἀρξάμενοι ἄνω πρὸς τὸ *
ἐγκάρσιον τεῖχος ἁπλοῦν, ὅπως οἱ Ἀθηναῖοι, εἰ μὴ δύναιντο
κωλῦσαι, μηκέτι οἷοί τε ὦσιν ἀποτειχίσαι. καὶ οἵ τε 2
25 Ἀθηναῖοι ἀνεβεβήκεσαν ἤδη ἄνω, τὸ ἐπὶ θαλάσσῃ τεῖχος
ἐπιτελέσαντες, καὶ ὁ Γύλιππος (ἦν γάρ τι τοῖς Ἀθηναίοις
τοῦ τείχους ἀσθενές) νυκτὸς ἀναλαβὼν τὴν στρατιὰν ἐπῄει
πρὸς αὐτό. οἱ δ' Ἀθηναῖοι (ἔτυχον γὰρ ἔξω αὐλιζόμενοι) 3
ὡς ᾔσθοντο, ἀντεπῇσαν· ὁ δὲ γνοὺς κατὰ τάχος ἀπήγαγε
30 τοὺς σφετέρους πάλιν. ἐποικοδομήσαντες δὲ αὐτὸ οἱ Ἀθηναῖοι ὑψηλότερον αὐτοὶ μὲν ταύτῃ ἐφύλασσον, τοὺς δὲ ἄλλους

2 τὸ B: om. cett.   3 προπέμπει A E F G M   4 ἐκ om. B
12 ἑαυτῶν B: ἑαυτοῦ cett.   20 post τᾷ add. μεγάλῳ B   22 *]
v. Rehm, Philologus, 1934, 133 sqq.

ξυμμάχους κατὰ τὸ ἄλλο τείχισμα ἤδη διέταξαν, ᾗπερ ἔμελλον·
ἕκαστοι φρουρεῖν.

4 Τῷ δὲ Νικίᾳ ἐδόκει τὸ Πλημμύριον καλούμενον τειχίσαι·
ἔστι δὲ ἄκρα ἀντιπέρας τῆς πόλεως, ἥπερ προύχουσα τοῦ
μεγάλου λιμένος τὸ στόμα στενὸν ποιεῖ, καὶ εἰ τειχισθείη, 5
ῥᾷων αὐτῷ ἐφαίνετο ἡ ἐσκομιδὴ τῶν ἐπιτηδείων ἔσεσθαι·
δι' ἐλάσσονος γὰρ πρὸς τῷ λιμένι τῷ τῶν Συρακοσίων
ἐφορμήσειν σφᾶς, καὶ οὐχ ὥσπερ νῦν ἐκ μυχοῦ τοῦ λιμένος
τὰς ἐπαναγωγὰς ποιήσεσθαι, ἤν τι ναυτικῷ κινῶνται. προσ-
εῖχέ τε ἤδη μᾶλλον τῷ κατὰ θάλασσαν πολέμῳ, ὁρῶν τὰ 10
ἐκ τῆς γῆς σφίσιν ἤδη, ἐπειδὴ Γύλιππος ἧκεν, ἀνελπιστότερα
5 ὄντα. διακομίσας οὖν στρατιὰν καὶ τὰς ναῦς ἐξετείχισε
τρία φρούρια· καὶ ἐν αὐτοῖς τά τε σκεύη τὰ πλεῖστα ἔκειτο
καὶ τὰ πλοῖα ἤδη ἐκεῖ τὰ μεγάλα ὥρμει καὶ αἱ ταχεῖαι νῆες.
6 ὥστε καὶ τῶν πληρωμάτων οὐχ ἥκιστα τότε πρῶτον κάκωσις 15
ἐγένετο· τῷ τε γὰρ ὕδατι σπανίῳ χρώμενοι καὶ οὐκ ἐγγύθεν,
καὶ ἐπὶ φρυγανισμὸν ἅμα ὁπότε ἐξέλθοιεν οἱ ναῦται, ὑπὸ
τῶν ἱππέων τῶν Συρακοσίων κρατούντων τῆς γῆς διεφθεί-
ροντο· τρίτον γὰρ μέρος τῶν ἱππέων τοῖς Συρακοσίοις διὰ
τοὺς ἐν τῷ Πλημμυρίῳ, ἵνα μὴ κακουργήσοντες ἐξίοιεν, ἐπὶ 20
7 τῇ ἐν τῷ Ὀλυμπιείῳ πολίχνῃ ἐτετάχατο. ἐπυνθάνετο δὲ
καὶ τὰς λοιπὰς τῶν Κορινθίων ναῦς προσπλεούσας ὁ Νικίας·
καὶ πέμπει ἐς φυλακὴν αὐτῶν εἴκοσι ναῦς, αἷς εἴρητο περί
τε Λοκροὺς καὶ Ῥήγιον καὶ τὴν προσβολὴν τῆς Σικελίας
ναυλοχεῖν αὐτάς. 25

5 Ὁ δὲ Γύλιππος ἅμα μὲν ἐτείχιζε τὸ διὰ τῶν Ἐπιπολῶν
τεῖχος, τοῖς λίθοις χρώμενος οὓς οἱ Ἀθηναῖοι προπαρε-
βάλοντο σφίσιν, ἅμα δὲ παρέτασσεν ἐξάγων αἰεὶ πρὸ τοῦ
τειχίσματος τοὺς Συρακοσίους καὶ τοὺς ξυμμάχους· καὶ οἱ
2 Ἀθηναῖοι ἀντιπαρετάσσοντο. ἐπειδὴ δὲ ἔδοξε τῷ Γυλίππῳ 30

---

6 ῥάων C : ῥᾷον cett.   9 ἐπαναγωγὰς B : ἐπαγωγὰς cett.
11 ἤδη B : om. cett.   post ἐπειδὴ add. ὁ B   14 ὡρμίζετο B
18 post γῆς add. οἱ πολλοὶ B   26 διετείχιζε B   30 τῷ B : om.
cett.

καιρὸς εἶναι, ἦρχε τῆς ἐφόδου· καὶ ἐν χερσὶ γενόμενοι
ἐμάχοντο μεταξὺ τῶν τειχισμάτων, ᾗ τῆς ἵππου τῶν Συρακοσίων οὐδεμία χρῆσις ἦν. καὶ νικηθέντων τῶν Συρακοσίων 3
καὶ τῶν ξυμμάχων καὶ νεκροὺς ὑποσπόνδους ἀνελομένων καὶ
5 τῶν Ἀθηναίων τροπαῖον στησάντων, ὁ Γύλιππος ξυγκαλέσας
τὸ στράτευμα οὐκ ἔφη τὸ ἁμάρτημα ἐκείνων, ἀλλ' ἑαυτοῦ
γενέσθαι· τῆς γὰρ ἵππου καὶ τῶν ἀκοντιστῶν τὴν ὠφελίαν
τῇ τάξει ἐντὸς λίαν τῶν τειχῶν ποιήσας ἀφελέσθαι· νῦν
οὖν αὖθις ἐπάξειν. καὶ διανοεῖσθαι οὕτως ἐκέλευεν αἰτοὺς 4
10 ὡς τῇ μὲν παρασκευῇ οὐκ ἔλασσον ἕξοντας, τῇ δὲ γνώμῃ
οὐκ ἀνεκτὸν ἐσόμενον εἰ μὴ ἀξιώσουσι Πελοποννήσιοί τε
ὄντες καὶ Δωριῆς Ἰώνων καὶ νησιωτῶν καὶ ξυγκλύδων
ἀνθρώπων κρατήσαντες ἐξελάσασθαι ἐκ τῆς χώρας. καὶ 6
μετὰ ταῦτα, ἐπειδὴ καιρὸς ἦν, αὖθις ἐπῆγεν αὐτούς. ὁ δὲ
15 Νικίας καὶ οἱ Ἀθηναῖοι νομίζοντες, καὶ εἰ ἐκεῖνοι μὴ ἐθέλοιεν
μάχης ἄρχειν, ἀναγκαῖον εἶναι σφίσι μὴ περιορᾶν παροι-
κοδομούμενον τὸ τεῖχος (ἤδη γὰρ καὶ ὅσον οὐ παρεληλύθει
τὴν τῶν Ἀθηναίων τοῦ τείχους τελευτὴν ἡ ἐκείνων τείχισις,
καί, εἰ προέλθοι, ταὐτὸν ἤδη ἐποίει αὐτοῖς νικᾶν τε μαχομένοις
20 διὰ παντὸς καὶ μηδὲ μάχεσθαι), ἀντεπῇσαν οὖν τοῖς Συρακοσίοις. καὶ ὁ Γύλιππος τοὺς μὲν ὁπλίτας ἔξω τῶν τειχῶν 2
μᾶλλον ἢ πρότερον προαγαγὼν ξυνέμισγεν αὐτοῖς, τοὺς δ'
ἱππέας καὶ τοὺς ἀκοντιστὰς ἐκ πλαγίου τάξας τῶν Ἀθηναίων
κατὰ τὴν εὐρυχωρίαν, ᾗ τῶν τειχῶν ἀμφοτέρων αἱ ἐργασίαι
25 ἔληγον. καὶ προσβαλόντες οἱ ἱππῆς ἐν τῇ μάχῃ τῷ εὐωνύμῳ 3
κέρᾳ τῶν Ἀθηναίων, ὅπερ κατ' αὐτοὺς ἦν, ἔτρεψαν· καὶ δι'
αὐτὸ καὶ τὸ ἄλλο στράτευμα νικηθὲν ὑπὸ τῶν Συρακοσίων
κατηράχθη ἐς τὰ τειχίσματα. καὶ τῇ ἐπιούσῃ νυκτὶ ἔφθασαν 4
παροικοδομήσαντες καὶ παρελθόντες τὴν τῶν Ἀθηναίων οἰκο-

---

2 post Συρακοσίων add. καὶ τῶν ξυμμάχων C G   5 post ὁ add.
μὲν B   6 ἑαυτοῦ B : αὐτοῦ vel αὑτοῦ cett.   14 ἐπεὶ B
16 σφίσιν εἶναι B   19 παρέλθοι Classen   τὸ αὐτὸ B
20 μάχεσθαι] ἀμύνεσθαι B   26 κέρατι B   δι' αὐτὸ] διὰ τοῦτο B
28 κατηράχθη C : κατερράχθη (-ηρρ- B) cett.

C

δομίαν, ὥστε μηκέτι μήτε αὐτοὶ κωλύεσθαι ὑπ' αὐτῶν, ἐκείνους τε καὶ παντάπασιν ἀπεστερηκέναι, εἰ καὶ κρατοῖεν, μὴ ἂν ἔτι σφᾶς ἀποτειχίσαι.

7 Μετὰ δὲ τοῦτο αἵ τε τῶν Κορινθίων νῆες καὶ Ἀμπρακιωτῶν καὶ Λευκαδίων ἐσέπλευσαν αἱ ὑπόλοιποι δώδεκα, λαθοῦσαι 5 τὴν τῶν Ἀθηναίων φυλακήν (ἦρχε δ' αὐτῶν Ἐρασινίδης Κορίνθιος), καὶ ξυνετείχισαν τὸ λοιπὸν τοῖς Συρακοσίοις
2 μέχρι * τοῦ ἐγκαρσίου τείχους. καὶ ὁ Γύλιππος ἐς τὴν ἄλλην Σικελίαν ἐπὶ στρατιάν τε ᾤχετο, καὶ ναυτικὴν καὶ πεζὴν ξυλλέξων, καὶ τῶν πόλεων ἅμα προσαξόμενος εἴ τις 10 ἢ μὴ πρόθυμος ἦν ἢ παντάπασιν ἔτι ἀφειστήκει τοῦ πολέμου.
3 πρέσβεις τε ἄλλοι τῶν Συρακοσίων καὶ Κορινθίων ἐς Λακεδαίμονα καὶ Κόρινθον ἀπεστάλησαν, ὅπως στρατιὰ ἔτι περαιωθῇ τρόπῳ ᾧ ἂν ἐν ὁλκάσιν ἢ πλοίοις ἢ ἄλλως ὅπως
4 ἂν προχωρῇ, ὡς καὶ τῶν Ἀθηναίων ἐπιμεταπεμπομένων. οἵ 15 τε Συρακόσιοι ναυτικὸν ἐπλήρουν καὶ ἀνεπειρῶντο ὡς καὶ τούτῳ ἐπιχειρήσοντες, καὶ ἐς τἆλλα πολὺ ἐπέρρωντο.

8 Ὁ δὲ Νικίας αἰσθόμενος τοῦτο καὶ ὁρῶν καθ' ἡμέραν ἐπιδιδοῦσαν τήν τε τῶν πολεμίων ἰσχὺν καὶ τὴν σφετέραν ἀπορίαν, ἔπεμπε καὶ αὐτὸς ἐς τὰς Ἀθήνας ἀγγέλλων πολλάκις 20 μὲν καὶ ἄλλοτε καθ' ἕκαστα τῶν γιγνομένων, μάλιστα δὲ καὶ τότε, νομίζων ἐν δεινοῖς τε εἶναι καί, εἰ μὴ ὡς τάχιστα ἢ σφᾶς μεταπέμψουσιν ἢ ἄλλους μὴ ὀλίγους ἀποστελοῦσιν,
2 οὐδεμίαν εἶναι σωτηρίαν. φοβούμενος δὲ μὴ οἱ πεμπόμενοι ἢ κατὰ τὴν τοῦ λέγειν ἀδυνασίαν ἢ καὶ μνήμης ἐλλιπεῖς 25 γιγνόμενοι ἢ τῷ ὄχλῳ πρὸς χάριν τι λέγοντες οὐ τὰ ὄντα ἀπαγγέλλωσιν, ἔγραψεν ἐπιστολήν, νομίζων οὕτως ἂν μάλιστα τὴν αὐτοῦ γνώμην μηδὲν ἐν τῷ ἀγγέλῳ ἀφανισθεῖσαν μαθόντας τοὺς Ἀθηναίους βουλεύσασθαι περὶ τῆς ἀληθείας.

6 Ἐρασινίδης] Θρασωνίδης B   8 *] v. c. 4 supra   10 πεζὴν B : πεζικὴν cett.   12 post ἐς add. τὴν B   14 πλοίῳ A E F M   20 ἀγγέλλοντας B : ἄγγελον C G (corr. G¹) : ἀγγέλων (sic) E   22 εἰ B : ἦν cett.   23 μεταπέμψωσιν B   25 τὴν B : om. cett.   μνήμης B : γνώμης cett.   26 γενόμενοι M   27 ἀπαγγείλωσιν C   28 μάλιστα] μόλις B

καὶ οἱ μὲν ᾤχοντο φέροντες, οὓς ἀπέστειλε, τὰ γράμματα 3
καὶ ὅσα ἔδει αὐτοὺς εἰπεῖν· ὁ δὲ τὰ κατὰ τὸ στρατόπεδον
διὰ φυλακῆς μᾶλλον ἤδη ἔχων ἢ δι᾽ ἑκουσίων κινδύνων
ἐπεμέλετο.

5   Ἐν δὲ τῷ αὐτῷ θέρει τελευτῶντι καὶ Εὐετίων στρατηγὸς 9
Ἀθηναίων μετὰ Περδίκκου στρατεύσας ἐπ᾽ Ἀμφίπολιν Θρᾳξὶ
πολλοῖς τὴν μὲν πόλιν οὐχ εἷλεν, ἐς δὲ τὸν Στρυμόνα περι-
κομίσας τριήρεις ἐκ τοῦ ποταμοῦ ἐπολιόρκει ὁρμώμενος ἐξ
Ἱμεραίου. καὶ τὸ θέρος ἐτελεύτα.

10   Τοῦ δ᾽ ἐπιγιγνομένου χειμῶνος ἥκοντες ἐς τὰς Ἀθήνας οἱ 10
παρὰ τοῦ Νικίου ὅσα τε ἀπὸ γλώσσης εἴρητο αὐτοῖς εἶπον,
καὶ εἴ τίς τι ἐπηρώτα ἀπεκρίνοντο, καὶ τὴν ἐπιστολὴν ἀπ-
έδοσαν. ὁ δὲ γραμματεὺς ὁ τῆς πόλεως παρελθὼν ἀνέγνω
τοῖς Ἀθηναίοις δηλοῦσαν τοιάδε.

15   ʻΤὰ μὲν πρότερον πραχθέντα, ὦ Ἀθηναῖοι, ἐν ἄλλαις 11
πολλαῖς ἐπιστολαῖς ἴστε· νῦν δὲ καιρὸς οὐχ ἧσσον μαθόντας
ὑμᾶς ἐν ᾧ ἐσμὲν βουλεύσασθαι. κρατησάντων γὰρ ἡμῶν 2
μάχαις ταῖς πλέοσι Συρακοσίους ἐφ᾽ οὓς ἐπέμφθημεν καὶ τὰ
τείχη οἰκοδομησαμένων ἐν οἷσπερ νῦν ἐσμέν, ἦλθε Γύλιππος
20 Λακεδαιμόνιος στρατιὰν ἔχων ἔκ τε Πελοποννήσου καὶ ἀπὸ
τῶν ἐν Σικελίᾳ πόλεων ἔστιν ὧν. καὶ μάχῃ τῇ μὲν πρώτῃ
νικᾶται ὑφ᾽ ἡμῶν, τῇ δ᾽ ὑστεραίᾳ ἱππεῦσί τε πολλοῖς καὶ
ἀκοντισταῖς βιασθέντες ἀνεχωρήσαμεν ἐς τὰ τείχη. νῦν οὖν 3
ἡμεῖς μὲν παυσάμενοι τοῦ περιτειχισμοῦ διὰ τὸ πλῆθος τῶν
25 ἐναντίων ἡσυχάζομεν (οὐδὲ γὰρ ξυμπάσῃ τῇ στρατιᾷ δυναίμεθ᾽
ἂν χρήσασθαι ἀπανηλωκυίας τῆς φυλακῆς τῶν τειχῶν μέρος
τι τοῦ ὁπλιτικοῦ)· οἱ δὲ παρῳκοδομήκασιν ἡμῖν τεῖχος ἁπλοῦν,
ὥστε μὴ εἶναι ἔτι περιτειχίσαι αὐτούς, ἢν μή τις τὸ παρατείχισμα τοῦτο πολλῇ στρατιᾷ ἐπελθὼν ἕλῃ. ξυμβέβηκέ 4

2 τὰ om. Β Μ   3 μᾶλλον Β : om. cett.   ἢ δι᾽ Β C : ἤδη
A E F : om. G M   9 post ἐτελεύτα add. τοῦτο Β C E G   12 ἐπηρώτα Β : ἠρώτα cett.   13 alterum ὁ Β : om. cett.   16 πολλαῖς
om. Β   19 νῦν om. C G M   post Γύλιππος add. ὁ Β   20 τε
Β : om. cett.   ἀπὸ om. Β   24 τὸ om. C   26 χρήσασθαι C :
χρήσεσθαι cett. (corr. G¹)   28 post prius μὴ add. δυνατὸν Β

τε πολιορκεῖν δοκοῦντας ἡμᾶς ἄλλους αὐτοὺς μᾶλλον, ὅσα γε
κατὰ γῆν, τοῦτο πάσχειν· οὐδὲ γὰρ τῆς χώρας ἐπὶ πολὺ διὰ
τοὺς ἱππέας ἐξερχόμεθα.

12   'Πεπόμφασι δὲ καὶ ἐς Πελοπόννησον πρέσβεις ἐπ' ἄλλην
στρατιάν, καὶ ἐς τὰς ἐν Σικελίᾳ πόλεις Γύλιππος οἴχεται, 5
τὰς μὲν καὶ πείσων ξυμπολεμεῖν ὅσαι νῦν ἡσυχάζουσιν, ἀπὸ
δὲ τῶν καὶ στρατιὰν ἔτι πεζὴν καὶ ναυτικοῦ παρασκευήν, ἢν
2 δύνηται, ἄξων. διανοοῦνται γάρ, ὡς ἐγὼ πυνθάνομαι, τῷ
τε πεζῷ ἅμα τῶν τειχῶν ἡμῶν πειρᾶν καὶ ταῖς ναυσὶ κατὰ
3 θάλασσαν. καὶ δεινὸν μηδενὶ ὑμῶν δόξῃ εἶναι ὅτι καὶ 10
κατὰ θάλασσαν. τὸ γὰρ ναυτικὸν ἡμῶν, ὅπερ κἀκεῖνοι
πυνθάνονται, τὸ μὲν πρῶτον ἤκμαζε καὶ τῶν νεῶν τῇ ξηρότητι
καὶ τῶν πληρωμάτων τῇ σωτηρίᾳ· νῦν δὲ αἵ τε νῆες διάβροχοι τοσοῦτον χρόνον ἤδη θαλασσεύουσαι, καὶ τὰ πληρώ-
4 ματα ἔφθαρται. τὰς μὲν γὰρ ναῦς οὐκ ἔστιν ἀνελκύσαντας 15
διαψῦξαι διὰ τὸ ἀντιπάλους τῷ πλήθει καὶ ἔτι πλείους τὰς
τῶν πολεμίων οὔσας αἰεὶ προσδοκίαν παρέχειν ὡς ἐπιπλεύ-
5 σονται. φανεραὶ δ' εἰσὶν ἀναπειρώμεναι, καὶ αἱ ἐπιχειρήσεις
ἐπ' ἐκείνοις καὶ ἀποξηρᾶναι τὰς σφετέρας μᾶλλον ἐξουσία·
13 οὐ γὰρ ἐφορμοῦσιν ἄλλοις. ἡμῖν δ' ἐκ πολλῆς ἂν περιουσίας 20
νεῶν μόλις τοῦτο ὑπῆρχε καὶ μὴ ἀναγκαζομένοις ὥσπερ
νῦν πάσαις φυλάσσειν· εἰ γὰρ ἀφαιρήσομέν τι καὶ βραχὺ
τῆς τηρήσεως, τὰ ἐπιτήδεια οὐχ ἕξομεν, παρὰ τὴν ἐκείνων
2 πόλιν χαλεπῶς καὶ νῦν ἐσκομιζόμενοι. τὰ δὲ πληρώματα
διὰ τόδε ἐφθάρη τε ἡμῖν καὶ ἔτι νῦν φθείρεται, τῶν ναυτῶν 25
[τῶν] μὲν διὰ φρυγανισμὸν καὶ ἁρπαγὴν καὶ ὑδρείαν μακρὰν
ὑπὸ τῶν ἱππέων ἀπολλυμένων· οἱ δὲ θεράποντες, ἐπειδὴ ἐς
ἀντίπαλα καθεστήκαμεν, αὐτομολοῦσι, καὶ οἱ ξένοι οἱ μὲν
ἀναγκαστοὶ ἐσβάντες εὐθὺς κατὰ τὰς πόλεις ἀποχωροῦσιν,

7 καὶ στρατιὰν ἔτι B: ἔτι καὶ στρατιὰν cett.   9 τε om. B
11 ὅπερ recc.: ἥπερ codd.   κἀκεῖνοι B: καὶ ἐκεῖνοι cett.   16 τῷ]
τῷ τε B: καὶ τῷ cett.   ἔτι recc.: ὅτι codd.   18 φανεραὶ B   ἀνα-
πειρόμεναι B: ἀποπειρόμεναι cett.   19 καὶ τὸ ξηρᾶναι B   ἐξουσία
om. M   26 τῶν secl. Poppo   ἁρπαγὴν μακρὰν (μικρὰν G¹) καὶ ὑδρείαν
A C E F G M Schol.

οἱ δὲ ὑπὸ μεγάλου μισθοῦ τὸ πρῶτον ἐπαρθέντες καὶ οἰόμενοι
χρηματιεῖσθαι μᾶλλον ἢ μαχεῖσθαι, ἐπειδὴ παρὰ γνώμην
ναυτικόν τε δὴ καὶ τἆλλα ἀπὸ τῶν πολεμίων ἀνθεστῶτα
ὁρῶσιν, οἱ μὲν ἐπ' αὐτομολίας προφάσει ἀπέρχονται, οἱ δὲ
5 ὡς ἕκαστοι δύνανται (πολλὴ δ' ἡ Σικελία), εἰσὶ δ' οἳ καὶ
αὐτοὶ ἐμπορευόμενοι ἀνδράποδα Ὑκκαρικὰ ἀντεμβιβάσαι ὑπὲρ
σφῶν πείσαντες τοὺς τριηράρχους τὴν ἀκρίβειαν τοῦ ναυτικοῦ
ἀφῄρηνται. ἐπισταμένοις δ' ὑμῖν γράφω ὅτι βραχεῖα ἀκμὴ 14
πληρώματος καὶ ὀλίγοι τῶν ναυτῶν οἱ ἐξορμῶντές τε ναῦν
10 καὶ ξυνέχοντες τὴν εἰρεσίαν. τούτων δὲ πάντων ἀπορώτατον 2
τό τε μὴ οἷόν τε εἶναι ταῦτα ἐμοὶ κωλῦσαι τῷ στρατηγῷ
(χαλεπαὶ γὰρ αἱ ὑμέτεραι φύσεις ἄρξαι) καὶ ὅτι οὐδ' ὁπόθεν
ἐπιπληρωσόμεθα τὰς ναῦς ἔχομεν, ὃ τοῖς πολεμίοις πολλα-
χόθεν ὑπάρχει, ἀλλ' ἀνάγκη ἀφ' ὧν ἔχοντες ἤλθομεν τά τε
15 ὄντα καὶ ἀπαναλισκόμενα γίγνεσθαι· αἱ γὰρ νῦν οὖσαι πόλεις
ξύμμαχοι ἀδύνατοι Νάξος καὶ Κατάνη. εἰ δὲ προσγενήσεται 3
ἓν ἔτι τοῖς πολεμίοις, ὥστε τὰ τρέφοντα ἡμᾶς χωρία τῆς
Ἰταλίας, ὁρῶντα ἐν ᾧ τ' ἐσμὲν καὶ ὑμῶν μὴ ἐπιβοηθούντων,
πρὸς ἐκείνους χωρῆσαι, διαπεπολεμήσεται αὐτοῖς ἀμαχεὶ
20 ἐκπολιορκηθέντων ἡμῶν [ὁ πόλεμος].

'Τούτων ἐγὼ ἡδίω μὲν ἂν εἶχον ὑμῖν ἕτερα ἐπιστέλλειν, 4
οὐ μέντοι χρησιμώτερά γε, εἰ δεῖ σαφῶς εἰδότας τὰ ἐνθάδε
βουλεύσασθαι. καὶ ἅμα τὰς φύσεις ἐπιστάμενος ὑμῶν,
βουλομένων μὲν τὰ ἥδιστα ἀκούειν, αἰτιωμένων δὲ ὕστερον,
25 ἤν τι ὑμῖν ἀπ' αὐτῶν μὴ ὅμοιον ἐκβῇ, ἀσφαλέστερον ἡγη-
σάμην τὸ ἀληθὲς δηλῶσαι. καὶ νῦν ὡς ἐφ' ἃ μὲν ἤλθομεν 15
τὸ πρῶτον καὶ τῶν στρατιωτῶν καὶ τῶν ἡγεμόνων ὑμῖν μὴ
μεμπτῶν γεγενημένων, οὕτω τὴν γνώμην ἔχετε· ἐπειδὴ δὲ
Σικελία τε ἅπασα ξυνίσταται καὶ ἐκ Πελοποννήσου ἄλλη

3 τὰ ἄλλα B   4 αὐτομολίας] αὐτονομίας Passow: alii alia
6 αὐτοὶ B : αὐτοῦ cett.   17 χωρία ἡμᾶς B   19 διαπολεμί-
σεται A C E F G M (corr. M¹)   20 ὁ πόλεμος. ut videtur, non legit
Schol., secl. Krüger (om. recc.)   22 post σαφῶς add. ὑμᾶς A C
E F G M   27 τὸ om. A E F M   28 post δὲ (om. B) add. ἢ C (G)

στρατιὰ προσδόκιμος αὐτοῖς, βουλεύεσθε ἤδη ὡς τῶν γ'
ἐνθάδε μηδὲ τοῖς παροῦσιν ἀνταρκούντων, ἀλλ' ἢ τούτους
μεταπέμπειν δέον ἢ ἄλλην στρατιὰν μὴ ἐλάσσω ἐπιπέμπειν
καὶ πεζὴν καὶ ναυτικὴν καὶ χρήματα μὴ ὀλίγα, ἐμοὶ δὲ
διάδοχόν τινα, ὡς ἀδύνατός εἰμι διὰ νόσον νεφρῖτιν παρα- 5
2 μένειν.　ἀξιῶ δ' ὑμῶν ξυγγνώμης τυγχάνειν· καὶ γὰρ ὅτ'
ἐρρώμην πολλὰ ἐν ἡγεμονίαις ὑμᾶς εὖ ἐποίησα.　ὅτι δὲ
μέλλετε, ἅμα τῷ ἦρι εὐθὺς καὶ μὴ ἐς ἀναβολὰς πράσσετε,
ὡς τῶν πολεμίων τὰ μὲν ἐν Σικελίᾳ δι' ὀλίγου ποριουμένων,
τὰ δ' ἐκ Πελοποννήσου σχολαίτερον μέν, ὅμως δ', ἢν μὴ 10
προσέχητε τὴν γνώμην, τὰ μὲν λήσουσιν ὑμᾶς, ὥσπερ καὶ
πρότερον, τὰ δὲ φθήσονται.'

16　Ἡ μὲν τοῦ Νικίου ἐπιστολὴ τοσαῦτα ἐδήλου, οἱ δὲ
Ἀθηναῖοι ἀκούσαντες αὐτῆς τὸν μὲν Νικίαν οὐ παρέλυσαν
τῆς ἀρχῆς, ἀλλ' αὐτῷ, ἕως ἂν ἕτεροι ξυνάρχοντες αἱρεθέντες 15
ἀφίκωνται, τῶν αὐτοῦ ἐκεῖ δύο προσείλοντο Μένανδρον
καὶ Εὐθύδημον, ὅπως μὴ μόνος ἐν ἀσθενείᾳ ταλαιπωροίη,
στρατιὰν δὲ ἄλλην ἐψηφίσαντο πέμπειν καὶ ναυτικὴν καὶ
2 πεζὴν Ἀθηναίων τε ἐκ καταλόγου καὶ τῶν ξυμμάχων.　καὶ
ξυνάρχοντας αὐτῷ εἵλοντο Δημοσθένη τε τὸν Ἀλκισθένους 20
καὶ Εὐρυμέδοντα τὸν Θουκλέους.　καὶ τὸν μὲν Εὐρυμέδοντα
εὐθὺς περὶ ἡλίου τροπὰς τὰς χειμερινὰς ἀποπέμπουσιν ἐς τὴν
Σικελίαν μετὰ δέκα νεῶν, ἄγοντα εἴκοσι ⟨καὶ ἑκατὸν⟩ τάλαντα
ἀργυρίου, καὶ ἅμα ἀγγελοῦντα τοῖς ἐκεῖ ὅτι ἥξει βοήθεια καὶ
17 ἐπιμέλεια αὐτῶν ἔσται· ὁ δὲ Δημοσθένης ὑπομένων παρε- 25
σκευάζετο τὸν ἔκπλουν ὡς ἅμα τῷ ἦρι ποιησόμενος, στρατιάν
τε ἐπαγγέλλων ἐς τοὺς ξυμμάχους καὶ χρήματα αὐτόθεν καὶ
2 ναῦς καὶ ὁπλίτας ἑτοιμάζων.　πέμπουσι δὲ καὶ περὶ τὴν
Πελοπόννησον οἱ Ἀθηναῖοι εἴκοσι ναῦς, ὅπως φυλάσσοιεν
μηδένα ἀπὸ Κορίνθου καὶ τῆς Πελοποννήσου ἐς τὴν Σικελίαν 30

1 αὐτοὶ βουλεύσασθε B　　　2 ἀνταρκούντων E F: αὐταρκούντων
cett.　　　τούτοις A B E M　　　4 πεζικὴν M　　　δὲ] τε B
18 ἐπεψηφίσαντο B　　prius καὶ om. B　　19 πεζὴν B: πεζικὴν
cett.　　23 καὶ ἑκατὸν add. recc.

περαιοῦσθαι. οἱ γὰρ Κορίνθιοι, ὡς αὐτοῖς οἱ πρέσβεις ἧκον 3
καὶ τὰ ἐν τῇ Σικελίᾳ βελτίω ἤγγελλον, νομίσαντες οὐκ
ἄκαιρον καὶ τὴν προτέραν πέμψιν τῶν νεῶν ποιήσασθαι,
πολλῷ μᾶλλον ἐπέρρωντο, καὶ ἐν ὁλκάσι παρεσκευάζοντο
5 αὐτοί τε ἀποστελοῦντες ὁπλίτας ἐς τὴν Σικελίαν καὶ ἐκ
τῆς ἄλλης Πελοποννήσου οἱ Λακεδαιμόνιοι τῷ αἰτῷ τρόπῳ
πέμψοντες· ναῦς τε οἱ Κορίνθιοι πέντε καὶ εἴκοσιν ἐπλήρουν, 4
ὅπως ναυμαχίας τε ἀποπειράσωσι πρὸς τὴν ἐν τῇ Ναυπάκτῳ
φυλακήν, καὶ τὰς ὁλκάδας αὐτῶν ἧσσον οἱ ἐν τῇ Ναυπάκτῳ
10 Ἀθηναῖοι κωλύοιεν ἀπαίρειν, πρὸς τὴν σφετέραν ἀντίταξιν
τῶν τριήρων τὴν φυλακὴν ποιούμενοι.

Παρεσκευάζοντο δὲ καὶ τὴν ἐς τὴν Ἀττικὴν ἐσβολὴν οἱ 18
Λακεδαιμόνιοι, ὥσπερ τε προυδέδοκτο αὐτοῖς καὶ τῶν Συρακοσίων καὶ Κορινθίων ἐναγόντων, ἐπειδὴ ἐπυνθάνοντο τὴν
15 ἀπὸ τῶν Ἀθηναίων βοήθειαν ἐς τὴν Σικελίαν, ὅπως δὴ
ἐσβολῆς γενομένης διακωλυθῇ. καὶ ὁ Ἀλκιβιάδης προσκείμενος ἐδίδασκε τὴν Δεκέλειαν τειχίζειν καὶ μὴ ἀνιέναι τὸν
πόλεμον. μάλιστα δὲ τοῖς Λακεδαιμονίοις ἐγεγένητό τις 2
ῥώμη, διότι τοὺς Ἀθηναίους ἐνόμιζον διπλοῦν τὸν πόλεμον
20 ἔχοντας, πρός τε σφᾶς καὶ Σικελιώτας, εὐκαθαιρετωτέρους
ἔσεσθαι, καὶ ὅτι τὰς σπονδὰς προτέρους λελυκέναι ἡγοῦντο
αὐτούς· ἐν γὰρ τῷ προτέρῳ πολέμῳ σφέτερον τὸ παρανό-
μημα μᾶλλον γενέσθαι, ὅτι τε ἐς Πλάταιαν ἦλθον Θηβαῖοι
ἐν σπονδαῖς, καὶ εἰρημένον ἐν ταῖς πρότερον ξυνθήκαις
25 ὅπλα μὴ ἐπιφέρειν, ἢν δίκας ἐθέλωσι διδόναι, αὐτοὶ οὐχ
ὑπήκουον ἐς δίκας προκαλουμένων τῶν Ἀθηναίων. καὶ διὰ
τοῦτο εἰκότως δυστυχεῖν τε ἐνόμιζον, καὶ ἐνεθυμοῦντο τήν
τε περὶ Πύλον ξυμφορὰν καὶ εἴ τις ἄλλη αὐτοῖς ἐγένετο.
ἐπειδὴ δὲ οἱ Ἀθηναῖοι ταῖς τριάκοντα ναυσὶν ἐξ Ἄργους 3

1 αὐτοῖς οἱ πρέσβεις B: οἵ τε πρέσβεις αὐτοῖς cett. 5 ἐς τὴν
Σικελίαν B: ἐν τῇ Σικελίᾳ cett. 7 πέμψαντες Λ Ε F M 14 post
καὶ add. τῶν C G 17 τὴν om. C G ἀνεῖναι B 23 τε
B: om. cett. 25 ἐθέλωσι recc.: θέλωσι codd. 28 ἐγένετο M:
ἐγεγένοιτο sic) B: γένοιτο cett. 29 ἐξ Ἄργους B: om. cett.

ὁρμώμενοι Ἐπιδαύρου τέ τι καὶ Πρασιῶν καὶ ἄλλα ἐδῄωσαν
καὶ ἐκ Πύλου ἅμα ἐλῃστεύοντο, καὶ ὁσάκις περί του δια-
φοραὶ γένοιντο τῶν κατὰ τὰς σπονδὰς ἀμφισβητουμένων,
ἐς δίκας προκαλουμένων τῶν Λακεδαιμονίων οὐκ ἤθελον
ἐπιτρέπειν, τότε δὴ οἱ Λακεδαιμόνιοι νομίσαντες τὸ παρα- 5
νόμημα, ὅπερ καὶ σφίσι πρότερον ἡμάρτητο, αὖθις ἐς τοὺς
Ἀθηναίους τὸ αὐτὸ περιεστάναι, πρόθυμοι ἦσαν ἐς τὸν
4 πόλεμον.   καὶ ἐν τῷ χειμῶνι τούτῳ σίδηρόν τε περιήγ-
γελλον κατὰ τοὺς ξυμμάχους καὶ τᾶλλα ἐργαλεῖα ἡτοίμαζον
ἐς τὸν ἐπιτειχισμόν, καὶ τοῖς ἐν τῇ Σικελίᾳ ἅμα ὡς ἀπο- 10
πέμψοντες ἐν ταῖς ὁλκάσιν ἐπικουρίαν αὐτοί τε ἐπόριζον καὶ
τοὺς ἄλλους Πελοποννησίους προσηνάγκαζον.   καὶ ὁ χειμὼν
ἐτελεύτα, καὶ ὄγδοον καὶ δέκατον ἔτος τῷ πολέμῳ ἐτελεύτα
τῷδε ὃν Θουκυδίδης ξυνέγραψεν.

19   Τοῦ δ' ἐπιγιγνομένου ἦρος εὐθὺς ἀρχομένου πρωίτατα δὴ 15
οἱ Λακεδαιμόνιοι καὶ οἱ ξύμμαχοι ἐς τὴν Ἀττικὴν ἐσέβαλον·
ἡγεῖτο δὲ Ἆγις ὁ Ἀρχιδάμου Λακεδαιμονίων βασιλεύς,
καὶ πρῶτον μὲν τῆς χώρας τὰ περὶ τὸ πεδίον ἐδῄωσαν,
ἔπειτα Δεκέλειαν ἐτείχιζον, κατὰ πόλεις διελόμενοι τὸ
2 ἔργον.   ἀπέχει δὲ ἡ Δεκέλεια σταδίους μάλιστα τῆς τῶν 20
Ἀθηναίων πόλεως εἴκοσι καὶ ἑκατόν, παραπλήσιον δὲ καὶ
οὐ πολλῷ πλέον καὶ ἀπὸ τῆς Βοιωτίας.   ἐπὶ δὲ τῷ πεδίῳ
καὶ τῆς χώρας τοῖς κρατίστοις ἐς τὸ κακουργεῖν ᾠκοδομεῖτο
3 τὸ τεῖχος, ἐπιφανὲς μέχρι τῆς τῶν Ἀθηναίων πόλεως.   καὶ
οἱ μὲν ἐν τῇ Ἀττικῇ Πελοποννήσιοι καὶ οἱ ξύμμαχοι ἐτεί- 25
χιζον, οἱ δ' ἐν τῇ Πελοποννήσῳ ἀπέστελλον περὶ τὸν αὐτὸν
χρόνον ταῖς ὁλκάσι τοὺς ὁπλίτας ἐς τὴν Σικελίαν, Λακεδαιμόνιοι μὲν τῶν τε Εἱλώτων ἐπιλεξάμενοι τοὺς βελτίστους
καὶ τῶν νεοδαμώδων, ξυναμφοτέρων ἐς ἑξακοσίους ὁπλίτας,

---

1 τέ B : om. cett.   2 ἐλῃστευον B   3 τὰς om. B
13 ἐτελεύτα τῷ πολέμῳ B   15 πρωιαίτατα B   δὴ οἱ om. B
21 alterum καὶ B et Schol. Patm. ad vi. 91 : om. cett.   22 ἀπὸ recc.
et Schol. Patm. : ἐπὶ codd.   28 βελτίους A E F M   29 τῶν B C :
om. cett.   ἐς B : om. cett.

καὶ Ἔκκριτον Σπαρτιάτην ἄρχοντα, Βοιωτοὶ δὲ τριακοσίους
ὁπλίτας, ὧν ἦρχον Ξένων τε καὶ Νίκων Θηβαῖοι καὶ Ἡγή-
σανδρος Θεσπιεύς.   οὗτοι μὲν οὖν ἐν τοῖς πρῶτοι ὁρμή- 4
σαντες ἀπὸ τοῦ Ταινάρου τῆς Λακωνικῆς ἐς τὸ πέλαγος
5 ἀφῆκαν· μετὰ δὲ τούτους Κορίνθιοι οὐ πολλῷ ὕστερον
πεντακοσίους ὁπλίτας, τοὺς μὲν ἐξ αὐτῆς Κορίνθου, τοὺς
δὲ προσμισθωσάμενοι Ἀρκάδων, καὶ ἄρχοντα Ἀλέξαρχον
Κορίνθιον προστάξαντες ἀπέπεμψαν.   ἀπέστειλαν δὲ καὶ
Σικυώνιοι διακοσίους ὁπλίτας ὁμοῦ τοῖς Κορινθίοις, ὧν ἦρχε
10 Σαργεὺς Σικυώνιος.   αἱ δὲ πέντε καὶ εἴκοσι νῆες τῶν 5
Κορινθίων αἱ τοῦ χειμῶνος πληρωθεῖσαι ἀνθώρμουν ταῖς ἐν
τῇ Ναυπάκτῳ εἴκοσιν Ἀττικαῖς, ἕωσπερ αὐτοῖς οὗτοι οἱ
ὁπλῖται ταῖς ὁλκάσιν ἀπὸ τῆς Πελοποννήσου ἀπῆραν· οὗπερ
ἕνεκα καὶ τὸ πρῶτον ἐπληρώθησαν, ὅπως μὴ οἱ Ἀθηναῖοι
15 πρὸς τὰς ὁλκάδας μᾶλλον ἢ πρὸς τὰς τριήρεις τὸν νοῦν
ἔχωσιν.

Ἐν δὲ τούτῳ καὶ οἱ Ἀθηναῖοι ἅμα τῆς Δεκελείας τῷ 20
τειχισμῷ καὶ τοῦ ἦρος εὐθὺς ἀρχομένου περί τε Πελοπόννησον ναῦς τριάκοντα ἔστειλαν καὶ Χαρικλέα τὸν Ἀπόλλο-
20 δώρου ἄρχοντα, ᾧ εἴρητο καὶ ἐς Ἄργος ἀφικομένῳ κατὰ τὸ
ξυμμαχικὸν παρακαλεῖν Ἀργείων [τε] ὁπλίτας ἐπὶ τὰς ναῦς,
καὶ τὸν Δημοσθένη ἐς τὴν Σικελίαν, ὥσπερ ἔμελλον, ἀπ- 2
έστελλον ἐξήκοντα μὲν ναυσὶν Ἀθηναίων καὶ πέντε Χίαις,
ὁπλίταις δὲ ἐκ καταλόγου Ἀθηναίων διακοσίοις καὶ χιλίοις,
25 καὶ νησιωτῶν ὅσοις ἑκασταχόθεν οἷόν τ᾽ ἦν πλείστοις χρήσασθαι, καὶ ἐκ τῶν ἄλλων ξυμμάχων τῶν ὑπηκόων, εἴ ποθέν
τι εἶχον ἐπιτήδειον ἐς τὸν πόλεμον, ξυμπορίσαντες.   εἴρητο
δ᾽ αὐτῷ πρῶτον μετὰ τοῦ Χαρικλέους ἅμα περιπλέοντα
ξυστρατεύεσθαι περὶ τὴν Λακωνικήν.   καὶ ὁ μὲν Δημο- 3
30 σθένης ἐς τὴν Αἴγιναν προσπλεύσας τοῦ στρατεύματός τε εἴ

3 πρῶτοι recc. : πρῶτοις codd.   6 ἐξ] ἀπ᾽ B   12 αὐτοῖς B : om.
cett.   14 πρῶτον B : πρότερον cett.   15 prius τὰς B : om. cett.
17 τῆς B : om. cett.   18 τε B : om. cett.   21 τε secl.
Reiske   29 ξυστρατεύσασθαι B   30 πλείσας A E F M

τι ὑπελέλειπτο περιέμενε καὶ τὸν Χαρικλέα τοὺς Ἀργείους
παραλαβεῖν.

21 Ἐν δὲ τῇ Σικελίᾳ ὑπὸ τοὺς αὐτοὺς χρόνους τούτου τοῦ
ἦρος καὶ ὁ Γύλιππος ἧκεν ἐς τὰς Συρακούσας, ἄγων ἀπὸ
τῶν πόλεων ὧν ἔπεισε στρατιὰν ὅσην ἑκασταχόθεν πλείστην 5
2 ἐδύνατο. καὶ ξυγκαλέσας τοὺς Συρακοσίους ἔφη χρῆναι
πληροῦν ναῦς ὡς δύνανται πλείστας καὶ ναυμαχίας ἀπό-
πειραν λαμβάνειν· ἐλπίζειν γὰρ ἀπ' αὐτοῦ τι ἔργον ἄξιον
3 τοῦ κινδύνου ἐς τὸν πόλεμον κατεργάσεσθαι. ξυνανέπειθε
δὲ καὶ ὁ Ἑρμοκράτης οὐχ ἥκιστα, τοῦ ταῖς ναυσὶ μὴ 10
ἀθυμεῖν ἐπιχειρῆσαι πρὸς τοὺς Ἀθηναίους, λέγων οὐδ' ἐκείνους πάτριον τὴν ἐμπειρίαν οὐδ' ἀίδιον τῆς θαλάσσης ἔχειν,
ἀλλ' ἠπειρώτας μᾶλλον τῶν Συρακοσίων ὄντας καὶ ἀναγ-
κασθέντας ὑπὸ Μήδων ναυτικοὺς γενέσθαι. καὶ πρὸς ἄνδρας
τολμηρούς, οἵους καὶ Ἀθηναίους, τοὺς ἀντιτολμῶντας χα- 15
λεπωτάτους ἂν [αὐτοῖς] φαίνεσθαι· ᾧ γὰρ ἐκεῖνοι τοὺς πέλας,
οὐ δυνάμει ἔστιν ὅτε προύχοντες, τῷ δὲ θράσει ἐπιχειροῦντες
καταφοβοῦσι, καὶ σφᾶς ἂν τὸ αὐτὸ ὁμοίως τοῖς ἐναντίοις
4 ὑποσχεῖν. καὶ Συρακοσίους εὖ εἰδέναι ἔφη τῷ τολμῆσαι
ἀπροσδοκήτως πρὸς τὸ Ἀθηναίων ναυτικὸν ἀντιστῆναι πλέον 20
τι διὰ τὸ τοιοῦτον ἐκπλαγέντων αὐτῶν περιγενησομένους ἢ
Ἀθηναίους τῇ ἐπιστήμῃ τὴν Συρακοσίων ἀπειρίαν βλάψοντας. ἰέναι οὖν ἐκέλευεν ἐς τὴν πεῖραν τοῦ ναυτικοῦ καὶ
μὴ ἀποκνεῖν.

5 Καὶ οἱ μὲν Συρακόσιοι, τοῦ τε Γυλίππου καὶ Ἑρμοκράτους 25
καὶ εἴ του ἄλλου πειθόντων, ὥρμηντό τε ἐς τὴν ναυμαχίαν
22 καὶ τὰς ναῦς ἐπλήρουν· ὁ δὲ Γύλιππος ἐπειδὴ παρεσκευάσατο

---

1 ὑπελέλειπτο Stahl : ὑπελείπετο codd.   9 κατεργάσεσθαι g :
κατεργάσασθαι codd.   ξυνανέπειθει B : ξυνέπειθε(ν) A E F M
10 τοῦ om. G M : αὐτοὺς Stahl   11 ἐπιχειρῆσαι recc., fort. legit
Schol. : ἐπιχειρήσειν codd.   ἐκείνους B : ἐκείνοις cett. (corr. G)
13 ἀλλ' om. B spatio relicto   τὼν om. B   16 ἂν B : om. cett.
αὐτοῖς secl. Badham   21 τι B : om. cett.   περιγενησομένους B :
περιεσομένους cett.   23 ἐκέλευεν om. C G   25 post alterum καὶ
add. τοῦ A C E F G M   27 παρεσκεύαστο recc.

τὸ ναυτικόν, ἀγαγὼν ὑπὸ νύκτα πᾶσαν τὴν στρατιὰν τὴν
πεζὴν αὐτὸς μὲν τοῖς ἐν τῷ Πλημμυρίῳ τείχεσι κατὰ γῆν
ἔμελλε προσβαλεῖν, αἱ δὲ τριήρεις τῶν Συρακοσίων ἅμα καὶ
ἀπὸ ξυνθήματος πέντε μὲν καὶ τριάκοντα ἐκ τοῦ μεγάλου
5 λιμένος ἐπέπλεον, αἱ δὲ πέντε καὶ τεσσαράκοντα ἐκ τοῦ
ἐλάσσονος, οὗ ἦν καὶ τὸ νεώριον αὐτοῖς, [καὶ] περιέπλεον
βουλόμενοι πρὸς τὰς ἐντὸς προσμεῖξαι καὶ ἅμα ἐπιπλεῖν τῷ
Πλημμυρίῳ, ὅπως οἱ Ἀθηναῖοι ἀμφοτέρωθεν θορυβῶνται.
οἱ δ' Ἀθηναῖοι διὰ τάχους ἀντιπληρώσαντες ἑξήκοντα ναῦς 2
10 ταῖς μὲν πέντε καὶ εἴκοσι πρὸς τὰς πέντε καὶ τριάκοντα τῶν
Συρακοσίων τὰς ἐν τῷ μεγάλῳ λιμένι ἐναυμάχουν, ταῖς δ'
ἐπιλοίποις ἀπήντων ἐπὶ τὰς ἐκ τοῦ νεωρίου περιπλεούσας.
καὶ εὐθὺς πρὸ τοῦ στόματος τοῦ μεγάλου λιμένος ἐναυμάχουν,
καὶ ἀντεῖχον ἀλλήλοις ἐπὶ πολύ, οἱ μὲν βιάσασθαι βουλό-
15 μενοι τὸν ἔσπλουν, οἱ δὲ κωλύειν. ἐν τούτῳ δ' ὁ Γύλιππος 23
τῶν ἐν τῷ Πλημμυρίῳ Ἀθηναίων πρὸς τὴν θάλασσαν ἐπι-
καταβάντων καὶ τῇ ναυμαχίᾳ τὴν γνώμην προσεχόντων
φθάνει προσπεσὼν ἅμα τῇ ἕῳ αἰφνιδίως τοῖς τείχεσι, καὶ
αἱρεῖ τὸ μέγιστον πρῶτον, ἔπειτα δὲ καὶ τὰ ἐλάσσω δύο,
20 οὐχ ὑπομεινάντων τῶν φυλάκων, ὡς εἶδον τὸ μέγιστον
ῥᾳδίως ληφθέν. καὶ ἐκ μὲν τοῦ πρώτου ἁλόντος χαλεπῶς οἱ 2
ἄνθρωποι, ὅσοι καὶ ἐς τὰ πλοῖα καὶ ὁλκάδα τινὰ κατέφυγον,
ἐς τὸ στρατόπεδον ἐξεκομίζοντο· τῶν γὰρ Συρακοσίων ταῖς
ἐν τῷ μεγάλῳ λιμένι ναυσὶ κρατούντων τῇ ναυμαχίᾳ ὑπὸ
25 τριήρους μιᾶς καὶ εὖ πλεούσης ἐπεδιώκοντο· ἐπειδὴ δὲ
τὰ δύο τειχίσματα ἡλίσκετο, ἐν τούτῳ καὶ οἱ Συρακόσιοι
ἐτύγχανον ἤδη νικώμενοι καὶ οἱ ἐξ αὐτῶν φεύγοντες ῥᾷον
παρέπλευσαν. αἱ γὰρ τῶν Συρακοσίων αἱ πρὸ τοῦ στόματος 3
νῆες ναυμαχοῦσαι βιασάμεναι τὰς τῶν Ἀθηναίων ναῦς οὐδενὶ
30 κόσμῳ ἐσέπλεον, καὶ ταραχθεῖσαι περὶ ἀλλήλας παρέδοσαν
τὴν νίκην τοῖς Ἀθηναίοις· ταύτας τε γὰρ ἔτρεψαν καὶ ὑφ'

2 πεζικὴν Μ   6 καὶ om. recc.   11 δ' om. Β   15 ἔκπλουν Β   23 ἐξεκομίζοντο ἐς τὸ στρατόπεδον C G   31 τε
om C

4 ὧν τὸ πρῶτον ἐνικῶντο ἐν τῷ λιμένι. καὶ ἔνδεκα μὲν ναῦς
τῶν Συρακοσίων κατέδυσαν, καὶ τοὺς πολλοὺς τῶν ἀνθρώπων
ἀπέκτειναν, πλὴν ὅσον ἐκ τριῶν νεῶν οὓς ἐζώγρησαν· τῶν
δὲ σφετέρων τρεῖς νῆες διεφθάρησαν. τὰ δὲ ναυάγια
ἀνελκύσαντες τῶν Συρακοσίων καὶ τροπαῖον ἐν τῷ νησιδίῳ 5
στήσαντες τῷ πρὸ τοῦ Πλημμυρίου, ἀνεχώρησαν ἐς τὸ ἑαυτῶν
στρατόπεδον.

24 Οἱ δὲ Συρακόσιοι κατὰ μὲν τὴν ναυμαχίαν οὕτως ἐπεπρά-
γεσαν, τὰ δ' ἐν τῷ Πλημμυρίῳ τείχη εἶχον, καὶ τροπαῖα
ἔστησαν αὐτῶν τρία. καὶ τὸ μὲν ἕτερον τοῖν δυοῖν τειχοῖν 10
τοῖν ὕστερον ληφθέντοιν κατέβαλον, τὰ δὲ δύο ἐπισκευά-
2 σαντες ἐφρούρουν. ἄνθρωποι δ' ἐν τῶν τειχῶν τῇ ἁλώσει
ἀπέθανον καὶ ἐζωγρήθησαν πολλοί, καὶ χρήματα πολλὰ τὰ
ξύμπαντα ἑάλω· ὥσπερ γὰρ ταμιείῳ χρωμένων τῶν Ἀθηναίων τοῖς τείχεσι πολλὰ μὲν ἐμπόρων χρήματα καὶ σῖτος 15
ἐνῆν, πολλὰ δὲ καὶ τῶν τριηράρχων, ἐπεὶ καὶ ἱστία τεσσαράκοντα τριήρων καὶ τἆλλα σκεύη ἐγκατελήφθη καὶ τριήρεις
3 ἀνειλκυσμέναι τρεῖς. μέγιστόν τε καὶ ἐν τοῖς πρῶτον
ἐκάκωσε τὸ στράτευμα τὸ τῶν Ἀθηναίων ἡ τοῦ Πλημμυρίου
λῆψις· οὐ γὰρ ἔτι οὐδ' οἱ ἔσπλοι ἀσφαλεῖς ἦσαν τῆς ἐπαγωγῆς 20
τῶν ἐπιτηδείων (οἱ γὰρ Συρακόσιοι ναυσὶν αὐτόθι ἐφορμοῦντες
ἐκώλυον, καὶ διὰ μάχης ἤδη ἐγίγνοντο αἱ ἐσκομιδαί), ἔς τε
τἆλλα κατάπληξιν παρέσχε καὶ ἀθυμίαν τῷ στρατεύματι.

25 Μετὰ δὲ τοῦτο ναῦς τε ἐκπέμπουσι δώδεκα οἱ Συρακόσιοι
καὶ Ἀγάθαρχον ἐπ' αὐτῶν Συρακόσιον ἄρχοντα. καὶ αὐτῶν 25
μία μὲν ἐς Πελοπόννησον ᾤχετο, πρέσβεις ἄγουσα οἵπερ τά
τε σφέτερα φράσουσιν ὅτι ἐν ἐλπίσιν εἰσὶ καὶ τὸν ἐκεῖ
πόλεμον ἔτι μᾶλλον ἐποτρυνοῦσι γίγνεσθαι· αἱ δ' ἔνδεκα
νῆες πρὸς τὴν Ἰταλίαν ἔπλευσαν, πυνθανόμεναι πλοῖα τοῖς

14 ὥσπερ recc. (cf. Joseph. A. J. xviii. 9. 1) : ἅτε B : ὥστε cett.
16 τῶν B : om. cett.   17 τὰ ἄλλα B   18 τε B : δὲ cett.
19 alterum τὸ om. B M   20 οἱ om. B   23 τἆλλα (sic) G : τὰ
ἄλλα cett.   παρεῖχε M   26 οἵπερ | ὥσπερ E : ὅπως B   27 τε
B : om. cett.   φράσουσιν c f g : φράσωσιν codd.   28 ἐποτρυνοῦσι
Dobree : ἐποτρύνωσι codd.   29 πυνθανόμεναι M

'Αθηναίοις γέμοντα χρημάτων προσπλεῖν. καὶ τῶν τε πλοίων 2
ἐπιτυχοῦσαι τὰ πολλὰ διέφθειραν καὶ ξύλα ναυπηγήσιμα ἐν
τῇ Καυλωνιάτιδι κατέκαυσαν, ἃ τοῖς Ἀθηναίοις ἑτοῖμα ἦν.
ἔς τε Λοκροὺς μετὰ ταῦτα ἦλθον, καὶ ὁρμουσῶν αὐτῶν κατ- 3
5 έπλευσε μία τῶν ὁλκάδων τῶν ἀπὸ Πελοποννήσου ἄγουσα
Θεσπιῶν ὁπλίτας· καὶ ἀναλαβόντες αὐτοὺς οἱ Συρακόσιοι 4
ἐπὶ τὰς ναῦς παρέπλεον ἐπ' οἴκου. φυλάξαντες δ' αὐτοὺς
οἱ Ἀθηναῖοι εἴκοσι ναυσὶ πρὸς τοῖς Μεγάροις μίαν μὲν ναῦν
λαμβάνουσιν αὐτοῖς ἀνδράσι, τὰς δ' ἄλλας οὐκ ἐδυνήθησαν,
10 ἀλλ' ἀποφεύγουσιν ἐς τὰς Συρακούσας.

'Εγένετο δὲ καὶ περὶ τῶν σταυρῶν ἀκροβολισμὸς ἐν τῷ 5
λιμένι, οὓς οἱ Συρακόσιοι πρὸ τῶν παλαιῶν νεωσοίκων κατέπηξαν ἐν τῇ θαλάσσῃ, ὅπως αὐτοῖς αἱ νῆες ἐντὸς ὁρμοῖεν
καὶ οἱ Ἀθηναῖοι ἐπιπλέοντες μὴ βλάπτοιεν ἐμβάλλοντες.
15 προσαγαγόντες γὰρ ναῦν μυριοφόρον αὐτοῖς οἱ Ἀθηναῖοι, 6
πύργους τε ξυλίνους ἔχουσαν καὶ παραφράγματα, ἔκ τε τῶν
ἀκάτων ὤνευον ἀναδούμενοι τοὺς σταυροὺς καὶ ἀνέκλων καὶ
κατακολυμβῶντες ἐξέπριον. οἱ δὲ Συρακόσιοι ἀπὸ τῶν
νεωσοίκων ἔβαλλον· οἱ δ' ἐκ τῆς ὁλκάδος ἀντέβαλλον, καὶ
20 τέλος τοὺς πολλοὺς τῶν σταυρῶν ἀνεῖλον οἱ Ἀθηναῖοι.
χαλεπωτάτη δ' ἦν τῆς σταυρώσεως ἡ κρύφιος· ἦσαν γὰρ 7
τῶν σταυρῶν οὓς οὐχ ὑπερέχοντας τῆς θαλάσσης κατέπηξαν,
ὥστε δεινὸν ἦν προσπλεῦσαι, μὴ οὐ προϊδών τις ὥσπερ περὶ
ἕρμα περιβάλῃ τὴν ναῦν. ἀλλὰ καὶ τούτους κολυμβηταὶ
25 δυόμενοι ἐξέπριον μισθοῦ. ὅμως δ' αὖθις οἱ Συρακόσιοι
ἐσταύρωσαν. πολλὰ δὲ καὶ ἄλλα πρὸς ἀλλήλους οἷον εἰκὸς 8
τῶν στρατοπέδων ἐγγὺς ὄντων καὶ ἀντιτεταγμένων ἐμηχα-
νῶντο καὶ ἀκροβολισμοῖς καὶ πείραις παντοίαις ἐχρῶντο.

Ἔπεμψαν δὲ καὶ ἐς τὰς πόλεις πρέσβεις οἱ Συρακόσιοι 9
30 Κορινθίων καὶ Ἀμπρακιωτῶν καὶ Λακεδαιμονίων, ἀγγέλλοντας
τήν τε τοῦ Πλημμυρίου λῆψιν καὶ τῆς ναυμαχίας πέρι ὡς

1 χρημάτων γέμοντα B   7 ἔπλεον B (γρ. παρενέπλεον)   11 σταυρωμάτων B   17 ἀνέκλων] ἀνεῖλον Widmann (fort. legit Schol.)

οὐ τῇ τῶν πολεμίων ἰσχύι μᾶλλον ἢ τῇ σφετέρᾳ ταραχῇ
ἡσσηθεῖεν, τά τε ἄλλα [αὖ] δηλώσοντας ὅτι ἐν ἐλπίσιν εἰσὶ
καὶ ἀξιώσοντας ξυμβοηθεῖν ἐπ' αὐτοὺς καὶ ναυσὶ καὶ πεζῷ,
ὡς καὶ τῶν Ἀθηναίων προσδοκίμων ὄντων ἄλλῃ στρατιᾷ
καί, ἢν φθάσωσιν αὐτοὶ πρότερον διαφθείραντες τὸ παρὸν 5
στράτευμα αὐτῶν, διαπεπολεμησόμενον. καὶ οἱ μὲν ἐν τῇ
Σικελίᾳ ταῦτα ἔπρασσον.

26 Ὁ δὲ Δημοσθένης, ἐπεὶ ξυνελέγη αὐτῷ τὸ στράτευμα ὃ
ἔδει ἔχοντα ἐς τὴν Σικελίαν βοηθεῖν, ἄρας ἐκ τῆς Αἰγίνης
καὶ πλεύσας πρὸς τὴν Πελοπόννησον τῷ τε Χαρικλεῖ καὶ 10
ταῖς τριάκοντα ναυσὶ τῶν Ἀθηναίων ξυμμίσγει, καὶ παρα-
λαβόντες τῶν Ἀργείων ὁπλίτας ἐπὶ τὰς ναῦς ἔπλεον ἐς τὴν
2 Λακωνικήν· καὶ πρῶτον μὲν τῆς Ἐπιδαύρου τι τῆς Λιμηρᾶς
ἐδῄωσαν, ἔπειτα σχόντες ἐς τὰ καταντικρὺ Κυθήρων τῆς
Λακωνικῆς, ἔνθα τὸ ἱερὸν τοῦ Ἀπόλλωνός ἐστι, τῆς τε γῆς 15
ἔστιν ἃ ἐδῄωσαν καὶ ἐτείχισαν ἰσθμῶδές τι χωρίον, ἵνα δὴ
οἵ τε Εἵλωτες τῶν Λακεδαιμονίων αὐτόσε αὐτομολῶσι καὶ
ἅμα λῃσταὶ ἐξ αὐτοῦ, ὥσπερ ἐκ τῆς Πύλου, ἁρπαγὴν ποιῶνται.
3 καὶ ὁ μὲν Δημοσθένης εὐθὺς ἐπειδὴ ξυγκατέλαβε τὸ χωρίον
παρέπλει ἐπὶ τῆς Κερκύρας, ὅπως καὶ τῶν ἐκεῖθεν ξυμμάχων 20
παραλαβὼν τὸν ἐς τὴν Σικελίαν πλοῦν ὅτι τάχιστα ποιῆται·
ὁ δὲ Χαρικλῆς περιμείνας ἕως τὸ χωρίον ἐξετείχισε καὶ
καταλιπὼν φυλακὴν αὐτοῦ ἀπεκομίζετο καὶ αὐτὸς ὕστερον
ταῖς τριάκοντα ναυσὶν ἐπ' οἴκου καὶ οἱ Ἀργεῖοι ἅμα.

27 Ἀφίκοντο δὲ καὶ Θρᾳκῶν τῶν μαχαιροφόρων τοῦ Διακοῦ 25
γένους ἐς τὰς Ἀθήνας πελτασταὶ ἐν τῷ αὐτῷ θέρει τούτῳ
τριακόσιοι καὶ χίλιοι, οὓς ἔδει τῷ Δημοσθένει ἐς τὴν Σικελίαν
2 ξυμπλεῖν. οἱ δ' Ἀθηναῖοι, ὡς ὕστεροι ἧκον, διενοοῦντο
αὐτοὺς πάλιν ὅθεν ἦλθον ἐς Θρᾴκην ἀποπέμπειν. τὸ γὰρ

2 αὖ om. BCM   6 διαπεπολεμησόμενον B : διαπολεμησόμενον
cett.   8 ἐπειδὴ B   18 ἅμα B : om. cett.   20 παρέπλει
recc. : ἐπιπαρέπλει B : ἐπέπλει cett.   ἐκεῖ B   22 ἕως B :
ὡς cett.   25 post καὶ add. τῶν ACEFM   τοῦ Διακοῦ] τῶν
Δακικοῦ C   26 τοῦ αὐτοῦ θέρους τούτου B   28 ὕστεροι Herwerden :
ὕστερον codd.

ἔχειν πρὸς τὸν ἐκ τῆς Δεκελείας πόλεμον αὐτοὺς πολυτελὲς
ἐφαίνετο· δραχμὴν γὰρ τῆς ἡμέρας ἕκαστος ἐλάμβανεν.
ἐπειδὴ γὰρ ἡ Δεκέλεια τὸ μὲν πρῶτον ὑπὸ πάσης τῆς 3
στρατιᾶς ἐν τῷ θέρει τούτῳ τειχισθεῖσα, ὕστερον δὲ φρουραῖς
5 ἀπὸ τῶν πόλεων κατὰ διαδοχὴν χρόνου ἐπιούσαις τῇ χώρᾳ
ἐπῳκεῖτο, πολλὰ ἔβλαπτε τοὺς Ἀθηναίους, καὶ ἐν τοῖς πρῶτον
χρημάτων τ' ὀλέθρῳ καὶ ἀνθρώπων φθορᾷ ἐκάκωσε τὰ πράγματα.   πρότερον μὲν γὰρ βραχεῖαι γιγνόμεναι αἱ ἐσβολαὶ 4
τὸν ἄλλον χρόνον τῆς γῆς ἀπολαύειν οὐκ ἐκώλυον· τότε δὲ
10 ξυνεχῶς ἐπικαθημένων, καὶ ὁτὲ μὲν καὶ πλεόνων ἐπιόντων,
ὁτὲ δ' ἐξ ἀνάγκης τῆς ἴσης φρουρᾶς καταθεούσης τε τὴν
χώραν καὶ λῃστείας ποιουμένης, βασιλέως τε παρόντος τοῦ
τῶν Λακεδαιμονίων Ἄγιδος, ὃς οὐκ ἐκ παρέργου τὸν πόλεμον
ἐποιεῖτο, μεγάλα οἱ Ἀθηναῖοι ἐβλάπτοντο.   τῆς τε γὰρ 5
15 χώρας ἁπάσης ἐστέρηντο, καὶ ἀνδραπόδων πλέον ἢ δύο
μυριάδες ηὐτομολήκεσαν, καὶ τούτων τὸ πολὺ μέρος χειροτέχναι, πρόβατά τε πάντα ἀπωλώλει καὶ ὑποζύγια ἵπποι τε,
ὁσημέραι ἐξελαυνόντων τῶν ἱππέων πρός τε τὴν Δεκέλειαν
καταδρομὰς ποιουμένων καὶ κατὰ τὴν χώραν φυλασσόντων,
20 οἱ μὲν ἀπεχωλοῦντο ἐν γῇ ἀποκρότῳ τε καὶ ξυνεχῶς ταλαι-
πωροῦντες, οἱ δ' ἐτιτρώσκοντο.   ἥ τε τῶν ἐπιτηδείων παρα- 28
κομιδὴ ἐκ τῆς Εὐβοίας, πρότερον ἐκ τοῦ Ὠρωποῦ κατὰ γῆν
διὰ τῆς Δεκελείας θᾶσσον οὖσα, περὶ Σούνιον κατὰ θάλασσαν
πολυτελὴς ἐγίγνετο· τῶν τε πάντων ὁμοίως ἐπακτῶν ἐδεῖτο
25 ἡ πόλις, καὶ ἀντὶ τοῦ πόλις εἶναι φρούριον κατέστη.   πρὸς 2
γὰρ τῇ ἐπάλξει τὴν μὲν ἡμέραν κατὰ διαδοχὴν οἱ Ἀθηναῖοι
φυλάσσοντες, τὴν δὲ νύκτα καὶ ξύμπαντες πλὴν τῶν ἱππέων,
οἱ μὲν ἐφ' ὅπλοις †ποιούμενοι†, οἱ δ' ἐπὶ τοῦ τείχους, καὶ
θέρους καὶ χειμῶνος ἐταλαιπωροῦντο.   μάλιστα δ' αὐτοὺς 3

2 ἕκαστος ἡμέρας ἐλάμβανον B   5 ἀπὸ B : ὑπὸ cett.   χρόνον B   6 πρῶτον recc. : πρώτοις codd.   11 post φρουρᾶς add.
καὶ B   16 τὸ B : om. cett.   17 ἀπωλώλει πάντα B
ὑποζύγια] ζεύγη B   22 γῆν recc. : γῆς codd.   23 θᾶσσον G M
28 ποιούμενοι] που B : fort. ἀναπαυόμενοι

ἐπίεζεν ὅτι δύο πολέμους ἅμα εἶχον, καὶ ἐς φιλονικίαν
καθέστασαν τοιαύτην ἣν πρὶν γενέσθαι ἠπίστησεν ἄν τις
ἀκούσας. τὸ γὰρ αὐτοὺς πολιορκουμένους ἐπιτειχισμῷ ὑπὸ
Πελοποννησίων μηδ᾽ ὡς ἀποστῆναι ἐκ Σικελίας, ἀλλ᾽ ἐκεῖ
Συρακούσας τῷ αὐτῷ τρόπῳ ἀντιπολιορκεῖν, πόλιν οὐδὲν 5
ἐλάσσω αὐτήν γε καθ᾽ αὑτὴν τῆς τῶν Ἀθηναίων, καὶ τὸν
παράλογον τοσοῦτον ποιῆσαι τοῖς Ἕλλησι τῆς δυνάμεως καὶ
τόλμης, ὅσον κατ᾽ ἀρχὰς τοῦ πολέμου οἱ μὲν ἐνιαυτόν, οἱ δὲ
δύο, οἱ δὲ τριῶν γε ἐτῶν οὐδεὶς πλείω χρόνον ἐνόμιζον
περιοίσειν αὐτούς, εἰ οἱ Πελοποννήσιοι ἐσβάλοιεν ἐς τὴν 10
χώραν, ὥστε ἔτει ἑπτακαιδεκάτῳ μετὰ τὴν πρώτην ἐσβολὴν
ἦλθον ἐς Σικελίαν ἤδη τῷ πολέμῳ κατὰ πάντα τετρυχωμένοι, καὶ πόλεμον οὐδὲν ἐλάσσω προσανείλοντο τοῦ πρότερον
4 ὑπάρχοντος ἐκ Πελοποννήσου. δι᾽ ἃ καὶ τότε ὑπό τε τῆς
Δεκελείας πολλὰ βλαπτούσης καὶ τῶν ἄλλων ἀναλωμάτων 15
μεγάλων προσπιπτόντων ἀδύνατοι ἐγένοντο τοῖς χρήμασιν.
καὶ τὴν εἰκοστὴν ὑπὸ τοῦτον τὸν χρόνον τῶν κατὰ θάλασσαν
ἀντὶ τοῦ φόρου τοῖς ὑπηκόοις ἐποίησαν, πλείω νομίζοντες
ἂν σφίσι χρήματα οὕτω προσιέναι. αἱ μὲν γὰρ δαπάναι
οὐχ ὁμοίως καὶ πρίν, ἀλλὰ πολλῷ μείζους καθέστασαν, ὅσῳ 20
καὶ μείζων ὁ πόλεμος ἦν· αἱ δὲ πρόσοδοι ἀπώλλυντο.

29 Τοὺς οὖν Θρᾷκας τοὺς τῷ Δημοσθένει ὑστερήσαντας διὰ
τὴν παροῦσαν ἀπορίαν τῶν χρημάτων οὐ βουλόμενοι δαπανᾶν
εὐθὺς ἀπέπεμπον, προστάξαντες κομίσαι αὐτοὺς Διειτρέφει,
καὶ εἰπόντες ἅμα ἐν τῷ παράπλῳ (ἐπορεύοντο γὰρ δι᾽ Εὐρίπου) 25
2 καὶ τοὺς πολεμίους, ἤν τι δύνηται, ἀπ᾽ αὐτῶν βλάψαι. ὁ δὲ
ἔς τε τὴν Τάναγραν ἀπεβίβασεν αὐτοὺς καὶ ἁρπαγήν τινα
ἐποιήσατο διὰ τάχους καὶ ἐκ Χαλκίδος τῆς Εὐβοίας ἀφ᾽
ἑσπέρας διέπλευσε τὸν Εὔριπον καὶ ἀποβιβάσας ἐς τὴν

3 γὰρ] γ᾽ Badham   5 οὐδὲν B : οὐδένα cett.   6 ἐλάσσω
recc. : ἐλάσσονα codd.   γε recc. : τε codd.   τῆς om. A C E F G M
τῶν om. B   11 ἑβδόμῳ καὶ δεκάτῳ Krüger   14 τε B : om.
cett.   17 ὑπὸ] κατὰ B   18 ἐπέθεσαν Badham   26 δύνηται B : δύνωνται cett.   27 τε B : om. cett.   Ταναγραίαν Classen
29 διαπλεύσας suprascr. διέπλευσεν B

Βοιωτίαν ἦγεν αὐτοὺς ἐπὶ Μυκαλησσόν. καὶ τὴν μὲν νύκτα 3
λαθὼν πρὸς τῷ Ἑρμαίῳ ηὐλίσατο (ἀπέχει δὲ τῆς Μυκαλησσοῦ
ἑκκαίδεκα μάλιστα σταδίους), ἅμα δὲ τῇ ἡμέρᾳ τῇ πόλει
προσέκειτο οὔσῃ οὐ μεγάλῃ, καὶ αἱρεῖ ἀφυλάκτοις τε ἐπι-
5 πεσὼν καὶ ἀπροσδοκήτοις μὴ ἄν ποτέ τινας σφίσιν ἀπὸ
θαλάσσης τοσοῦτον ἐπαναβάντας ἐπιθέσθαι, τοῦ τείχους
ἀσθενοῦς ὄντος καὶ ἔστιν ᾗ καὶ πεπτωκότος, τοῦ δὲ βραχέος
ᾠκοδομημένου, καὶ πυλῶν ἅμα διὰ τὴν ἄδειαν ἀνεῳγμένων.
ἐσπεσόντες δὲ οἱ Θρᾷκες ἐς τὴν Μυκαλησσὸν τάς τε οἰκίας 4
10 καὶ τὰ ἱερὰ ἐπόρθουν καὶ τοὺς ἀνθρώπους ἐφόνευον φειδόμενοι
οὔτε πρεσβυτέρας οὔτε νεωτέρας ἡλικίας, ἀλλὰ πάντας ἑξῆς,
ὅτῳ ἐντύχοιεν, καὶ παῖδας καὶ γυναῖκας κτείνοντες, καὶ
προσέτι καὶ ὑποζύγια καὶ ὅσα ἄλλα ἔμψυχα ἴδοιεν· τὸ γὰρ
γένος τὸ τῶν Θρᾳκῶν ὁμοῖα τοῖς μάλιστα τοῦ βαρβαρικοῦ,
15 ἐν ᾧ ἂν θαρσήσῃ, φονικώτατόν ἐστιν. καὶ τότε ἄλλη τε 5
ταραχὴ οὐκ ὀλίγη καὶ ἰδέα πᾶσα καθειστήκει ὀλέθρου, καὶ
ἐπιπεσόντες διδασκαλείῳ παίδων, ὅπερ μέγιστον ἦν αὐτόθι
καὶ ἄρτι ἔτυχον οἱ παῖδες ἐσεληλυθότες, κατέκοψαν πάντας·
καὶ ξυμφορὰ τῇ πόλει πάσῃ οὐδεμιᾶς ἥσσων μᾶλλον ἑτέρας
20 ἀδόκητός τε ἐπέπεσεν αὕτη καὶ δεινή. οἱ δὲ Θηβαῖοι αἰσθό- 30
μενοι ἐβοήθουν, καὶ καταλαβόντες προκεχωρηκότας ἤδη τοὺς
Θρᾷκας οὐ πολὺ τήν τε λείαν ἀφείλοντο καὶ αὐτοὺς φοβή-
σαντες καταδιώκουσιν ἐπὶ τὸν Εὔριπον καὶ τὴν θάλασσαν,
οὗ αὐτοῖς τὰ πλοῖα ἃ ἤγαγεν ὥρμει. καὶ ἀποκτείνουσιν 2
25 αὐτῶν ἐν τῇ ἐσβάσει τοὺς πλείστους οὔτε ἐπισταμένους νεῖν
τῶν τε ἐν τοῖς πλοίοις, ὡς ἑώρων τὰ ἐν τῇ γῇ, ὁρμισάντων
ἔξω τοξεύματος τὰ πλοῖα, ἐπεὶ ἔν γε τῇ ἄλλῃ ἀναχωρήσει
οὐκ ἀτόπως οἱ Θρᾷκες πρὸς τὸ τῶν Θηβαίων ἱππικόν, ὅπερ
πρῶτον προσέκειτο, προεκθέοντές τε καὶ ξυστρεφόμενοι ἐν

2 ηὐλίσατο B : ηὐλίζετο cett. γρ. B   4 οὐ B : om. cett. γρ. B
5 τινας B : τινα cett.   6 ἐπαναβάντα C G suprascr B   12 γυναῖκας καὶ παῖδας B   14 τὸ om. B   18 ἐσεληλυθότες οἱ παῖδες B
19 πάσῃ πόλει B   ἥσσον recc.   μᾶλλον ἑτέρας secl. Heilmann
26 τὰ ἐν τῇ γῇ] τὴν φυγὴν B   27 τοξεύματος recc. (extra ictum
sagittarum Valla) : τοῦ ζεύγματος (ζεύματος B G) codd.   29 τε B :
om. cett.

D

ἐπιχωρίῳ τάξει τὴν φυλακὴν ἐποιοῦντο, καὶ ὀλίγοι αὐτῶν
ἐν τούτῳ διεφθάρησαν. μέρος δέ τι καὶ ἐν τῇ πόλει αὐτῇ
δι' ἁρπαγὴν ἐγκαταληφθὲν ἀπώλετο. οἱ δὲ ξύμπαντες τῶν
Θρᾳκῶν πεντήκοντα καὶ διακόσιοι ἀπὸ τριακοσίων καὶ χιλίων
3 ἀπέθανον. διέφθειραν δὲ καὶ τῶν Θηβαίων καὶ τῶν ἄλλων 5
οἳ ξυνεβοήθησαν ἐς εἴκοσι μάλιστα ἱππέας τε καὶ ὁπλίτας
ὁμοῦ καὶ Θηβαίων τῶν βοιωταρχῶν Σκιρφώνδαν· τῶν δὲ
Μυκαλησσίων μέρος τι ἀπανηλώθη. τὰ μὲν κατὰ τὴν
Μυκαλησσὸν πάθει χρησαμένην οὐδενὸς ὡς ἐπὶ μεγέθει
τῶν κατὰ τὸν πόλεμον ἦσσον ὀλοφύρασθαι ἀξίῳ τοιαῦτα 10
ξυνέβη.

31   Ὁ δὲ Δημοσθένης τότε ἀποπλέων ἐπὶ τῆς Κερκύρας μετὰ
τὴν ἐκ τῆς Λακωνικῆς τείχισιν, ὁλκάδα ὁρμοῦσαν ἐν Φειᾷ
τῇ Ἠλείων εὑρών, ἐν ᾗ οἱ Κορίνθιοι ὁπλῖται ἐς τὴν Σικελίαν
ἔμελλον περαιοῦσθαι, αὐτὴν μὲν διαφθείρει, οἱ δ' ἄνδρες 15
2 ἀποφυγόντες ὕστερον λαβόντες ἄλλην ἔπλεον. καὶ μετὰ
τοῦτο ἀφικόμενος ὁ Δημοσθένης ἐς τὴν Ζάκυνθον καὶ Κεφαλληνίαν ὁπλίτας τε παρέλαβε καὶ ἐκ τῆς Ναυπάκτου τῶν
Μεσσηνίων μετεπέμψατο καὶ ἐς τὴν ἀντιπέρας ἤπειρον τῆς
Ἀκαρνανίας διέβη, ἐς Ἀλύζιάν τε καὶ Ἀνακτόριον, ὃ αὐτοὶ 20
3 εἶχον. ὄντι δ' αὐτῷ περὶ ταῦτα ὁ Εὐρυμέδων ἀπαντᾷ ἐκ τῆς
Σικελίας ἀποπλέων, ὃς τότε τοῦ χειμῶνος τὰ χρήματα ἄγων
τῇ στρατιᾷ ἀπεπέμφθη, καὶ ἀγγέλλει τά τε ἄλλα καὶ ὅτι
πύθοιτο κατὰ πλοῦν ἤδη ὢν τὸ Πλημμύριον ὑπὸ τῶν Συρα-
4 κοσίων ἑαλωκός. ἀφικνεῖται δὲ καὶ Κόνων παρ' αὐτούς, ὃς 25
ἦρχε Ναυπάκτου, ἀγγέλλων ὅτι αἱ πέντε καὶ εἴκοσι νῆες
τῶν Κορινθίων αἱ σφίσιν ἀνθορμοῦσαι οὔτε καταλύουσι τὸν
πόλεμον ναυμαχεῖν τε μέλλουσιν· πέμπειν οὖν ἐκέλευεν
αὐτοὺς ναῦς, ὡς οὐχ ἱκανὰς οὔσας δυοῖν δεούσας εἴκοσι τὰς

3 ἐγκαταλειφθὲν recc.   τῶν Θρᾳκῶν secl. Herwerden   6 τε
om. B M   9 χρησαμένην Reiske : χρησαμένων codd.   12 ἐπὶ
B : ἐκ cett.   14 εὑρών B : om. cett.   17 τὴν] τε B   24 post
Συρακοσίων add. ἤδη B   27 τὸν πόλεμον secl. Madvig   29 οὔσας]
εἶναι B (γρ. οὔσας)   δεούσας B : δεούσαις vel δὲ οὔσαις cett. γρ. B   τὰς
B : ταῖς cett. γρ. B

ἑαυτῶ·, πρὸς τὰς ἐκείνων πέντε καὶ εἴκοσι ναυμαχεῖν. τῷ 5
μὲν οὖν Κόνωνι δέκα ναῦς ὁ Δημοσθένης καὶ ὁ Εὐρυμέδων
τὰς ἄριστα σφίσι πλεούσας ἀφ' ὧν αὐτοὶ εἶχον ξυμπέμπουσι
πρὸς τὰς ἐν τῇ Ναυπάκτῳ· αὐτοὶ δὲ τὰ περὶ τῆς στρατιᾶς
5 τὸν ξύλλογον ἡτοιμάζοντο, Εὐρυμέδων μὲν ἐς τὴν Κέρκυραν
πλεύσας καὶ πέντε καὶ δέκα τε ναῦς πληροῦν κελεύσας αὐτοὺς
καὶ ὁπλίτας καταλεγόμενος (ξυνῆρχε γὰρ ἤδη Δημοσθένει
ἀποτραπόμενος, ὥσπερ καὶ ᾑρέθη), Δημοσθένης δ' ἐκ τῶν
περὶ τὴν Ἀκαρνανίαν χωρίων σφενδονήτας τε καὶ ἀκοντιστὰς
10 ξυναγείρων.

Οἱ δ' ἐκ τῶν Συρακουσῶν τότε μετὰ τὴν τοῦ Πλημμυρίου 32
ἅλωσιν πρέσβεις οἰχόμενοι ἐς τὰς πόλεις ἐπειδὴ ἔπεισάν
τε καὶ ξυναγείραντες ἔμελλον ἄξειν τὸν στρατόν, ὁ Νικίας
προπυθόμενος πέμπει ἐς τῶν Σικελῶν τοὺς τὴν δίοδον ἔχοντας
15 καὶ σφίσι ξυμμάχους, Κεντόριπάς τε καὶ Ἁλικυαίους καὶ
ἄλλους, ὅπως μὴ διαφρήσωσι τοὺς πολεμίους, ἀλλὰ ξυστρα-
φέντες κωλύσωσι διελθεῖν· ἄλλῃ γὰρ αὐτοὺς οὐδὲ πειράσειν·
Ἀκραγαντῖνοι γὰρ οὐκ ἐδίδοσαν διὰ τῆς ἑαυτῶν ὁδόν.
πορευομένων δ' ἤδη τῶν Σικελιωτῶν οἱ Σικελοί, καθάπερ 2
20 ἐδέοντο οἱ Ἀθηναῖοι, ἐνέδραν τινὰ τριχῇ ποιησάμενοι, ἀφυλάκτοις τε καὶ ἐξαίφνης ἐπιγενόμενοι διέφθειραν ἐς ὀκτακο-
σίους μάλιστα καὶ τοὺς πρέσβεις πλὴν ἑνὸς τοῦ Κορινθίου
πάντας· οὗτος δὲ τοὺς διαφυγόντας ἐς πεντακοσίους καὶ
χιλίους ἐκόμισεν ἐς τὰς Συρακούσας. καὶ περὶ τὰς αὐτὰς 33
25 ἡμέρας καὶ οἱ Καμαριναῖοι ἀφικνοῦνται αὐτοῖς βοηθοῦντες,
πεντακόσιοι μὲν ὁπλῖται, τριακόσιοι δὲ ἀκοντισταὶ καὶ τοξόται
τριακόσιοι. ἔπεμψαν δὲ καὶ οἱ Γελῷοι ναυτικόν τε ἐς πέντε
ναῦς καὶ ἀκοντιστὰς τετρακοσίους καὶ ἱππέας διακοσίους.
σχεδὸν γάρ τι ἤδη πᾶσα ἡ Σικελία πλὴν Ἀκραγαντίνων 2
30 (οὗτοι δ' οὐδὲ μεθ' ἑτέρων ἦσαν), οἱ δ' ἄλλοι ἐπὶ τοὺς

6 τε om. B. habet γρ. B   11 τοῦ om. A E F M   14 πυθό-
μενος B   15 σφίσι B : om. cett.   16 διαφρήσωσι (ita in M scriptum
ratus) Stahl : διαφήσωσι C M : διαφήσουσι cett.   18 α τῶν B
20 τινὰ τριχῇ] τριχῇ B : τινὰ cett. γρ. B   29 ἅπασα B

Ἀθηναίους μετὰ τῶν Συρακοσίων οἱ πρότερον περιορώμενοι ξυστάντες ἐβοήθουν.

3   Καὶ οἱ μὲν Συρακόσιοι, ὡς αὐτοῖς τὸ ἐν τοῖς Σικελοῖς πάθος ἐγένετο, ἐπέσχον τὸ εὐθέως τοῖς Ἀθηναίοις ἐπιχειρεῖν· ὁ δὲ Δημοσθένης καὶ Εὐρυμέδων, ἑτοίμης ἤδη τῆς στρατιᾶς 5 οὔσης ἔκ τε τῆς Κερκύρας καὶ ἀπὸ τῆς ἠπείρου, ἐπεραιώθησαν 4 ξυμπάσῃ τῇ στρατιᾷ τὸν Ἰόνιον ἐπ' ἄκραν Ἰαπυγίαν· καὶ ὁρμηθέντες αὐτόθεν κατίσχουσιν ἐς τὰς Χοιράδας νήσους Ἰαπυγίας, καὶ ἀκοντιστάς τέ τινας τῶν Ἰαπύγων πεντήκοντα καὶ ἑκατὸν τοῦ Μεσσαπίου ἔθνους ἀναβιβάζονται ἐπὶ τὰς 10 ναῦς, καὶ τῷ Ἄρτᾳ, ὅσπερ καὶ τοὺς ἀκοντιστὰς δυνάστης ὢν παρέσχετο αὐτοῖς, ἀνανεωσάμενοί τινα παλαιὰν φιλίαν 5 ἀφικνοῦνται ἐς Μεταπόντιον τῆς Ἰταλίας.   καὶ τοὺς Μεταποντίους πείσαντες κατὰ τὸ ξυμμαχικὸν ἀκοντιστάς τε ξυμπέμπειν τριακοσίους καὶ τριήρεις δύο καὶ ἀναλαβόντες 15 ταῦτα παρέπλευσαν ἐς Θουρίαν.   καὶ καταλαμβάνουσι νεωστὶ 6 στάσει τοὺς τῶν Ἀθηναίων ἐναντίους ἐκπεπτωκότας· καὶ βουλόμενοι τὴν στρατιὰν αὐτόθι πᾶσαν ἀθροίσαντες εἴ τις ὑπελέλειπτο ἐξετάσαι, καὶ τοὺς Θουρίους πεῖσαι σφίσι ξυστρατεύειν τε ὡς προθυμότατα καί, ἐπειδήπερ ἐν τούτῳ 20 τύχης εἰσί, τοὺς αὐτοὺς ἐχθροὺς καὶ φίλους τοῖς Ἀθηναίοις νομίζειν, περιέμενον ἐν τῇ Θουρίᾳ καὶ ἔπρασσον ταῦτα.

34   Οἱ δὲ Πελοποννήσιοι περὶ τὸν αὐτὸν χρόνον τοῦτον οἱ ἐν ταῖς πέντε καὶ εἴκοσι ναυσίν, οἵπερ τῶν ὁλκάδων ἕνεκα τῆς 25 ἐς Σικελίαν κομιδῆς ἀνθώρμουν πρὸς τὰς ἐν Ναυπάκτῳ ναῦς, παρασκευασάμενοι ὡς ἐπὶ ναυμαχίᾳ καὶ προσπληρώσαντες ἔτι ναῦς ὥστε ὀλίγῳ ἐλάσσους εἶναι αὐτοῖς τῶν Ἀττικῶν νεῶν, ὁρμίζονται κατὰ Ἐρινεὸν τῆς Ἀχαίας ἐν τῇ Ῥυπικῇ. 2 καὶ αὐτοῖς τοῦ χωρίου μηνοειδοῦς ὄντος ἐφ' ᾧ ὥρμουν, ὁ μὲν 30

4 ἐπέσχον τὸ C M : ἐπέσχοντο cett.   6 τε B : om. cett.
11 ὅσπερ A E F M   12 παρέσχεν A B E F M   16 ταῦτα] αὑτὰς B
24 post Πελοποννήσιοι add. καὶ οἱ A C E F G M   25 οἵπερ] οἱ περὶ B
30 ἐφ'] ἐν B

πεζὸς ἑκατέρωθεν προσβεβοηθηκὼς τῶν τε Κορινθίων καὶ
τῶν αὐτόθεν ξυμμάχων ἐπὶ ταῖς προανεχούσαις ἄκραις παρε-
τέτακτο, αἱ δὲ νῆες τὸ μεταξὺ εἶχον ἐμφάρξασαι· ἦρχε δὲ
τοῦ ναυτικοῦ Πολυάνθης Κορίνθιος.   οἱ δ' Ἀθηναῖοι ἐκ τῆς 3
5 Ναυπάκτου τριάκοντα ναυσὶ καὶ τρισίν (ἦρχε δὲ αὐτῶν
Δίφιλος) ἐπέπλευσαν αὐτοῖς.   καὶ οἱ Κορίνθιοι τὸ μὲν 4
πρῶτον ἡσύχαζον, ἔπειτα ἀρθέντος αὐτοῖς τοῦ σημείου, ἐπεὶ
καιρὸς ἐδόκει εἶναι, ὥρμησαν ἐπὶ τοὺς Ἀθηναίους καὶ ἐναυμάχουν.   καὶ χρόνον ἀντεῖχον πολὺν ἀλλήλοις.   καὶ τῶν 5
10 μὲν Κορινθίων τρεῖς νῆες διαφθείρονται, τῶν δ' Ἀθηναίων
κατέδυ μὲν οὐδεμία ἁπλῶς, ἑπτὰ δέ τινες ἄπλοι ἐγένοντο
ἀντίπρῳροι ἐμβαλλόμεναι καὶ ἀναρραγεῖσαι τὰς παρεξειρεσίας
ὑπὸ τῶν Κορινθίων νεῶν ἐπ' αὐτὸ τοῦτο παχυτέρας τὰς
ἐπωτίδας ἐχουσῶν.   ναυμαχήσαντες δὲ ἀντίπαλα μὲν καὶ 6
15 ὡς αὐτοὺς ἑκατέρους ἀξιοῦν νικᾶν, ὅμως δὲ τῶν ναυαγίων
κρατησάντων τῶν Ἀθηναίων διά τε τὴν τοῦ ἀνέμου ἄπωσιν
αὐτῶν ἐς τὸ πέλαγος καὶ διὰ τὴν τῶν Κορινθίων οὐκέτι
ἐπαναγωγήν, διεκρίθησαν ἀπ' ἀλλήλων, καὶ δίωξις οὐδεμία
ἐγένετο, οὐδ' ἄνδρες οὐδετέρων ἑάλωσαν· οἱ μὲν γὰρ Κορίνθιοι
20 καὶ Πελοποννήσιοι πρὸς τῇ γῇ ναυμαχοῦντες ῥᾳδίως διεσῴ-
ζοντο, τῶν δὲ Ἀθηναίων οὐδεμία κατέδυ ναῦς.   ἀποπλευ- 7
σάντων δὲ τῶν Ἀθηναίων ἐς τὴν Ναύπακτον οἱ Κορίνθιοι
εὐθὺς τροπαῖον ἔστησαν ὡς νικῶντες, ὅτι πλείους τῶν
ἐναντίων ναῦς ἄπλους ἐποίησαν καὶ νομίσαντες αὐτοὶ οὐχ
25 ἡσσᾶσθαι δι' ὅπερ οὐδ' οἱ ἕτεροι νικᾶν· οἵ τε γὰρ Κορίνθιοι
ἡγήσαντο κρατεῖν εἰ μὴ καὶ πολὺ ἐκρατοῦντο, οἵ τ' Ἀθηναῖοι
ἐνόμιζον ἡσσᾶσθαι ὅτι οὐ πολὺ ἐνίκων.   ἀποπλευσάντων δὲ 8
τῶν Πελοποννησίων καὶ τοῦ πεζοῦ διαλυθέντος οἱ Ἀθηναῖοι
ἔστησαν τροπαῖον καὶ αὐτοὶ ἐν τῇ Ἀχαΐᾳ ὡς νικήσαντες,

1 προσβεβοηθηκὼς B : προσβεβοηθηκότες cett. γρ. B   2 προανεχούσαις B : ἀνεχούσαις cett.   13 αὐτῷ τούτῳ A B   18 ἐπαναγωγήν
M : ἐπαναγωγωγήν B : ἐπαγωγήν cett.   20 ῥᾳδίως B : καὶ cett.
24 αὐτοὶ Stahl : αὐτὸ B : δι' αὐτὸ cett.   26 καὶ B : om. cett.   πολλοὶ
B   27 ὅτι οὐ B : εἰ μὴ cett. γρ. B

ἀπέχον τοῦ Ἐρινεοῦ, ἐν ᾧ οἱ Κορίνθιοι ὥρμουν, ὡς εἴκοσι σταδίους. καὶ ἡ μὲν ναυμαχία οὕτως ἐτελεύτα.

35 Ὁ δὲ Δημοσθένης καὶ Εὐρυμέδων, ἐπειδὴ ξυστρατεύειν αὐτοῖς οἱ Θούριοι παρεσκευάσθησαν ἑπτακοσίοις μὲν ὁπλί- ταις, τριακοσίοις δὲ ἀκοντισταῖς, τὰς μὲν ναῦς παραπλεῖν 5 ἐκέλευον ἐπὶ τῆς Κροτωνιάτιδος, αὐτοὶ δὲ τὸν πεζὸν πάντα ἐξετάσαντες πρῶτον ἐπὶ τῷ Συβάρει ποταμῷ ἦγον διὰ τῆς 2 Θουριάδος γῆς. καὶ ὡς ἐγένοντο ἐπὶ τῷ Ὑλίᾳ ποταμῷ καὶ αὐτοῖς οἱ Κροτωνιᾶται προσπέμψαντες εἶπον οὐκ ἂν σφίσι βουλομένοις εἶναι διὰ τῆς γῆς σφῶν τὸν στρατὸν 10 ἰέναι, ἐπικαταβάντες ηὐλίσαντο πρὸς τὴν θάλασσαν καὶ τὴν ἐκβολὴν τοῦ Ὑλίου· καὶ αἱ νῆες αὐτοῖς ἐς τὸ αὐτὸ ἀπήντων. τῇ δ' ὑστεραίᾳ ἀναβιβασάμενοι παρέπλεον, ἴσχοντες πρὸς ταῖς πόλεσι πλὴν Λοκρῶν, ἕως ἀφίκοντο ἐπὶ Πέτραν τῆς Ῥηγίνης. 15

36 Οἱ δὲ Συρακόσιοι ἐν τούτῳ πυνθανόμενοι αὐτῶν τὸν ἐπίπλουν αὖθις ταῖς ναυσὶν ἀποπειρᾶσαι ἐβούλοντο καὶ τῇ ἄλλῃ παρασκευῇ τοῦ πεζοῦ, ἥνπερ ἐπ' αὐτὸ τοῦτο πρὶν 2 ἐλθεῖν αὐτοὺς φθάσαι βουλόμενοι ξυνέλεγον. παρεσκευά- σαντο δὲ τό τε ἄλλο ναυτικὸν ὡς ἐκ τῆς προτέρας ναυμαχίας 20 τι πλέον ἐνεῖδον σχήσοντες, καὶ τὰς πρῴρας τῶν νεῶν ξυντεμόντες ἐς ἔλασσον στεριφωτέρας ἐποίησαν, καὶ τὰς ἐπωτίδας ἐπέθεσαν ταῖς πρῴραις παχείας, καὶ ἀντηρίδας ἀπ' αὐτῶν ὑπέτειναν πρὸς τοὺς τοίχους ὡς ἐπὶ ἓξ πήχεις ἐντός τε καὶ ἔξωθεν· ᾧπερ τρόπῳ καὶ οἱ Κορίνθιοι πρὸς 25 τὰς ἐν τῇ Ναυπάκτῳ ναῦς ἐπισκευασάμενοι πρῴραθεν ἐναυ- 3 μάχουν. ἐνόμισαν γὰρ οἱ Συρακόσιοι πρὸς τὰς τῶν Ἀθη- ναίων ναῦς οὐχ ὁμοίως ἀντινεναυπηγημένας, ἀλλὰ λεπτὰ τὰ πρῴραθεν ἐχούσας διὰ τὸ μὴ ἀντιπρῴροις μᾶλλον αὐτοὺς ἢ ἐκ περίπλου ταῖς ἐμβολαῖς χρῆσθαι, οὐκ ἔλασσον σχήσειν, 30 καὶ τὴν ἐν τῷ μεγάλῳ λιμένι ναυμαχίαν, οὐκ ἐν πολλῷ

πολλαῖς ναυσὶν οὖσαν, πρὸς ἑαυτῶν ἔσεσθαι· ἀντιπρώροις
γὰρ ταῖς ἐμβολαῖς χρώμενοι ἀναρρήξειν τὰ πρώραθεν αὐτοῖς,
στερίφοις καὶ παχέσι πρὸς κοῖλα καὶ ἀσθενῆ παίοντες
τοῖς ἐμβόλοις. τοῖς δὲ Ἀθηναίοις οὐκ ἔσεσθαι σφῶν ἐν 4
5 στενοχωρίᾳ οὔτε περίπλουν οὔτε διέκπλουν, ᾧπερ τῆς
τέχνης μάλιστα ἐπίστευον· αὐτοὶ γὰρ κατὰ τὸ δυνατὸν τὸ
μὲν οὐ δώσειν διεκπλεῖν, τὸ δὲ τὴν στενοχωρίαν κωλύσειν
ὥστε μὴ περιπλεῖν. τῇ τε πρότερον ἀμαθίᾳ τῶν κυβερνη- 5
τῶν δοκούσῃ εἶναι, τὸ ἀντίπρωρον ξυγκροῦσαι, μάλιστ' ἂν
10 αὐτοὶ χρήσασθαι· πλεῖστον γὰρ ἐν αὐτῷ σχήσειν· τὴν γὰρ
ἀνάκρουσιν οὐκ ἔσεσθαι τοῖς Ἀθηναίοις ἐξωθουμένοις ἄλλοσε
ἢ ἐς τὴν γῆν, καὶ ταύτην δι' ὀλίγου καὶ ἐς ὀλίγον, κατ'
αὐτὸ τὸ στρατόπεδον τὸ ἑαυτῶν· τοῦ δ' ἄλλου λιμένος αὐτοὶ
κρατήσειν, καὶ ξυμφερομένους αὐτούς, ἤν πῃ βιάζωνται, ἐς 6
15 ὀλίγον τε καὶ πάντας ἐς τὸ αὐτό, προσπίπτοντας ἀλλήλοις
ταράξεσθαι (ὅπερ καὶ ἔβλαπτε μάλιστα τοὺς Ἀθηναίους
ἐν ἁπάσαις ταῖς ναυμαχίαις, οὐκ οὔσης αὐτοῖς ἐς πάντα
τὸν λιμένα τῆς ἀνακρούσεως, ὥσπερ τοῖς Συρακοσίοις)·
περιπλεῦσαι δὲ ἐς τὴν εὐρυχωρίαν, σφῶν ἐχόντων τὴν
20 ἐπίπλευσιν ἀπὸ τοῦ πελάγους τε καὶ ἀνάκρουσιν, οὐ δυνή-
σεσθαι αὐτούς, ἄλλως τε καὶ τοῦ Πλημμυρίου πολεμίου τε
αὐτοῖς ἐσομένου καὶ τοῦ στόματος οὐ μεγάλου ὄντος τοῦ
λιμένος.

Τοιαῦτα οἱ Συρακόσιοι πρὸς τὴν ἑαυτῶν ἐπιστήμην τε 37
25 καὶ δύναμιν ἐπινοήσαντες καὶ ἅμα τεθαρσηκότες μᾶλλον
ἤδη ἀπὸ τῆς προτέρας ναυμαχίας, ἐπεχείρουν τῷ τε πεζῷ
ἅμα καὶ ταῖς ναυσίν. καὶ τὸν μὲν πεζὸν ὀλίγῳ πρότερον 2
τὸν ἐκ τῆς πόλεως Γύλιππος προεξαγαγὼν προσῆγε τῷ
τείχει τῶν Ἀθηναίων, καθ' ὅσον πρὸς τὴν πόλιν αὐτοῦ

1 ἀντιπρώροις Reiske : ἀντίπρωροι codd.   3 παίοντες B : παρέχοντες cett.   4 δὲ om. B   7 διέκπλουν suprascr. διεκπλεῖν B
9 τὸ] τὸν A F γρ. B : τῷ Dobree   ξυγκροῦσαι B : ξυγκρούσει vel
συγκρούσει cett. γρ. B   μάλιστ' ἂν αὐτοί! μάλιστα αὐτοῖς B (γρ.
μάλιστ' ἂν αὐτοί)   10 χρήσεσθαι B (γρ χρήσασθαι)   15 πάντα B
18 τῆς B : om. cett.   κρούσεως A C E (G) M   24 ταῦτα B

ἑώρα· καὶ οἱ ἀπὸ τοῦ Ὀλυμπιείου, οἵ τε ὁπλῖται ὅσοι ἐκεῖ
ἦσαν καὶ οἱ ἱππῆς καὶ ἡ γυμνητεία τῶν Συρακοσίων ἐκ
τοῦ ἐπὶ θάτερα προσῄει τῷ τείχει· αἱ δὲ νῆες μετὰ τοῦτο
3 εὐθὺς ἐπεξέπλεον τῶν Συρακοσίων καὶ ξυμμάχων. καὶ οἱ
Ἀθηναῖοι τὸ πρῶτον αὐτοὺς οἰόμενοι τῷ πεζῷ μόνῳ πειρά- 5
σειν, ὁρῶντες δὲ καὶ τὰς ναῦς ἐπιφερομένας ἄφνω, ἐθορυ-
βοῦντο, καὶ οἱ μὲν ἐπὶ τὰ τείχη καὶ πρὸ τῶν τειχῶν τοῖς
προσιοῦσιν ἀντιπαρετάσσοντο, οἱ δὲ πρὸς τοὺς ἀπὸ τοῦ
Ὀλυμπιείου καὶ τῶν ἔξω κατὰ τάχος χωροῦντας ἱππέας τε
πολλοὺς καὶ ἀκοντιστὰς ἀντεπεξῇσαν, ἄλλοι δὲ τὰς ναῦς 10
ἐπλήρουν καὶ ἅμα ἐπὶ τὸν αἰγιαλὸν παρεβοήθουν, καὶ ἐπειδὴ
πλήρεις ἦσαν, ἀντανῆγον πέντε καὶ ἑβδομήκοντα ναῦς·
38 καὶ τῶν Συρακοσίων ἦσαν ὀγδοήκοντα μάλιστα. τῆς δὲ
ἡμέρας ἐπὶ πολὺ προσπλέοντες καὶ ἀνακρουόμενοι καὶ
πειράσαντες ἀλλήλων καὶ οὐδέτεροι δυνάμενοι ἄξιόν τι 15
λόγου παραλαβεῖν, εἰ μὴ ναῦν μίαν ἢ δύο τῶν Ἀθηναίων
οἱ Συρακόσιοι καταδύσαντες, διεκρίθησαν· καὶ ὁ πεζὸς ἅμα
ἀπὸ τῶν τειχῶν ἀπῆλθεν.

2   Τῇ δ' ὑστεραίᾳ οἱ μὲν Συρακόσιοι ἡσύχαζον, οὐδὲν
δηλοῦντες ὁποῖόν τι τὸ μέλλον ποιήσουσιν· ὁ δὲ Νικίας 20
ἰδὼν ἀντίπαλα τὰ τῆς ναυμαχίας γενόμενα καὶ ἐλπίζων
αὐτοὺς αὖθις ἐπιχειρήσειν τούς τε τριηράρχους ἠνάγκαζεν
ἐπισκευάζειν τὰς ναῦς, εἴ τίς τι ἐπεπονήκει, καὶ ὁλκάδας
προώρμισε πρὸ τοῦ σφετέρου σταυρώματος, ὃ αὐτοῖς πρὸ
τῶν νεῶν ἀντὶ λιμένος κλῃστοῦ ἐν τῇ θαλάσσῃ ἐπεπήγει. 25
3 διαλειπούσας δὲ τὰς ὁλκάδας ὅσον δύο πλέθρα ἀπ' ἀλλήλων
κατέστησεν, ὅπως, εἴ τις βιάζοιτο ναῦς, εἴη κατάφευξις
ἀσφαλὴς καὶ πάλιν καθ' ἡσυχίαν ἔκπλους. παρασκευαζό-
μενοι δὲ ταῦτα ὅλην τὴν ἡμέραν διετέλεσαν οἱ Ἀθηναῖοι
μέχρι νυκτός.
                                          30

4 ἐπεξέπλεον Β : ἐξέπλεον cett.   8 post δὲ add. 'Αθηναῖοι
A C E F G M   13 post καὶ add. αἱ C E G   14 alterum καὶ secl.
Classen   17 οἱ Β : om. cett.   διεκρίθη]σαν . . . 24 σ[φετέρου Π¹⁶
21 τὰ Β Π¹⁶ : om. cett.   24 προώρμησε A E F M [Π¹⁶]   26 διαλειπούσας recc. : διαλιπούσας codd.

Τῇ δ' ὑστεραίᾳ οἱ Συρακόσιοι τῆς μὲν ὥρας πρωίτερον, 39
τῇ δ' ἐπιχειρήσει τῇ αὐτῇ τοῦ τε πεζοῦ καὶ τοῦ ναυτικοῦ
προσέμισγον τοῖς Ἀθηναίοις, καὶ ἀντικαταστάντες ταῖς 2
ναυσὶ τὸν αὐτὸν τρόπον αὖθις ἐπὶ πολὺ διῆγον τῆς ἡμέρας
5 πειρώμενοι ἀλλήλων, πρὶν δὴ Ἀρίστων ὁ Πυρρίχου Κορίνθιος, ἄριστος ὢν κυβερνήτης τῶν μετὰ Συρακοσίων, πείθει
τοὺς σφετέρους τοῦ ναυτικοῦ ἄρχοντας, πέμψαντας ὡς τοὺς
ἐν τῇ πόλει ἐπιμελομένους, κελεύειν ὅτι τάχιστα τὴν ἀγορὰν
τῶν πωλουμένων παρὰ τὴν θάλασσαν μεταστῆσαι κομίσαντας,
10 καὶ ὅσα τις ἔχει ἐδώδιμα, πάντας ἐκεῖσε φέροντας ἀναγκάσαι
πωλεῖν, ὅπως αὐτοῖς ἐκβιβάσαντες τοὺς ναύτας εὐθὺς παρὰ
τὰς ναῦς ἀριστοποιήσωνται, καὶ δι' ὀλίγου αὖθις καὶ αὐθη-
μερὸν ἀπροσδοκήτοις τοῖς Ἀθηναίοις ἐπιχειρῶσιν. καὶ οἱ 40
μὲν πεισθέντες ἔπεμψαν ἄγγελον, καὶ ἡ ἀγορὰ παρεσκευά-
15 σθη, καὶ οἱ Συρακόσιοι ἐξαίφνης πρύμναν κρουσάμενοι
πάλιν πρὸς τὴν πόλιν ἔπλευσαν καὶ εὐθὺς ἐκβάντες αὐτοῦ
ἄριστον ἐποιοῦντο· οἱ δ' Ἀθηναῖοι νομίσαντες αὐτοὺς ὡς 2
ἡσσημένους σφῶν πρὸς τὴν πόλιν ἀνακρούσασθαι, καθ'
ἡσυχίαν ἐκβάντες τά τε ἄλλα διεπράσσοντο καὶ τὰ ἀμφὶ
20 τὸ ἄριστον ὡς τῆς γε ἡμέρας ταύτης οὐκέτι οἰόμενοι ἂν
ναυμαχῆσαι. ἐξαίφνης δὲ οἱ Συρακόσιοι πληρώσαντες τὰς 3
ναῦς ἐπέπλεον αὖθις· οἱ δὲ διὰ πολλοῦ θορύβου καὶ ἄσιτοι
οἱ πλείους οὐδενὶ κόσμῳ ἐσβάντες μόλις ποτὲ ἀνταγήγοντο.
καὶ χρόνον μέν τινα ἀπέσχοντο ἀλλήλων φυλασσόμενοι· 4
25 ἔπειτα οὐκ ἐδόκει τοῖς Ἀθηναίοις ὑπὸ σφῶν αὐτῶν διαμέλ-
λοντας κόπῳ ἁλίσκεσθαι, ἀλλ' ἐπιχειρεῖν ὅτι τάχιστα,
καὶ ἐπιφερόμενοι ἐκ παρακελεύσεως ἐναυμάχουν. οἱ δὲ 5
Συρακόσιοι δεξάμενοι καὶ ταῖς [τε] ναυσὶν ἀντιπρῴροις
χρώμενοι, ὥσπερ διενοήθησαν, τῶν ἐμβόλων τῇ παρασκευῇ

1 πρωίτερον B : πρότερον cett.   post πρωίτερον add. ἢ τὸ πρότερον B   9 παρὰ . . . κομίσαντας] μεταναστήσαντας ἐπὶ τὴν
θάλασσαν κομίσαι B   12 ἄριστον ποιήσωνται B : ἀριστοποιήσονται A F
αὖθις καὶ bis habent A C F G M   23 μόλις B : μόγις cett.   28 τε
om. A F G M   29 ἐμβόλων Abresch : ἐμβολὰν codd.

ἀνερρήγνυσαν τὰς τῶν Ἀθηναίων ναῦς ἐπὶ πολὺ τῆς παρεξειρεσίας, καὶ οἱ ἀπὸ τῶν καταστρωμάτων αὐτοῖς ἀκοντίζοντες μεγάλα ἔβλαπτον τοὺς Ἀθηναίους, πολὺ δ' ἔτι μείζω
οἱ ἐν τοῖς λεπτοῖς πλοίοις περιπλέοντες τῶν Συρακοσίων
καὶ ἔς τε τοὺς ταρσοὺς ὑποπίπτοντες τῶν πολεμίων νεῶν 5
καὶ ἐς τὰ πλάγια παραπλέοντες καὶ ἐξ αὐτῶν ἐς τοὺς
41 ναύτας ἀκοντίζοντες. τέλος δὲ τούτῳ τῷ τρόπῳ κατὰ
κράτος ναυμαχοῦντες οἱ Συρακόσιοι ἐνίκησαν, καὶ οἱ Ἀθηναῖοι τραπόμενοι διὰ τῶν ὁλκάδων τὴν κατάφευξιν ἐποιοῦντο
2 ἐς τὸν ἑαυτῶν ὅρμον. αἱ δὲ τῶν Συρακοσίων νῆες μέχρι 10
μὲν τῶν ὁλκάδων ἐπεδίωκον· ἔπειτα αὐτοὺς αἱ κεραῖαι ὑπὲρ
τῶν ἔσπλων αἱ ἀπὸ τῶν ὁλκάδων δελφινοφόροι ἠρμέναι
3 ἐκώλυον. δύο δὲ νῆες τῶν Συρακοσίων ἐπαιρόμεναι τῇ
νίκῃ προσέμειξαν αὐτῶν ἐγγὺς καὶ διεφθάρησαν, καὶ ἡ
4 ἑτέρα αὐτοῖς ἀνδράσιν ἑάλω. καταδύσαντες δ' οἱ Συρακό- 15
σιοι τῶν Ἀθηναίων ἑπτὰ ναῦς καὶ κατατραυματίσαντες
πολλὰς ἄνδρας τε τοὺς μὲν πολλοὺς ζωγρήσαντες, τοὺς
δὲ ἀποκτείναντες ἀπεχώρησαν, καὶ τροπαῖά τε ἀμφοτέρων
τῶν ναυμαχιῶν ἔστησαν, καὶ τὴν ἐλπίδα ἤδη ἐχυρὰν εἶχον
ταῖς μὲν ναυσὶ καὶ πολὺ κρείσσους εἶναι, ἐδόκουν δὲ καὶ 20
τὸν πεζὸν χειρώσεσθαι.

42 Καὶ οἱ μὲν ὡς ἐπιθησόμενοι κατ' ἀμφότερα παρεσκευάζοντο αὖθις, ἐν τούτῳ δὲ Δημοσθένης καὶ Εὐρυμέδων ἔχοντες
τὴν ἀπὸ τῶν Ἀθηνῶν βοήθειαν. παραγίγνονται, ναῦς τε
τρεῖς καὶ ἑβδομήκοντα μάλιστα ξὺν ταῖς ξενικαῖς καὶ 25
ὁπλίτας περὶ πεντακισχιλίους ἑαυτῶν τε καὶ τῶν ξυμμάχων,
ἀκοντιστάς τε βαρβάρους καὶ Ἕλληνας οὐκ ὀλίγους, καὶ
σφενδονήτας καὶ τοξότας καὶ τὴν ἄλλην παρασκευὴν
2 ἱκανήν. καὶ τοῖς μὲν Συρακοσίοις καὶ ξυμμάχοις κατάπληξις ἐν τῷ αὐτίκα οὐκ ὀλίγη ἐγένετο, εἰ πέρας μηδὲν 30
ἔσται σφίσι τοῦ ἀπαλλαγῆναι τοῦ κινδύνου, ὁρῶντες οὔτε

11 ὑπὲρ] ὑπὸ B   17 πολλοὺς om. B   20 prius καὶ B : om. cett.
δοκεῖν B   25 μάλιστα om. B

διὰ τὴν Δεκέλειαν τειχιζομένην οὐδὲν ἦσσον στρατὸν ἴσον
καὶ παραπλήσιον τῷ προτέρῳ ἐπεληλυθότα τήν τε τῶν
Ἀθηναίων δύναμιν πανταχόσε πολλὴν φαινομένην· τῷ δὲ
προτέρῳ στρατεύματι τῶν Ἀθηναίων ὡς ἐκ κακῶν ῥώμη
5 τις ἐγεγένητο. ὁ δὲ Δημοσθένης ἰδὼν ὡς εἶχε τὰ πράγματα 3
καὶ νομίσας οὐχ οἷόν τε εἶναι διατρίβειν οὐδὲ παθεῖν ὅπερ
ὁ Νικίας ἔπαθεν (ἀφικόμενος γὰρ τὸ πρῶτον ὁ Νικίας
φοβερός, ὡς οὐκ εὐθὺς προσέκειτο ταῖς Συρακούσαις, ἀλλ᾽
ἐν Κατάνῃ διεχείμαζεν, ὑπερώφθη τε καὶ ἔφθασεν αὐτὸν
10 ἐκ τῆς Πελοποννήσου στρατιᾷ ὁ Γύλιππος ἀφικόμενος, ἣν
οὐδ᾽ ἂν μετέπεμψαν οἱ Συρακόσιοι, εἰ ἐκεῖνος εὐθὺς ἐπέκειτο·
ἱκανοὶ γὰρ αὐτοὶ οἰόμενοι εἶναι ἅμα τ᾽ ἂν ἔμαθον ἥσσους
ὄντες καὶ ἀποτετειχισμένοι ἂν ἦσαν, ὥστε μηδ᾽ εἰ μετέπεμψαν ἔτι ὁμοίως ἂν αὐτοὺς ὠφελεῖν), ταῦτα οὖν ἀνα-
15 σκοπῶν ὁ Δημοσθένης, καὶ γιγνώσκων ὅτι καὶ αὐτὸς ἐν τῷ
παρόντι τῇ πρώτῃ ἡμέρᾳ μάλιστα δεινότατός ἐστι τοῖς
ἐναντίοις, ἐβούλετο ὅτι τάχος ἀποχρήσασθαι τῇ παρούσῃ
τοῦ στρατεύματος ἐκπλήξει. καὶ ὁρῶν τὸ παρατείχισμα 4
τῶν Συρακοσίων, ᾧ ἐκώλυσαν περιτειχίσαι σφᾶς τοὺς
20 Ἀθηναίους, ἁπλοῦν ὂν καί, εἰ κρατήσειέ τις τῶν τε Ἐπιπολῶν τῆς ἀναβάσεως καὶ αὖθις τοῦ ἐν αὐταῖς στρατοπέδου,
ῥᾳδίως ἂν αὐτὸ ληφθέν (οὐδὲ γὰρ ὑπομεῖναι ἂν σφᾶς
οὐδένα), ἠπείγετο ἐπιθέσθαι τῇ πείρᾳ, καί οἱ ξυντομωτάτην 5
ἡγεῖτο διαπολέμησιν· ἢ γὰρ κατορθώσας ἕξειν Συρακούσας,
25 ἢ ἀπάξειν τὴν στρατιὰν καὶ οὐ τρίψεσθαι ἄλλως Ἀθηναίους
τε τοὺς ξυστρατευομένους καὶ τὴν ξύμπασαν πόλιν.

Πρῶτον μὲν οὖν τήν τε γῆν ἐξελθόντες τῶν Συρακοσίων 6
ἔτεμον οἱ Ἀθηναῖοι περὶ τὸν Ἄναπον, καὶ τῷ στρατεύματι
ἐπεκράτουν ὥσπερ τὸ πρῶτον, τῷ τε πεζῷ καὶ ταῖς ναυσίν

20 post ἁπλοῦν add. τε A C E F G M   post εἰ add. μὴ B
ἐπικρατήσειε B   τε B: om. cett.   23 οἱ B: om. cett. γρ. B
post ξυντομωτάτην add. ταύτην Madvig   25 τρίψεσθαι B: τρί-
βεσθαι cett.   26 post τε add. καὶ B   28 ἔτεμνον C G   29 τε
om. C

(οὐδὲ γὰρ καθ' ἕτερα οἱ Συρακόσιοι ἀντεπεξῆσαν ὅτι μὴ
43 τοῖς ἱππεῦσι καὶ ἀκοντισταῖς ἀπὸ τοῦ Ὀλυμπιείου)· ἔπειτα
μηχαναῖς ἔδοξε τῷ Δημοσθένει πρότερον ἀποπειρᾶσαι τοῦ
παρατειχίσματος. ὡς δὲ αὐτῷ προσαγαγόντι κατεκαύθησάν
τε ὑπὸ τῶν ἐναντίων ἀπὸ τοῦ τείχους ἀμυνομένων αἱ 5
μηχαναὶ καὶ τῇ ἄλλῃ στρατιᾷ πολλαχῇ προσβάλλοντες
ἀπεκρούοντο, οὐκέτι ἐδόκει διατρίβειν, ἀλλὰ πείσας τόν τε
Νικίαν καὶ τοὺς ἄλλους ξυνάρχοντας, ὡς ἐπενόει, τὴν
2 ἐπιχείρησιν τῶν Ἐπιπολῶν ἐποιεῖτο. καὶ ἡμέρας μὲν
ἀδύνατα ἐδόκει εἶναι λαθεῖν προσελθόντας τε καὶ ἀνα- 10
βάντας, παραγγείλας δὲ πέντε ἡμερῶν σιτία καὶ τοὺς
λιθολόγους καὶ τέκτονας πάντας λαβὼν καὶ ἄλλην παρασκευὴν τοξευμάτων τε καὶ ὅσα ἔδει, ἢν κρατῶσι, τειχίζοντας
ἔχειν, αὐτὸς μὲν ἀπὸ πρώτου ὕπνου καὶ Εὐρυμέδων καὶ
Μένανδρος ἀναλαβὼν τὴν πᾶσαν στρατιὰν ἐχώρει πρὸς 15
τὰς Ἐπιπολάς, Νικίας δὲ ἐν τοῖς τείχεσιν ὑπελέλειπτο.
3 καὶ ἐπειδὴ ἐγένοντο πρὸς αὐταῖς κατὰ τὸν Εὐρύηλον, ᾗπερ
καὶ ἡ προτέρα στρατιὰ τὸ πρῶτον ἀνέβη, λανθάνουσί τε
τοὺς φύλακας τῶν Συρακοσίων, καὶ προσβάντες τὸ τείχισμα
ὃ ἦν αὐτόθι τῶν Συρακοσίων αἱροῦσι καὶ ἄνδρας τῶν 20
4 φυλάκων ἀποκτείνουσιν. οἱ δὲ πλείους διαφυγόντες εὐθὺς
πρὸς τὰ στρατόπεδα, ἃ ἦν ἐπὶ τῶν Ἐπιπολῶν τρία ἐν
προτειχίσμασιν, ἐν μὲν τῶν Συρακοσίων, ἐν δὲ τῶν ἄλλων
Σικελιωτῶν, ἐν δὲ τῶν ξυμμάχων, ἀγγέλλουσι τὴν ἔφοδον
καὶ τοῖς ἑξακοσίοις τῶν Συρακοσίων, οἳ καὶ πρῶτοι κατὰ 25
5 τοῦτο τὸ μέρος τῶν Ἐπιπολῶν φύλακες ἦσαν, ἔφραζον. οἱ
δ' ἐβοήθουν τ' εὐθύς, καὶ αὐτοῖς ὁ Δημοσθένης καὶ οἱ
Ἀθηναῖοι ἐντυχόντες ἀμυνομένους προθύμως ἔτρεψαν. καὶ
αὐτοὶ μὲν εὐθὺς ἐχώρουν ἐς τὸ πρόσθεν, ὅπως τῇ παρούσῃ

1 ἑκάτερα B   5 post ἀπὸ add. τε B   8 ὡς B : om. cett.
γρ. B   post ἐπενόει add. καὶ A C E F G M γρ. B   10 ἀδύνατα B :
ἀδύνατον cett.   15 πᾶσαν] πρότην B (γρ. πᾶσαν) : πεζὴν Wölfflin
16 ὑπελείπετο B   20 post ἄνδρας add. τινὰς B   22 ἐν προτειχίσμασιν B : om. cett.

ὁρμῇ τοῦ περαίνεσθαι ὧν ἕνεκα ἦλθον μὴ βραδεῖς γένωνται·
ἄλλοι δὲ ἀπὸ τῆς πρώτης τὸ παρατείχισμα τῶν Συρακοσίων
οὐχ ὑπομενόντων τῶν φυλάκων ᾕρουν τε καὶ τὰς ἐπάλξεις
ἀπέσυρον. οἱ δὲ Συρακόσιοι καὶ οἱ ξύμμαχοι καὶ ὁ Γύλιπ- 6
5 πος καὶ οἱ μετ' αὐτοῦ ἐβοήθουν ἐκ τῶν προτειχισμάτων,
καὶ ἀδοκήτου τοῦ τολμήματος σφίσιν ἐν νυκτὶ γενομένου
προσέβαλόν τε τοῖς Ἀθηναίοις ἐκπεπληγμένοι καὶ βιασθέντες ὑπ' αὐτῶν τὸ πρῶτον ὑπεχώρησαν. προϊόντων δὲ 7
τῶν Ἀθηναίων ἐν ἀταξίᾳ μᾶλλον ἤδη ὡς κεκρατηκότων καὶ
10 βουλομένων διὰ παντὸς τοῦ μήπω μεμαχημένου τῶν ἐναντίων
ὡς τάχιστα διελθεῖν, ἵνα μὴ ἀνέντων σφῶν τῆς ἐφόδου
αὖθις ξυστραφῶσιν, οἱ Βοιωτοὶ πρῶτοι αὐτοῖς ἀντέσχον καὶ
προσβαλόντες ἔτρεψάν τε καὶ ἐς φυγὴν κατέστησαν.

Καὶ ἐνταῦθα ἤδη ἐν πολλῇ ταραχῇ καὶ ἀπορίᾳ ἐγίγνοντο 44
15 οἱ Ἀθηναῖοι, ἣν οὐδὲ πυθέσθαι ῥᾴδιον ἦν οὐδ' ἀφ' ἑτέρων
ὅτῳ τρόπῳ ἕκαστα ξυνηνέχθη. ἐν μὲν γὰρ ἡμέρᾳ σαφέ-
στερα μέν, ὅμως δὲ οὐδὲ ταῦτα οἱ παραγενόμενοι πάντα
πλὴν τὸ καθ' ἑαυτὸν ἕκαστος μόλις οἶδεν· ἐν δὲ νυκτομαχίᾳ, ἣ μόνη δὴ στρατοπέδων μεγάλων ἔν γε τῷδε τῷ πολέμῳ
20 ἐγένετο, πῶς ἄν τις σαφῶς τι ᾔδει; ἦν μὲν γὰρ σελήνη 2
λαμπρά, ἑώρων δὲ οὕτως ἀλλήλους ὡς ἐν σελήνῃ εἰκὸς τὴν
μὲν ὄψιν τοῦ σώματος προορᾶν, τὴν δὲ γνῶσιν τοῦ οἰκείου
ἀπιστεῖσθαι. ὁπλῖται δὲ ἀμφοτέρων οὐκ ὀλίγοι ἐν στενοχωρίᾳ ἀνεστρέφοντο. καὶ τῶν Ἀθηναίων οἱ μὲν ἤδη ἐνι- 3
25 κῶντο, οἱ δ' ἔτι τῇ πρώτῃ ἐφόδῳ ἀήσσητοι ἐχώρουν. πολὺ
δὲ καὶ τοῦ ἄλλου στρατεύματος αὐτοῖς τὸ μὲν ἄρτι ἀνε-
βεβήκει, τὸ δ' ἔτι προσανῄει, ὥστ' οὐκ ἠπίσταντο πρὸς
ὅτι χρὴ χωρῆσαι. ἤδη γὰρ τὰ πρόσθεν τῆς τροπῆς
γεγενημένης ἐτετάρακτο πάντα καὶ χαλεπὰ ἦν ὑπὸ τῆς
30 βοῆς διαγνῶναι. οἵ τε γὰρ Συρακόσιοι καὶ οἱ ξύμμαχοι 4

2 τὸ post δὲ habent codd.: transp. Göller   6 ἐν νυκτὶ σφίσι
ACEFGM   7 προσέβαλον E: προσέβαλλον cett.   12 πρῶτοι]
πρότεροι B   18 μόγις B   19 γε B: om. cett.   28 τὰ]
τὸ B   29 γενομένης M

ὡς κρατοῦντες παρεκελεύοντό τε κραυγῇ οὐκ ὀλίγῃ χρώμενοι,
ἀδύνατον ὂν ἐν νυκτὶ ἄλλῳ τῳ σημῆναι, καὶ ἅμα τοὺς
προσφερομένους ἐδέχοντο· οἵ τε Ἀθηναῖοι ἐζήτουν τε σφᾶς
αὐτοὺς καὶ πᾶν τὸ ἐξ ἐναντίας, καὶ εἰ φίλιον εἴη τῶν ἤδη
πάλιν φευγόντων, πολέμιον ἐνόμιζον, καὶ τοῖς ἐρωτήμασι 5
τοῦ ξυνθήματος πυκνοῖς χρώμενοι διὰ τὸ μὴ εἶναι ἄλλῳ τῳ
γνωρίσαι σφίσι τε αὐτοῖς θόρυβον πολὺν παρεῖχον ἅμα
πάντες ἐρωτῶντες καὶ τοῖς πολεμίοις σαφὲς αὐτὸ κατέστη-
5 σαν· τὸ δ' ἐκείνων οὐχ ὁμοίως ἠπίσταντο διὰ τὸ κρατοῦντας
αὐτοὺς καὶ μὴ διεσπασμένους ἧσσον ἀγνοεῖσθαι, ὥστ' εἰ 10
μὲν ἐντύχοιέν τισι κρείσσους ὄντες τῶν πολεμίων, διέφευγον
αὐτοὺς ἅτε ἐκείνων ἐπιστάμενοι τὸ ξύνθημα, εἰ δ' αὐτοὶ μὴ
6 ἀποκρίνοιντο, διεφθείροντο. μέγιστον δὲ καὶ οὐχ ἥκιστα
ἔβλαψε καὶ ὁ παιανισμός· ἀπὸ γὰρ ἀμφοτέρων παραπλή-
σιος ὢν ἀπορίαν παρεῖχεν. οἵ τε γὰρ Ἀργεῖοι καὶ οἱ 15
Κερκυραῖοι καὶ ὅσον Δωρικὸν μετ' Ἀθηναίων ἦν, ὁπότε
παιανίσειαν, φόβον παρεῖχε τοῖς Ἀθηναίοις, οἵ τε πολέμιοι
7 ὁμοίως. ὥστε τέλος ξυμπεσόντες αὑτοῖς κατὰ πολλὰ τοῦ
στρατοπέδου, ἐπεὶ ἅπαξ ἐταράχθησαν, φίλοι τε φίλοις καὶ
πολῖται πολίταις, οὐ μόνον ἐς φόβον κατέστησαν, ἀλλὰ 20
8 καὶ ἐς χεῖρας ἀλλήλοις ἐλθόντες μόλις ἀπελύοντο. καὶ
διωκόμενοι κατά τε τῶν κρημνῶν [οἱ] πολλοὶ ῥίπτοντες ἑαυ-
τοὺς ἀπώλλυντο, στενῆς οὔσης τῆς ἀπὸ τῶν Ἐπιπολῶν
πάλιν καταβάσεως, καὶ ἐπειδὴ ἐς τὸ ὁμαλὸν οἱ σῳζόμενοι
ἄνωθεν καταβαῖεν, οἱ μὲν πολλοὶ αὐτῶν καὶ ὅσοι ἦσαν τῶν 25
προτέρων στρατιωτῶν ἐμπειρίᾳ μᾶλλον τῆς χώρας ἐς τὸ
στρατόπεδον διεφύγγανον, οἱ δὲ ὕστερον ἥκοντες εἰσὶν οἳ
διαμαρτόντες τῶν ὁδῶν κατὰ τὴν χώραν ἐπλανήθησαν· οὕς,

---

1 ὡς B: om. cett.　　2 ἀδύνατα ἦν C ? G　　ὂν] οὖν A F　　4 ἐξ
ἐναντίας B: ἐναντίον cett.　　12 ἐπισταμένων B: ἐπιστάντων C
13 κρίνοιντο B　　14 καὶ om. B　　παιανισμός f: παιωνισμός codd.
17 παιανίσειαν f: παιωνίσειαν codd.　　18 αὑτοῖς recc.: αὐτοῖς codd.
20 καθίστησαν (sic) B　　21 μόγις B　　22 οἱ secl. Bloom-
field　ῥιπτοῦντες B　　25 καταβαῖεν, οἱ μὲν B: καταβαίνοιεν cett.
γρ. B

ἐπειδὴ ἡμέρα ἐγένετο, οἱ ἱππῆς τῶν Συρακοσίων περιελά-
σαντες διέφθειραν.

Τῇ δ' ὑστεραίᾳ οἱ μὲν Συρακόσιοι δύο τροπαῖα ἔστησαν, 45
ἐπί τε ταῖς Ἐπιπολαῖς ᾗ ἡ πρόσβασις καὶ κατὰ τὸ χωρίον
5 ᾗ οἱ Βοιωτοὶ πρῶτον ἀντέστησαν, οἱ δ' Ἀθηναῖοι τοὺς νεκροὺς ὑποσπόνδους ἐκομίσαντο.   ἀπέθανον δὲ οὐκ ὀλίγοι 2
αὐτῶν τε καὶ τῶν ξυμμάχων, ὅπλα μέντοι ἔτι πλείω ἢ κατὰ
τοὺς νεκροὺς ἐλήφθη· οἱ γὰρ κατὰ τῶν κρημνῶν βιασθέντες
ἅλλεσθαι ψιλοὶ [ἄνευ τῶν ἀσπίδων] οἱ μὲν ἀπώλλυντο, οἱ
10 δ' ἐσώθησαν.

Μετὰ δὲ τοῦτο οἱ μὲν Συρακόσιοι ὡς ἐπὶ ἀπροσδοκήτῳ 46
εὐπραγίᾳ πάλιν αὖ ἀναρρωσθέντες, ὥσπερ καὶ πρότερον, ἐς
μὲν Ἀκράγαντα στασιάζοντα πέντε καὶ δέκα ναυσὶ Σικανὸν
ἀπέστειλαν, ὅπως ὑπαγάγοιτο τὴν πόλιν, εἰ δύναιτο· Γύ-
15 λιππος δὲ κατὰ γῆν ἐς τὴν ἄλλην Σικελίαν ᾤχετο αὖθις,
ἄξων στρατιὰν ἔτι, ὡς ἐν ἐλπίδι ὢν καὶ τὰ τείχη τῶν
Ἀθηναίων αἱρήσειν βίᾳ, ἐπειδὴ τὰ ἐν ταῖς Ἐπιπολαῖς οὕτω
ξυνέβη.

Οἱ δὲ τῶν Ἀθηναίων στρατηγοὶ ἐν τούτῳ ἐβουλεύοντο 47
20 πρός τε τὴν γεγενημένην ξυμφορὰν καὶ πρὸς τὴν παροῦσαν
ἐν τῷ στρατοπέδῳ κατὰ πάντα ἀρρωστίαν.   τοῖς τε γὰρ
ἐπιχειρήμασιν ἑώρων οὐ κατορθοῦντες καὶ τοὺς στρατιώτας
ἀχθομένους τῇ μονῇ· νόσῳ τε γὰρ ἐπιέζοντο κατ' ἀμφότερα, 2
τῆς τε ὥρας τοῦ ἐνιαυτοῦ ταύτης οὔσης ἐν ᾗ ἀσθενοῦσιν
25 ἄνθρωποι μάλιστα, καὶ τὸ χωρίον ἅμα ἐν ᾧ ἐστρατοπεδεύ-
οντο ἑλῶδες καὶ χαλεπὸν ἦν, τά τε ἄλλα ὅτι ἀνέλπιστα
αὐτοῖς ἐφαίνετο.   τῷ οὖν Δημοσθένει οὐκ ἐδόκει ἔτι χρῆναι 3
μένειν, ἀλλ' ἅπερ καὶ διανοηθεὶς ἐς τὰς Ἐπιπολὰς διεκιν-
δύνευσεν, ἐπειδὴ ἔσφαλτο, ἀπιέναι ἐψηφίζετο καὶ μὴ δια-

2 διέφθειρον A E F M   5 πρῶτον om. B   9 ἄνευ τῶν
ἀσπίδων secl. Pluygers   ἀπώλοντο Cobet   14 ἐπαγάγοιτο
Pluygers   15 ἄλλην B: om. cett.   22 κατορθοῦντες G M: κατορ-
θοῦντας cett.   26 ἦν om. B   ἄλλα ὅτι om. A   ἀνελπιστότατα
Reiske   28 διακινδυνεῦσαι A E F M   29 ἀπιέναι B: ἐξιέναι
cett.

τρίβειν, ἕως ἔτι τὸ πέλαγος οἶόν τε. περαιοῦσθαι καὶ τοῦ
4 στρατεύματος ταῖς γοῦν ἐπελθούσαις ναυσὶ κρατεῖν. καὶ
τῇ πόλει ὠφελιμώτερον ἔφη εἶναι πρὸς τοὺς ἐν τῇ χώρᾳ
σφῶν ἐπιτειχίζοντας τὸν πόλεμον ποιεῖσθαι ἢ Συρακοσίους,
οὓς οὐκέτι ῥᾴδιον εἶναι χειρώσασθαι· οὐδ' αὖ ἄλλως χρήματα 5
πολλὰ δαπανῶντας εἰκὸς εἶναι προσκαθῆσθαι.

48   Καὶ ὁ μὲν Δημοσθένης τοιαῦτα ἐγίγνωσκεν· ὁ δὲ
Νικίας ἐνόμιζε μὲν καὶ αὐτὸς πόνηρα σφῶν τὰ πράγματα
εἶναι, τῷ δὲ λόγῳ οὐκ ἐβούλετο αὐτὰ ἀσθενῆ ἀποδεικνύναι,
οὐδ' ἐμφανῶς σφᾶς ψηφιζομένους μετὰ πολλῶν τὴν ἀναχώ- 10
ρησιν τοῖς πολεμίοις καταγγέλτους γίγνεσθαι· λαθεῖν γὰρ
2 ἄν, ὁπότε βούλοιντο, τοῦτο ποιοῦντες πολλῷ ἧσσον. τὸ δέ
τι καὶ τὰ τῶν πολεμίων, ἀφ' ὧν ἐπὶ πλέον ἢ οἱ ἄλλοι
ᾐσθάνετο αὐτῶν, ἐλπίδος τι ἔτι παρεῖχε πονηρότερα τῶν
σφετέρων ἔσεσθαι, ἢν καρτερῶσι προσκαθήμενοι· χρημάτων 15
γὰρ ἀπορίᾳ αὐτοὺς ἐκτρυχώσειν, ἄλλως τε καὶ ἐπὶ πλέον
ἤδη ταῖς ὑπαρχούσαις ναυσὶ θαλασσοκρατούντων. καὶ ἦν
γάρ τι καὶ ἐν ταῖς Συρακούσαις βουλόμενον τοῖς Ἀθηναίοις
τὰ πράγματα ἐνδοῦναι, ἐπεκηρυκεύετο ὡς αὐτὸν καὶ οὐκ εἴα
3 ἀπανίστασθαι. ἃ ἐπιστάμενος τῷ μὲν ἔργῳ ἔτι ἐπ' ἀμφό- 20
τερα ἔχων καὶ διασκοπῶν ἀνεῖχε, τῷ δ' ἐμφανεῖ τότε λόγῳ
οὐκ ἔφη ἀπάξειν τὴν στρατιάν. εὖ γὰρ εἰδέναι ὅτι Ἀθηναῖοι σφῶν ταῦτα οὐκ ἀποδέξονται, ὥστε μὴ αὐτῶν ψηφισα-
μένων ἀπελθεῖν. καὶ γὰρ οὐ τοὺς αὐτοὺς ψηφιεῖσθαί τε
περὶ σφῶν [αὐτῶν] καὶ τὰ πράγματα ὥσπερ καὶ αὐτοὶ 25
ὁρῶντας καὶ οὐκ ἄλλων ἐπιτιμήσει ἀκούσαντας γνώσεσθαι,
ἀλλ' ἐξ ὧν ἄν τις εὖ λέγων διαβάλλοι, ἐκ τούτων αὐτοὺς
4 πείσεσθαι. τῶν τε παρόντων στρατιωτῶν πολλοὺς καὶ
τοὺς πλείους ἔφη, οἳ νῦν βοῶσιν ὡς ἐν δεινοῖς ὄντες, ἐκεῖσε
ἀφικομένους τἀναντία βοήσεσθαι ὡς ὑπὸ χρημάτων κατα- 30

   2 ἐπελθοῦσι(ν) A E F M   12 δ' ἔτι A B E F M   14 ἐλπίδας τε
B (ἐλπίδος τι γρ. B)   22 post ὅτι add. οἱ G   25 αὐτῶν secl. Bekker
26 ἀκούοντας B M   27 διαβάλλῃ Stahl   30 τἀναντία B : τὰ
ἐναντία cett.

προδόντες οἱ στρατηγοὶ ἀπῆλθον. οὔκουν βούλεσθαι αὐτός γε
ἐπιστάμενος τὰς Ἀθηναίων φύσεις ἐπ' αἰσχρᾷ τε αἰτίᾳ καὶ
ἀδίκως ὑπ' Ἀθηναίων ἀπολέσθαι μᾶλλον ἢ ὑπὸ τῶν πολεμίων,
εἰ δεῖ, κινδυνεύσας τοῦτο παθεῖν ἰδίᾳ. τά τε Συρακοσίων 5
5 ἔφη ὅμως ἔτι ἥσσω τῶν σφετέρων εἶναι· καὶ χρήμασι γὰρ
αὐτοὺς ξενοτροφοῦντας καὶ ἐν περιπολίοις ἅμα ἀναλίσκον-
τας καὶ ναυτικὸν πολὺ ἔτι ἐνιαυτὸν ἤδη βόσκοντας τὰ μὲν
ἀπορεῖν, τὰ δ' ἔτι ἀμηχανήσειν· δισχίλιά τε γὰρ τάλαντα
ἤδη ἀνηλωκέναι καὶ ἔτι πολλὰ προσοφείλειν, ἤν τε καὶ
10 ὁτιοῦν ἐκλίπωσι τῆς νῦν παρασκευῆς τῷ μὴ διδόναι τροφήν,
φθερεῖσθαι αὐτῶν τὰ πράγματα, ἐπικουρικὰ μᾶλλον ἢ δι'
ἀνάγκης ὥσπερ τὰ σφέτερα ὄντα. τρίβειν οὖν ἔφη χρῆναι 6
προσκαθημένους καὶ μὴ χρήμασιν, ὧν πολὺ κρείσσους εἰσί,
νικηθέντας ἀπιέναι.

15 Ὁ μὲν Νικίας τοσαῦτα λέγων ἰσχυρίζετο, αἰσθόμενος τὰ 49
ἐν ταῖς Συρακούσαις ἀκριβῶς καὶ τὴν τῶν χρημάτων ἀπορίαν καὶ ὅτι ἦν αὐτόθι πολὺ τὸ βουλόμενον τοῖς Ἀθηναίοις
γίγνεσθαι τὰ πράγματα καὶ ἐπικηρυκευόμενον πρὸς αὐτὸν
ὥστε μὴ ἀπανίστασθαι, καὶ ἅμα ταῖς γοῦν ναυσὶ μᾶλλον
20 ἢ πρότερον ἐθάρσησε κρατήσειν. ὁ δὲ Δημοσθένης περὶ 2
μὲν τοῦ προσκαθῆσθαι οὐδ' ὁπωσοῦν ἐνεδέχετο· εἰ δὲ δεῖ
μὴ ἀπάγειν τὴν στρατιὰν ἄνευ Ἀθηναίων ψηφίσματος, ἀλλὰ
τρίβειν αὐτοῦ, ἔφη χρῆναι ἢ ἐς τὴν Θάψον ἀναστάντας
τοῦτο ποιεῖν ἢ ἐς τὴν Κατάνην, ὅθεν τῷ τε πεζῷ ἐπὶ
25 πολλὰ τῆς χώρας ἐπιόντες θρέψονται πορθοῦντες τὰ τῶν
πολεμίων καὶ ἐκείνους βλάψουσι, ταῖς τε ναυσὶν ἐν πελάγει
καὶ οὐκ ἐν στενοχωρίᾳ, ἢ πρὸς τῶν πολεμίων μᾶλλόν ἐστι,
τοὺς ἀγῶνας ποιήσονται, ἀλλ' ἐν εὐρυχωρίᾳ, ἐν ᾗ τά τε

8 τε B : om. cett.   13 ὧν B : ὡς cett. γρ. B : οἶς recc.
17 πολὺ Linwood : του B : om. cett.   19 γοῦν] γ' ἂν Ε Μ : γὰρ
Α F   μᾶλλον Herwerden : θαρρῶν B : om. cett.   20 ἐθάρσησε B : θαρσήσει cett.   κρατήσειν Herwerden : κρατηθεὶς codd.
22 ἐπάγειν B   23 αὐτοῦ Krüger : αὐτοὺς codd.   25 θρέψονται
B : τρέψονται codd.   τὰ BC : τὰς cett.   27 ἐστι] ἐστιν ὥσπερ
νῦν B

E

τῆς ἐμπειρίας χρήσιμα σφῶν ἔσται καὶ ἀναχωρήσεις καὶ
ἐπίπλους οὐκ ἐκ βραχέος καὶ περιγραπτοῦ ὁρμώμενοί τε
3 καὶ καταίροντες ἕξουσιν. τό τε ξύμπαν εἰπεῖν, οὐδενὶ
τρόπῳ οἱ ἔφη ἀρέσκειν ἐν τῷ αὐτῷ ἔτι μένειν, ἀλλ' ὅτι
τάχιστα ἤδη ἐξανίστασθαι καὶ μὴ μέλλειν. καὶ ὁ Εὐρυμέδων 5
4 αὐτῷ ταῦτα ξυνηγόρευεν. ἀντιλέγοντος δὲ τοῦ Νικίου ὄκνος
τις καὶ μέλλησις ἐνεγένετο καὶ ἅμα ὑπόνοια μή τι καὶ πλέον
εἰδὼς ὁ Νικίας ἰσχυρίζηται. καὶ οἱ μὲν Ἀθηναῖοι τούτῳ
τῷ τρόπῳ διεμέλλησάν τε καὶ κατὰ χώραν ἔμενον.

50 Ὁ δὲ Γύλιππος καὶ ὁ Σικανὸς ἐν τούτῳ παρῆσαν ἐς τὰς 10
Συρακούσας, ὁ μὲν Σικανὸς ἁμαρτὼν τοῦ Ἀκράγαντος (ἐν
Γέλᾳ γὰρ ὄντος αὐτοῦ ἔτι ἡ τοῖς Συρακοσίοις στάσις [ἐς]
φιλία ἐξεπεπτώκει)· ὁ δὲ Γύλιππος ἄλλην τε στρατιὰν
πολλὴν ἔχων ἦλθεν ἀπὸ τῆς Σικελίας καὶ τοὺς ἐκ τῆς
Πελοποννήσου τοῦ ἦρος ἐν ταῖς ὁλκάσιν ὁπλίτας ἀποστα- 15
2 λέντας, ἀφικομένους ἀπὸ τῆς Λιβύης ἐς Σελινοῦντα. ἀπενεχθέντες γὰρ ἐς Λιβύην, καὶ δόντων Κυρηναίων τριήρεις δύο
καὶ τοῦ πλοῦ ἡγεμόνας, καὶ ἐν τῷ παράπλῳ Εὐεσπερίταις
πολιορκουμένοις ὑπὸ Λιβύων ξυμμαχήσαντες καὶ νικήσαντες
τοὺς Λίβυς, καὶ αὐτόθεν παραπλεύσαντες ἐς Νέαν πόλιν 20
Καρχηδονιακὸν ἐμπόριον, ὅθενπερ Σικελία ἐλάχιστον δυοῖν
ἡμερῶν καὶ νυκτὸς πλοῦν ἀπέχει, καὶ ἀπ' αὐτοῦ περαιω-
3 θέντες ἀφίκοντο ἐς Σελινοῦντα. καὶ οἱ μὲν Συρακόσιοι
εὐθὺς αὐτῶν ἐλθόντων παρεσκευάζοντο ὡς ἐπιθησόμενοι κατ'
ἀμφότερα αὖθις τοῖς Ἀθηναίοις καὶ ναυσὶ καὶ πεζῷ· οἱ δὲ 25
τῶν Ἀθηναίων στρατηγοὶ ὁρῶντες στρατιάν τε ἄλλην προσ-
γεγενημένην αὐτοῖς καὶ τὰ ἑαυτῶν ἅμα οὐκ ἐπὶ τὸ βέλτιον
χωροῦντα, ἀλλὰ καθ' ἡμέραν τοῖς πᾶσι χαλεπώτερον ἴσχοντα,
μάλιστα δὲ τῇ ἀσθενείᾳ τῶν ἀνθρώπων πιεζόμενα, μετε-

5 ἐξανίστασθαι (ἐξίστασθαι B) post μέλλειν habent codd., transp.
Haase   7 ἐγένετο A B F M   12 ἐς secl. Bauer   13 φιλία B :
φιλίαν G : φίλια cett. G¹ (sine acc. C)   τε om. B   14 ἔχων πολλὴν B
16 ἀπενεχθέντες B : ἀπενεχθέντων cett.   21 ὅθενπερ Σικελία Böhme :
ὅθεν πρὸς Σικελίαν codd.   δυοῖν B : δύο cett.   22 πλοῦν B :
πλοῦς cett.

μέλοντό τε πρότερον οὐκ ἀναστάντες καὶ ὡς αὐτοῖς οὐδὲ ὁ
Νικίας ἔτι ὁμοίως ἐνηντιοῦτο, ἀλλ' ἢ μὴ φανερῶς γε ἀξιῶν
ψηφίζεσθαι, προεῖπον ὡς ἐδύναντο ἀδηλότατα ἔκπλουν ἐκ τοῦ
στρατοπέδου πᾶσι, καὶ παρασκευάσασθαι ὅταν τις σημήνῃ.
5 καὶ μελλόντων αὐτῶν, ἐπειδὴ ἑτοῖμα ἦν, ἀποπλεῖν ἡ σελήνη 4
ἐκλείπει· ἐτύγχανε γὰρ πασσέληνος οὖσα. καὶ οἱ Ἀθηναῖοι οἵ τε πλείους ἐπισχεῖν ἐκέλευον τοὺς στρατηγοὺς
ἐνθύμιον ποιούμενοι, καὶ ὁ Νικίας (ἦν γάρ τι καὶ ἄγαν
θειασμῷ τε καὶ τῷ τοιούτῳ προσκείμενος) οὐδ' ἂν διαβου-
10 λεύσασθαι ἔτι ἔφη πρίν, ὡς οἱ μάντεις ἐξηγοῦντο, τρὶς
ἐννέα ἡμέρας μεῖναι, ὅπως ἂν πρότερον κινηθείη. καὶ τοῖς
μὲν Ἀθηναίοις μελλήσασι διὰ τοῦτο ἡ μονὴ ἐγεγένητο.

Οἱ δὲ Συρακόσιοι καὶ αὐτοὶ τοῦτο πυθόμενοι πολλῷ μᾶλ- 51
λον ἐπηρμένοι ἦσαν μὴ ἀνιέναι τὰ τῶν Ἀθηναίων, ὡς καὶ
15 αὐτῶν κατεγνωκότων ἤδη μηκέτι κρεισσόνων εἶναι σφῶν
μήτε ταῖς ναυσὶ μήτε τῷ πεζῷ (οὐ γὰρ ἂν τὸν ἔκπλουν
ἐπιβουλεῦσαι), καὶ ἅμα οὐ βουλόμενοι αὐτοὺς ἄλλοσέ ποι
τῆς Σικελίας καθεζομένους χαλεπωτέρους εἶναι προσπολε-
μεῖν, ἀλλ' αὐτοῦ ὡς τάχιστα καὶ ἐν ᾧ σφίσι ξυμφέρει
20 ἀναγκάσαι αὐτοὺς ναυμαχεῖν. τὰς οὖν ναῦς ἐπλήρουν καὶ 2
ἀνεπειρῶντο ἡμέρας ὅσαι αὐτοῖς ἐδόκουν ἱκαναὶ εἶναι.
ἐπειδὴ δὲ καιρὸς ἦν, τῇ μὲν προτέρᾳ πρὸς τὰ τείχη τῶν
Ἀθηναίων προσέβαλλον, καὶ ἐπεξελθόντος μέρους τινὸς οὐ
πολλοῦ καὶ τῶν ὁπλιτῶν καὶ τῶν ἱππέων κατά τινας πύλας
25 ἀπολαμβάνουσί τε τῶν ὁπλιτῶν τινὰς καὶ τρεψάμενοι κατα-
διώκουσιν· οὔσης δὲ στενῆς τῆς ἐσόδου οἱ Ἀθηναῖοι ἵππους
τε ἑβδομήκοντα ἀπολλύασι καὶ τῶν ὁπλιτῶν οὐ πολλούς.

Καὶ ταύτῃ μὲν τῇ ἡμέρᾳ ἀπεχώρησεν ἡ στρατιὰ τῶν 52
Συρακοσίων· τῇ δ' ὑστεραίᾳ ταῖς τε ναυσὶν ἐκπλέουσιν

2 ἀλλ' ἢ recc. : ἄλλο εἰ codd.   post ἀξιῶν add. μὴ codd. : om. recc.
4 παρεσκευάσθαι Abresch   10 post πρίν add. ἃς B : ἃς pro ὡς recc.
14 ἐπηρμένοι B : ἐγηγερμένοι cett. γρ. B   15 post σφῶν add. τε B
16 ταῖς B : om. cett. τῷ om. C ? suprascr. (G)   17 βουλόμενος B
21 ἀνεπειρῶντο B : ἀνεπαύοντο cett.   ὅσας B   εἶναι om. C G   22
προτεραίᾳ B   26 ἐσόδου B : ἐφόδου cett.

οὔσαις ἐξ καὶ ἐβδομήκοντα καὶ τῷ πεζῷ ἅμα πρὸς τὰ τείχη
ἐχώρουν. οἱ δ᾽ Ἀθηναῖοι ἀντανῆγον ναυσὶν ἐξ καὶ ὀγδοή-
2 κοντα καὶ προσμείξαντες ἐναυμάχουν. καὶ τὸν Εὐρυμέδοντα
ἔχοντα τὸ δεξιὸν κέρας τῶν Ἀθηναίων καὶ βουλόμενον
περικλῄσασθαι τὰς ναῦς τῶν ἐναντίων καὶ ἐπεξάγοντα τῷ 5
πλῷ πρὸς τὴν γῆν μᾶλλον, νικήσαντες οἱ Συρακόσιοι καὶ οἱ
ξύμμαχοι τὸ μέσον πρῶτον τῶν Ἀθηναίων ἀπολαμβάνουσι
κἀκεῖνον ἐν τῷ κοίλῳ καὶ μυχῷ τοῦ λιμένος καὶ αὐτόν τε
διαφθείρουσι καὶ τὰς μετ᾽ αὐτοῦ ναῦς ἐπισπομένας· ἔπει-α
δὲ καὶ τὰς πάσας ἤδη ναῦς τῶν Ἀθηναίων κατεδίωκόν τε 10
καὶ ἐξεώθουν ἐς τὴν γῆν.

53 Ὁ δὲ Γύλιππος ὁρῶν τὰς ναῦς τῶν πολεμίων νικωμένας
καὶ ἔξω τῶν σταυρωμάτων καὶ τοῦ ἑαυτῶν στρατοπέδου
καταφερομένας, βουλόμενος διαφθείρειν τοὺς ἐκβαίνοντας καὶ
τὰς ναῦς ῥᾷον τοὺς Συρακοσίους ἀφέλκειν τῆς γῆς φιλίας 15
οὔσης, παρεβοήθει ἐπὶ τὴν χηλὴν μέρος τι ἔχων τῆς στρατιᾶς.
2 καὶ αὐτοὺς οἱ Τυρσηνοί (οὗτοι γὰρ ἐφύλασσον τοῖς Ἀθηναίοις
ταύτῃ) ὁρῶντες ἀτάκτως προσφερομένους, ἐπεκβοηθήσαντες
καὶ προσπεσόντες τοῖς πρώτοις τρέπουσι καὶ ἐσβάλλουσιν
3 ἐς τὴν λίμνην τὴν Λυσιμέλειαν καλουμένην. ὕστερον δὲ 20
πλέονος ἤδη τοῦ στρατεύματος παρόντος τῶν Συρακοσίων
καὶ ξυμμάχων καὶ οἱ Ἀθηναῖοι ἐπιβοηθήσαντες καὶ δείσαντες
περὶ ταῖς ναυσὶν ἐς μάχην τε κατέστησαν πρὸς αὐτοὺς καὶ
νικήσαντες ἐπεδίωξαν καὶ ὁπλίτας τε οὐ πολλοὺς ἀπέκτειναν
καὶ τὰς ναῦς τὰς μὲν πολλὰς διέσωσάν τε καὶ ξυνήγαγον 25
κατὰ τὸ στρατόπεδον, δυοῖν δὲ δεούσας εἴκοσιν οἱ Συρακόσιοι
καὶ οἱ ξύμμαχοι ἔλαβον αὐτῶν καὶ τοὺς ἄνδρας πάντας
4 ἀπέκτειναν. καὶ ἐπὶ τὰς λοιπὰς ἐμπρῆσαι βουλόμενοι
ὁλκάδα παλαιὰν κληματίδων καὶ δᾳδὸς γεμίσαντες (ἦν γὰρ

1 τῷ τείχει Β   5 ἐπεξάγοντα Β : ἐξάγοντα cett.   7 τῶν Ἀθηναίων πρῶτον Α Β   8 prius καὶ om. C   10 ἤδη ναῦς Β : ναῦς ἤδη
cett.   11 ἐξώθουν Β   18 ταύτῃ Β : om. cett.   22 καὶ δείσαντες om. C   26 δὲ Β : om. cett. γρ. Β   post εἴκοσιν add. ἃς
ACEFGM γρ. Β   28 βουλόμενοι ἐμπρῆσαι Β

ἐπὶ τοὺς Ἀθηναίους ὁ ἄνεμος οὔριος) ἀφεῖσαν [τὴν ναῦν] πῦρ
ἐμβαλόντες. καὶ οἱ Ἀθηναῖοι δείσαντες περὶ ταῖς ναυσὶν
ἀντεμηχανήσαντό τε σβεστήρια κωλύματα καὶ παύσαντες
τήν τε φλόγα καὶ τὸ μὴ προσελθεῖν ἐγγὺς τὴν ὁλκάδα
5 τοῦ κινδύνου ἀπηλλάγησαν. μετὰ δὲ τοῦτο Συρακόσιοι 54
μὲν τῆς τε ναυμαχίας τροπαῖον ἔστησαν καὶ τῆς ἄνω τῆς
πρὸς τῷ τείχει ἀπολήψεως τῶν ὁπλιτῶν, ὅθεν καὶ τοὺς
ἵππους ἔλαβον, Ἀθηναῖοι δὲ ἧς τε οἱ Τυρσηνοὶ τροπῆς
ἐποιήσαντο τῶν πεζῶν ἐς τὴν λίμνην καὶ ἧς αὐτοὶ τῷ ἄλλῳ
10 στρατοπέδῳ.

Γεγενημένης δὲ τῆς νίκης τοῖς Συρακοσίοις λαμπρᾶς ἤδη 55
καὶ τοῦ ναυτικοῦ (πρότερον μὲν γὰρ ἐφοβοῦντο τὰς μετὰ τοῦ
Δημοσθένους ναῦς ἐπελθούσας) οἱ μὲν Ἀθηναῖοι ἐν παντὶ δὴ
ἀθυμίας ἦσαν καὶ ὁ παράλογος αὐτοῖς μέγας ἦν, πολὺ δὲ
15 μείζων ἔτι τῆς στρατείας ὁ μετάμελος. πόλεσι γὰρ ταύταις 2
μόναις ἤδη ὁμοιοτρόποις ἐπελθόντες, δημοκρατουμέναις τε,
ὥσπερ καὶ αὐτοί, καὶ ναῦς καὶ ἵππους καὶ μεγέθη ἐχούσαις,
οὐ δυνάμενοι ἐπενεγκεῖν οὔτ' ἐκ πολιτείας τι μεταβολῆς τὸ
διάφορον αὐτοῖς, ᾧ προσήγοντο ἄν, οὔτ' ἐκ παρασκευῆς πολλῷ
20 κρείσσονος, σφαλλόμενοι δὲ τὰ πλείω, τά τε πρὸ αὐτῶν
ἠπόρουν, καὶ ἐπειδή γε καὶ ταῖς ναυσὶν ἐκρατήθησαν, ὃ οὐκ
ἂν ᾤοντο, πολλῷ δὴ μᾶλλον ἔτι. οἱ δὲ Συρακόσιοι τόν τε 56
λιμένα εὐθὺς παρέπλεον ἀδεῶς καὶ τὸ στόμα αὐτοῦ διενοοῦντο
κλῄσειν, ὅπως μηκέτι, μηδ' εἰ βούλοιντο, λάθοιεν αὐτοὺς οἱ
25 Ἀθηναῖοι ἐκπλεύσαντες. οὐ γὰρ περὶ τοῦ αὐτοὶ σωθῆναι 2
μόνον ἔτι τὴν ἐπιμέλειαν ἐποιοῦντο, ἀλλὰ καὶ ὅπως ἐκείνους
κωλύσουσι, νομίζοντες ὅπερ ἦν, ἀπό τε τῶν παρόντων πολὺ

1 secl. Bothe   4 τε B : om. cett.   5 οἱ Συρακόσιοι A C
E F G M   7 δ]θεν incipit Π¹⁸   9 τῷ πεζῷ Π¹⁸   12 καὶ om.
B   μὲν om. Π¹⁸   13 δὴ] ἤδη B (γρ. δὴ) ! Π¹⁸   15 στρατείας Π¹⁸ :
στρατιᾶς cett.   16 ἤδη] δὴ ! Π¹⁸   ὁμ[οτ]ρό[πο]ι[ς] Π¹⁸   17 ναυσὶ καὶ
ἵπποις καὶ μεγέθει A C (-θη) E F G M (suprascr. -θη)   ἰσχνούσαις Duker
20 κρείσσονος Schol.: κρείσσους ὄντες B : κρείσσους cett. [Π¹⁸]   πρὸς
B [Π¹⁸]   25 αὐτοὶ B : αὐτοῦ cett. [Π¹⁸]   σωθῆναι B : ἡσσηθῆναι G :
ἡσσωθῆναι cett. [Π¹⁸]   27 κωλύσουσι C Π¹⁸ : κωλύσωσι cett.

σφῶν καθυπέρτερα τὰ πράγματα εἶναι καί, εἰ δύναιντο
κρατῆσαι Ἀθηναίων τε καὶ τῶν ξυμμάχων καὶ κατὰ γῆν καὶ
κατὰ θάλασσαν, καλὸν σφίσιν ἐς τοὺς Ἕλληνας τὸ ἀγώνισμα
φανεῖσθαι· τούς τε γὰρ ἄλλους Ἕλληνας εὐθὺς τοὺς μὲν
ἐλευθεροῦσθαι, τοὺς δὲ φόβου ἀπολύεσθαι (οὐ γὰρ ἔτι δυνατὴν 5
ἔσεσθαι τὴν ὑπόλοιπον Ἀθηναίων δύναμιν τὸν ὕστερον ἐπ-
ενεχθησόμενον πόλεμον ἐνεγκεῖν), καὶ αὐτοὶ δόξαντες αὐτῶν
αἴτιοι εἶναι ὑπό τε τῶν ἄλλων ἀνθρώπων καὶ ὑπὸ τῶν ἔπειτα
3 πολὺ θαυμασθήσεσθαι. καὶ ἦν δὲ ἄξιος ὁ ἀγὼν κατά τε
ταῦτα καὶ ὅτι οὐχὶ Ἀθηναίων μόνον περιεγίγνοντο, ἀλλὰ 10
καὶ τῶν ἄλλων πολλῶν ξυμμάχων, καὶ οὐδ᾽ αὐτοὶ αὖ μόνον,
ἀλλὰ καὶ μετὰ τῶν ξυμβοηθησάντων σφίσιν, ἡγεμόνες τε
γενόμενοι μετὰ Κορινθίων καὶ Λακεδαιμονίων καὶ τὴν
σφετέραν πόλιν ἐμπαρασχόντες προκινδυνεῦσαί τε καὶ τοῦ
4 ναυτικοῦ μέγα μέρος προκόψαντες. ἔθνη γὰρ πλεῖστα δὴ 15
ἐπὶ μίαν πόλιν ταύτην ξυνῆλθε, πλήν γε δὴ τοῦ ξύμπαντος
λόγου τοῦ ἐν τῷδε τῷ πολέμῳ πρὸς τὴν Ἀθηναίων τε πόλιν
καὶ Λακεδαιμονίων.

57 Τοσοίδε γὰρ ἑκάτεροι ἐπὶ Σικελίαν τε καὶ περὶ Σικελίας,
τοῖς μὲν ξυγκτησόμενοι τὴν χώραν ἐλθόντες, τοῖς δὲ ξυνδια- 20
σώσοντες, ἐπὶ Συρακούσας ἐπολέμησαν, οὐ κατὰ δίκην τι
μᾶλλον οὐδὲ κατὰ ξυγγένειαν μετ᾽ ἀλλήλων στάντες, ἀλλ᾽
ὡς ἑκάστοις τῆς ξυντυχίας ἢ κατὰ τὸ ξυμφέρον ἢ ἀνάγκη
2 ἔσχεν. Ἀθηναῖοι μὲν αὐτοὶ Ἴωνες ἐπὶ Δωριᾶς Συρακοσίους
ἑκόντες ἦλθον, καὶ αὐτοῖς τῇ αὐτῇ φωνῇ καὶ νομίμοις ἔτι 25
χρώμενοι Λήμνιοι καὶ Ἴμβριοι καὶ Αἰγινῆται, οἳ τότε Αἴγιναν
εἶχον, καὶ ἔτι Ἑστιαιῆς οἱ ἐν Εὐβοίᾳ Ἑστίαιαν οἰκοῦντες
3 ἄποικοι ὄντες ξυνεστράτευσαν. τῶν δ᾽ ἄλλων οἱ μὲν ὑπήκοοι,

1 τὰ om. B   5 φόβῳ A B E F M   7 ἀνενεγκεῖν Π¹⁸ : ἐπενεγκεῖν
M   αἴτιοι αὐτῶν (suprascr.) B   8 alt. ὑπὸ om. C ⟨G⟩ Π¹⁸   9 ἐπὶ
πολὺ Π¹⁸   10 μόνων Stahl [Π¹⁸]   11 μόνοι Madvig [Π¹⁸]   14 τε
? om. Π¹⁸   16 δὴ om. B ? Π¹⁸   17 λόγου) ὄχλου Krüger : ξυλλόγου
Heilmann [Π¹⁸]   20 ξυνδιασώσοντες E (-σώσ-) G suprascr. B Π¹⁸ :
ξυνδιασώσαντες cett.   21 Συρακούσαις Bauer   23 ἕκαστοι suprascr.
ἑκάστοις B   ἀνάγκης suprascr. ἀνάγκη B ⟨Π¹⁸]   24 ἔσχον recc. [Π¹⁸]
27 οἱ M

οἱ δ' ἀπὸ ξυμμαχίας αὐτόνομοι, εἰσὶ δὲ καὶ οἱ μισθοφόροι
ξυνεστράτευον. καὶ τῶν μὲν ὑπηκόων καὶ φόρου ὑποτελῶν 4
Ἐρετριῆς καὶ Χαλκιδῆς καὶ Στυρῆς καὶ Καρύστιοι ἀπ' Εὐβοίας
ἦσαν, ἀπὸ δὲ νήσων Κεῖοι καὶ Ἄνδριοι καὶ Τήνιοι, ἐκ δ'
5 Ἰωνίας Μιλήσιοι καὶ Σάμιοι καὶ Χῖοι. τούτων Χῖοι οὐχ
ὑποτελεῖς ὄντες φόρου, ναῦς δὲ παρέχοντες αὐτόνομοι ξυν-
έσποντο. καὶ τὸ πλεῖστον Ἴωνες ὄντες οὗτοι πάντες καὶ ἀπ'
Ἀθηναίων πλὴν Καρυστίων (οὗτοι δ' εἰσὶ Δρύοπες), ὑπήκοοι
δ' ὄντες καὶ ἀνάγκῃ ὅμως Ἴωνές γε ἐπὶ Δωριᾶς ἠκολούθουν.
10 πρὸς δ' αὐτοῖς Αἰολῆς, Μηθυμναῖοι μὲν ναυσὶ καὶ οὐ φόρῳ 5
ὑπήκοοι, Τενέδιοι δὲ καὶ Αἴνιοι ὑποτελεῖς. οὗτοι δὲ Αἰολῆς
Αἰολεῦσι τοῖς κτίσασι Βοιωτοῖς ⟨τοῖς⟩ μετὰ Συρακοσίων κατ'
ἀνάγκην ἐμάχοντο, Πλαταιῆς δὲ καταντικρὺ Βοιωτοὶ Βοιωτοῖς
μόνοι εἰκότως κατὰ τὸ ἔχθος. Ῥόδιοι δὲ καὶ Κυθήριοι Δωριῆς 6
15 ἀμφότεροι, οἱ μὲν Λακεδαιμονίων ἄποικοι Κυθήριοι ἐπὶ Λακε-
δαιμονίους τοὺς ἅμα Γυλίππῳ μετ' Ἀθηναίων ὅπλα ἔφερον,
Ῥόδιοι δὲ Ἀργεῖοι γένος Συρακοσίοις μὲν Δωριεῦσι, Γελῴοις
δὲ καὶ ἀποίκοις ἑαυτῶν οὖσι μετὰ Συρακοσίων στρατευομένοις
ἠναγκάζοντο πολεμεῖν. τῶν τε περὶ Πελοπόννησον νησιωτῶν 7
20 Κεφαλλῆνες μὲν καὶ Ζακύνθιοι αὐτόνομοι μέν, κατὰ δὲ τὸ
νησιωτικὸν μᾶλλον κατειργόμενοι, ὅτι θαλάσσης ἐκράτουν
οἱ Ἀθηναῖοι, ξυνείποντο· Κερκυραῖοι δὲ οὐ μόνον Δωριῆς,
ἀλλὰ καὶ Κορίνθιοι σαφῶς ἐπὶ Κορινθίους τε καὶ Συρακοσίους, τῶν μὲν ἄποικοι ὄντες, τῶν δὲ ξυγγενεῖς, ἀνάγκῃ
25 μὲν ἐκ τοῦ εὐπρεποῦς, βουλήσει δὲ κατὰ ἔχθος τὸ Κορινθίων
οὐχ ἧσσον εἵποντο. καὶ οἱ Μεσσήνιοι νῦν καλούμενοι ἐκ 8
Ναυπάκτου καὶ ἐκ Πύλου τότε ὑπ' Ἀθηναίων ἐχομένης ἐς
τὸν πόλεμον παρελήφθησαν. καὶ ἔτι Μεγαρέων φυγάδες
οὐ πολλοὶ Μεγαρεῦσι Σελινουντίοις οὖσι κατὰ ξυμφορὰν

---

1 οἱ καὶ BGM: καὶ om. E [Π¹⁸]   4 Τήνιοι B : Τήλιοι vel Τηλίοι cett.
⸘Π¹⁸   5 φόρου οὐχ ὑποτελεῖς ὄντες B   6 ξυνείποντο recc.   9 γε
B Π¹⁸ : τε cett.   12 τοῖς add. Lindau   13 καταντικρὺ] καὶ ἀντικρυς
Böhme   Βοιωτοὶ om. Π¹⁸   14 τὸ B M. om. cett. Π¹⁸   16 ἐπέ-
φερον B Π¹⁸   17 Δωριῆς Δωρι[εῦσι Π¹⁸   19 τε] δὲ B Π¹⁸ m. 1
22 οἱ om. C [Π¹⁸]   26 ἐκ Ναυπάκτου B Π¹⁸ : ἐν Ναυπάκτῳ cett.

9 ἐμάχοντο. τῶν δὲ ἄλλων ἑκούσιος μᾶλλον ἢ στρατεία
ἐγίγνετο ἤδη. Ἀργεῖοι μὲν γὰρ οὐ τῆς ξυμμαχίας ἕνεκα
μᾶλλον ἢ τῆς Λακεδαιμονίων τε ἔχθρας καὶ τῆς παραυτίκα
ἕκαστοι ἰδίας ὠφελίας Δωριῆς ἐπὶ Δωριᾶς μετὰ Ἀθηναίων
Ἰώνων ἠκολούθουν, Μαντινῆς δὲ καὶ ἄλλοι Ἀρκάδων μισθο- 5
φόροι ἐπὶ τοὺς αἰεὶ πολεμίους σφίσιν ἀποδεικνυμένους ἰέναι
εἰωθότες καὶ τότε τοὺς μετὰ Κορινθίων ἐλθόντας Ἀρκάδας
οὐδὲν ἧσσον διὰ κέρδος ἡγούμενοι πολεμίους, Κρῆτες δὲ καὶ
Αἰτωλοὶ μισθῷ καὶ οὗτοι πεισθέντες· ξυνέβη δὲ τοῖς Κρησὶ
τὴν Γέλαν Ῥοδίοις ξυγκτίσαντας μὴ ξὺν τοῖς ἀποίκοις, 10
10 ἀλλ' ἐπὶ τοὺς ἀποίκους ἑκόν.ας μετὰ μισθοῦ ἐλθεῖν. καὶ
Ἀκαρνάνων τινὲς ἅμα μὲν κέρδει, τὸ δὲ πλέον Δημοσθένους
φιλίᾳ καὶ Ἀθηναίων εὐνοίᾳ ξύμμαχοι ὄντες ἐπεκούρησαν.
11 καὶ οἵδε μὲν τῷ Ἰονίῳ κόλπῳ ὁριζόμενοι· Ἰταλιωτῶν δὲ
Θούριοι καὶ Μεταπόντιοι ἐν τοιαύταις ἀνάγκαις τότε στασιω- 15
τικῶν καιρῶν κατειλημμένοι ξυνεστράτευον, καὶ Σικελιωτῶν
Νάξιοι καὶ Καταναῖοι, βαρβάρων δὲ Ἐγεσταῖοί τε, οἵπερ
ἐπηγάγοντο, καὶ Σικελῶν τὸ πλέον, καὶ τῶν ἔξω Σικελίας
Τυρσηνῶν τέ τινες κατὰ διαφορὰν Συρακοσίων καὶ Ἰάπυγες
μισθοφόροι. τοσάδε μὲν μετὰ Ἀθηναίων ἔθνη ἐστράτευον. 20
58 Συρακοσίοις δὲ ἀντεβοήθησαν Καμαριναῖοι μὲν ὅμοροι
ὄντες καὶ Γελῷοι οἰκοῦντες μετ' αὐτούς, ἔπειτα Ἀκραγαντίνων ἡσυχαζόντων ἐν τῷ ἐπ' ἐκεῖνα ἱδρυμένοι Σελινούντιοι.
2 καὶ οἵδε μὲν τῆς Σικελίας τὸ πρὸς Λιβύην μέρος τετραμμένον
νεμόμενοι, Ἱμεραῖοι δὲ ἀπὸ τοῦ πρὸς τὸν Τυρσηνικὸν πόντον 25
μορίου, ἐν ᾧ καὶ μόνοι Ἕλληνες οἰκοῦσιν· οὗτοι δὲ καὶ ἐξ
3 αὐτοῦ μόνοι ἐβοήθησαν. καὶ Ἑλληνικὰ μὲν ἔθνη τῶν ἐν
Σικελίᾳ τοσάδε, Δωριῆς τε καὶ [οἱ] αὐτόνομοι πάντες, ξυνεμάχουν, βαρβάρων δὲ Σικελοὶ μόνοι ὅσοι μὴ ἀφέστασαν

2 γὰρ B : om. cett.   4 ὠφελίας a Π¹⁸ : ὠφελείας B : om. cett.
6 αἰεὶ πολεμίους] λειπομένους B   εἰωθότες ἰέναι B Π¹⁸   11 ἐποίκους
B [Π¹⁸]   ἑκόντας B : ἄκοντας cett. [Π¹⁸]   15 Μεταπον]τίνοι (sic)...
19 Συρακοσίων Π³⁰   στασιωτικῶν B C † Π³⁰ : στασιαστικῶν G : στρατιω-
τικῶν cett. [Π¹⁸]   16 κατειλημμένοι Π³⁰ : κατειλημμένων cett.   Σικε-
λιωτῶν] ες Σικελιω[ν] Π³⁰   17 καὶ om. B [Π¹⁸]   τε B Π³⁰ : om. cett.
[Π¹⁸]   18 Σικελῶν B Π³⁰ : Σικελιωτῶν cett. [Π¹⁸]   22 post
Γελῷοι add. οἱ C   27 ἐν om. B [Π¹⁸]   28 οἱ secl. Bekker [Π¹⁸]

πρὸς τοὺς Ἀθηναίους· τῶν δ' ἔξω Σικελίας Ἑλλήνων Λακεδαιμόνιοι μὲν ἡγεμόνα Σπαρτιάτην παρεχόμενοι, νεοδαμώδεις
δὲ τοὺς ἄλλους καὶ Εἵλωτας [δύναται δὲ τὸ νεοδαμῶδες
ἐλεύθερον ἤδη εἶναι], Κορίνθιοι δὲ καὶ ναυσὶ καὶ πεζῷ μόνοι
5 παραγενόμενοι καὶ Λευκάδιοι καὶ Ἀμπρακιῶται κατὰ τὸ
ξυγγενές, ἐκ δὲ Ἀρκαδίας μισθοφόροι ὑπὸ Κορινθίων ἀπο-
σταλέντες καὶ Σικυώνιοι ἀναγκαστοὶ στρατεύοντες, καὶ τῶν
ἔξω Πελοποννήσου Βοιωτοί. πρὸς δὲ τοὺς ἐπελθόντας 4
τούτους οἱ Σικελιῶται αὐτοὶ πλῆθος πλέον κατὰ πάντα παρέ-
10 σχοντο ἅτε μεγάλας πόλεις οἰκοῦντες· καὶ γὰρ ὁπλῖται
πολλοὶ καὶ νῆες καὶ ἵπποι καὶ ὁ ἄλλος ὅμιλος ἄφθονος
ξυνελέγη. καὶ πρὸς ἅπαντας αὖθις ὡς εἰπεῖν τοὺς ἄλλους
Συρακόσιοι αὐτοὶ πλείω ἐπορίσαντο διὰ μέγεθός τε πόλεως
καὶ ὅτι ἐν μεγίστῳ κινδύνῳ ἦσαν. καὶ αἱ μὲν ἑκατέρων 59
15 ἐπικουρίαι τοσαίδε ξυνελέγησαν, καὶ τότε ἤδη πᾶσαι ἀμφοτέροις παρῆσαν καὶ οὐκέτι οὐδὲν οὐδετέροις ἐπῆλθεν.

Οἱ δ' οὖν Συρακόσιοι καὶ οἱ ξύμμαχοι εἰκότως ἐνόμισαν 2
καλὸν ἀγώνισμα σφίσιν εἶναι ἐπὶ τῇ γεγενημένῃ νίκῃ τῆς
ναυμαχίας ἑλεῖν τε τὸ στρατόπεδον ἅπαν τῶν Ἀθηναίων
20 τοσοῦτον ὄν, καὶ μηδὲ καθ' ἕτερα αὐτούς, μήτε διὰ θαλάσσης
μήτε τῷ πεζῷ, διαφυγεῖν. ἔκλῃον οὖν τόν τε λιμένα εὐθὺς 3
τὸν μέγαν, ἔχοντα τὸ στόμα ὀκτὼ σταδίων μάλιστα, τριήρεσι
πλαγίαις καὶ πλοίοις καὶ ἀκάτοις ἐπ' ἀγκυρῶν ὁρμίζοντες,
καὶ τἆλλα, ἢν ἔτι ναυμαχεῖν οἱ Ἀθηναῖοι τολμήσωσι,
25 παρεσκευάζοντο, καὶ ὀλίγον οὐδὲν ἐς οὐδὲν ἐπενόουν. τοῖς 60
δὲ Ἀθηναίοις τήν τε ἀπόκλῃσιν ὁρῶσι καὶ τὴν ἄλλην διάνοιαν
αὐτῶν αἰσθομένοις βουλευτέα ἐδόκει. καὶ ξυνελθόντες οἵ 2
τε στρατηγοὶ καὶ οἱ ταξίαρχοι πρὸς τὴν παροῦσαν ἀπορίαν
τῶν τε ἄλλων καὶ ὅτι τὰ ἐπιτήδεια οὔτε αὐτίκα ἔτι εἶχον

3, 4 δύναται ... εἶναι, ut videtur, non legit Schol., secl. Aem. Portus
[Π¹⁸]   11 ὁ Β Π¹⁸: om. cett.   13 Συρακόσιοι Β : Συρακο(υ)σίους
cett. [Π¹⁸]   τε Β : om. cett. [Π¹⁸]   14 post ὅτι add. γὰρ Β [Π¹⁸]
17 δ' Krüger : τε codd. [Π¹⁸]   καὶ οἱ ξύμμαχοι Β : om. cett. [Π¹⁸]
18 ἀγώνισμα Β : ἀγῶνα cett. [Π¹⁸]   20 καθ' ἕτερα Β : κακάτερα (sic)
C : καθ' ἑκάτερα cett. [Π¹⁸]

(προπέμψαντες γὰρ ἐς Κατάνην ὡς ἐκπλευσόμενοι ἀπεῖπον μὴ
ἐπάγειν) οὔτε τὸ λοιπὸν ἔμελλον ἕξειν, εἰ μὴ ναυκρατήσουσιν,
ἐβουλεύσαντο τὰ μὲν τείχη τὰ ἄνω ἐκλιπεῖν, πρὸς δ' αὐταῖς
ταῖς ναυσὶν ἀπολαβόντες διατειχίσματι ὅσον οἷόν τε ἐλάχιστον τοῖς τε σκεύεσι καὶ τοῖς ἀσθενοῦσιν ἱκανὸν γενέσθαι, 5
τοῦτο μὲν φρουρεῖν, ἀπὸ δὲ τοῦ ἄλλου πεζοῦ τὰς ναῦς ἁπάσας,
ὅσαι ἦσαν καὶ δυναταὶ καὶ ἀπλοώτεραι, πάντα τινὰ ἐσβιβά-
ζοντες πληρῶσαι, καὶ διαναυμαχήσαντες, ἢν μὲν νικῶσιν, ἐς
Κατάνην κομίζεσθαι, ἢν δὲ μή, ἐμπρήσαντες τὰς ναῦς πεζῇ
ξυνταξάμενοι ἀποχωρεῖν ᾗ ἂν τάχιστα μέλλωσί τινος χωρίου 10
3 ἢ βαρβαρικοῦ ἢ Ἑλληνικοῦ φιλίου ἀντιλήψεσθαι. καὶ οἱ
μέν, ὡς ἔδοξεν αὐτοῖς ταῦτα, καὶ ἐποίησαν· ἔκ τε γὰρ τῶν
ἄνω τειχῶν ὑποκατέβησαν καὶ τὰς ναῦς ἐπλήρωσαν πάσας,
ἀναγκάσαντες ἐσβαίνειν ὅστις καὶ ὁπωσοῦν ἐδόκει ἡλικίας
4 μετέχων ἐπιτήδειος εἶναι. καὶ ξυνεπληρώθησαν νῆες αἱ 15
πᾶσαι δέκα μάλιστα καὶ ἑκατόν· τοξότας τε ἐπ' αὐτὰς
πολλοὺς καὶ ἀκοντιστὰς τῶν τε Ἀκαρνάνων καὶ τῶν ἄλλων
ξένων ἐσεβίβαζον, καὶ τἆλλα ὡς οἷόν τ' ἦν ἐξ ἀναγκαίου τε
5 καὶ τοιαύτης διανοίας ἐπορίσαντο. ὁ δὲ Νικίας, ἐπειδὴ τὰ
πολλὰ ἑτοῖμα ἦν, ὁρῶν τοὺς στρατιώτας τῷ τε παρὰ τὸ εἰωθὸς 20
πολὺ ταῖς ναυσὶ κρατηθῆναι ἀθυμοῦντας καὶ διὰ τὴν τῶν
ἐπιτηδείων σπάνιν ὡς τάχιστα βουλομένους διακινδυνεύειν,
ξυγκαλέσας ἅπαντας παρεκελεύσατό τε πρῶτον καὶ ἔλεξε
τοιάδε.

61   'Ἄνδρες στρατιῶται Ἀθηναίων τε καὶ τῶν ἄλλων ξυμ- 25
μάχων, ὁ μὲν ἀγὼν ὁ μέλλων ὁμοίως κοινὸς ἅπασιν ἔσται
περί τε σωτηρίας καὶ πατρίδος ἑκάστοις οὐχ ἧσσον ἢ τοῖς
πολεμίοις· ἢν γὰρ κρατήσωμεν νῦν ταῖς ναυσίν, ἔστι τῳ
2 τὴν ὑπάρχουσάν που οἰκείαν πόλιν ἐπιδεῖν. ἀθυμεῖν δὲ οὐ
χρὴ οὐδὲ πάσχειν ὅπερ οἱ ἀπειρότατοι τῶν ἀνθρώπων, οἳ 30

3 alt. τὰ] τῶν C [Π¹⁸]   5 ἀσθενοῦσιν B : ἀσθενέσιν cett. γρ. B [Π¹⁸]
6 ἁπάσας B : πάσας cett. [Π¹⁸]   7 ἐσβιάζοντες A E F M [Π¹⁸]   14 ante
ἐσβαίνειν add. ?πάντας Π¹⁸   15 αἱ πᾶσαι] ἅπασαι Π¹⁸ m. 1   18 ὡς]
ὅσα suprascr. ὡς B [Π¹⁸]   post ἦν add. καὶ ὡς Π¹⁸   20 post ὁρῶν
add. καὶ A C E F G M [Π¹⁸]   23 τε] τότε C [Π¹⁸]   25 στρατιῶται
om. C [Π¹⁸]   27 ἑκάστῳ suprascr. οις B [Π¹⁸]

τοῖς πρώτοις ἀγῶσι σφαλέντες ἔπειτα διὰ παντὸς τὴν ἐλπίδα τοῦ φόβου ὁμοίαν ταῖς ξυμφοραῖς ἔχουσιν. ἀλλ' ὅσοι 3
τε Ἀθηναίων πάρεστε, πολλῶν ἤδη πολέμων ἔμπειροι ὄντες,
καὶ ὅσοι τῶν ξυμμάχων, ξυστρατευόμενοι αἰεί, μνήσθητε
5 τῶν ἐν τοῖς πολέμοις παραλόγων, καὶ τὸ τῆς τύχης κἂν
μεθ' ἡμῶν ἐλπίσαντες στῆναι καὶ ὡς ἀναμαχούμενοι
ἀξίως τοῦδε τοῦ πλήθους, ὅσον αὐτοὶ ὑμῶν αὐτῶν ἐφορᾶτε,
παρασκευάζεσθε.

'Ἃ δὲ ἀρωγὰ ἐνείδομεν ἐπὶ τῇ τοῦ λιμένος στενότητι 62
10 πρὸς τὸν μέλλοντα ὄχλον τῶν νεῶν ἔσεσθαι καὶ πρὸς τὴν
ἐκείνων ἐπὶ τῶν καταστρωμάτων παρασκευήν, οἷς πρότερον
ἐβλαπτόμεθα, πάντα καὶ ἡμῖν νῦν ἐκ τῶν παρόντων μετὰ
τῶν κυβερνητῶν ἐσκεμμένα ἡτοίμασται. καὶ γὰρ τοξόται 2
πολλοὶ καὶ ἀκοντισταὶ ἐπιβήσονται καὶ ὄχλος, ᾧ ναυμαχίαν
15 μὲν ποιούμενοι ἐν πελάγει οὐκ ἂν ἐχρώμεθα διὰ τὸ βλάπτειν
ἂν τὸ τῆς ἐπιστήμης τῇ βαρύτητι τῶν νεῶν, ἐν δὲ τῇ ἐνθάδε
ἠναγκασμένῃ ἀπὸ τῶν νεῶν πεζομαχίᾳ πρόσφορα ἔσται.
ηὕρηται δ' ἡμῖν ὅσα χρὴ ἀντιναυπηγῆσαι, καὶ πρὸς τὰς τῶν 3
ἐπωτίδων αὐτοῖς παχύτητας, ᾧπερ δὴ μάλιστα ἐβλαπτόμεθα,
20 χειρῶν σιδηρῶν ἐπιβολαί, αἳ σχήσουσι τὴν πάλιν ἀνάκρουσιν τῆς προσπεσούσης νεώς, ἢν τὰ ἐπὶ τούτοις οἱ
ἐπιβάται ὑπουργῶσιν. ἐς τοῦτο γὰρ δὴ ἠναγκάσμεθα ὥστε 4
πεζομαχεῖν ἀπὸ τῶν νεῶν, καὶ τὸ μήτε αὐτοὺς ἀνακρούεσθαι
μήτ' ἐκείνους ἐᾶν ὠφέλιμον φαίνεται, ἄλλως τε καὶ τῆς
25 γῆς, πλὴν ὅσον ἂν ὁ πεζὸς ἡμῶν ἐπέχῃ, πολεμίας οὔσης.

'Ὧν χρὴ μεμνημένους διαμάχεσθαι ὅσον ἂν δύνησθε καὶ 63
μὴ ἐξωθεῖσθαι ἐς αὐτήν, ἀλλὰ ξυμπεσούσης νηὶ νεὼς μὴ
πρότερον ἀξιοῦν ἀπολύεσθαι ἢ τοὺς ἀπὸ τοῦ πολεμίου καταστρώματος ὁπλίτας ἀπαράξητε. καὶ ταῦτα τοῖς ὁπλίταις 2

12 ὑμῖν Α Β Ε F Μ [Π¹⁸]   18 χρὴ Β Π¹⁸ : μὴ cett.   ἀντιναυπηγῆσαι
Β ? Π¹⁸ : ἀντιναυπηγεῖσθαι cett. γρ. Β   19 δὴ Β : om. cett. [Π¹⁸]
23 ἀνακρούεσθαι Α Ε F   24 ἐὰν Α Β F   φαίνηται Α Β Μ   25 ἐσο-
μένης suprascr. οὔσης Β   28 ἀξιοῦν Β : ἄξιον cett. [Π¹⁸]   ἢ Β : ἢν
vel ἢν cett. γρ. Β [Π¹⁸]

οὐχ ἧσσον τῶν ναυτῶν παρακελεύομαι, ὅσῳ τῶν ἄνωθεν
μᾶλλον τὸ ἔργον τοῦτο· ὑπάρχει δ' ἡμῖν ἔτι νῦν γε τὰ
3 πλείω τῷ πεζῷ ἐπικρατεῖν. τοῖς δὲ ναύταις παραινῶ καὶ
ἐν τῷ αὐτῷ τῷδε καὶ δέομαι μὴ ἐκπεπλῆχθαί τι ταῖς
ξυμφοραῖς ἄγαν, τήν τε παρασκευὴν ἀπὸ τῶν καταστρω- 5
μάτων βελτίω νῦν ἔχοντας καὶ τὰς ναῦς πλείους, ἐκείνην
τε τὴν ἡδονὴν ἐνθυμεῖσθαι ὡς ἀξία ἐστὶ διασώσασθαι, οἳ
τέως Ἀθηναῖοι νομιζόμενοι καὶ μὴ ὄντες ἡμῶν τῆς τε φωνῆς
τῇ ἐπιστήμῃ καὶ τῶν τρόπων τῇ μιμήσει ἐθαυμάζεσθε κατὰ
τὴν Ἑλλάδα, καὶ τῆς ἀρχῆς τῆς ἡμετέρας οὐκ ἔλασσον 10
κατὰ τὸ ὠφελεῖσθαι ἔς τε τὸ φοβερὸν τοῖς ὑπηκόοις καὶ τὸ
4 μὴ ἀδικεῖσθαι πολὺ πλέον μετείχετε. ὥστε κοινωνοὶ μόνοι
ἐλευθέρως ἡμῖν τῆς ἀρχῆς ὄντες δικαίως [ἂν] αὐτὴν νῦν
μὴ καταπροδίδοτε, καταφρονήσαντες δὲ Κορινθίων τε, οὓς
πολλάκις νενικήκατε, καὶ Σικελιωτῶν, ὧν οὐδ' ἀντιστῆναι 15
οὐδεὶς ἕως ἤκμαζε τὸ ναυτικὸν ἡμῖν ἠξίωσεν, ἀμύνασθε
αὐτούς, καὶ δείξατε ὅτι καὶ μετ' ἀσθενείας καὶ ξυμφορῶν
ἡ ὑμετέρα ἐπιστήμη κρείσσων ἐστὶν ἑτέρας εὐτυχούσης
64 ῥώμης. τούς τε Ἀθηναίους ὑμῶν πάλιν αὖ καὶ τάδε
ὑπομιμνήσκω, ὅτι οὔτε ναῦς ἐν τοῖς νεωσοίκοις ἄλλας ὁμοίας 20
ταῖσδε οὔτε ὁπλιτῶν ἡλικίαν ὑπελίπετε, εἴ τε ξυμβήσεταί
τι ἄλλο ἢ τὸ κρατεῖν ὑμῖν, τούς τε ἐνθάδε πολεμίους εὐθὺς
ἐπ' ἐκεῖνα πλευσομένους καὶ τοὺς ἐκεῖ ὑπολοίπους ἡμῶν
ἀδυνάτους ἐσομένους τούς τε αὐτοῦ καὶ τοὺς ἐπελθόντας
ἀμύνασθαι. καὶ οἱ μὲν ἂν ὑπὸ Συρακοσίοις εὐθὺς γίγνοισθε, 25
οἷς αὐτοὶ ἴστε οἵᾳ γνώμῃ ἐπήλθετε, οἱ δὲ ἐκεῖ ὑπὸ Λακε-
2 δαιμονίοις. ὥστε ἐν ἑνὶ τῷδε ὑπὲρ ἀμφοτέρων ἀγῶνι
καθεστῶτες καρτερήσατε, εἴπερ ποτέ, καὶ ἐνθυμεῖσθε καθ'
ἑκάστους τε καὶ ξύμπαντες ὅτι οἱ ἐν ταῖς ναυσὶν ὑμῶν
νῦν ἐσόμενοι καὶ πεζοὶ τοῖς Ἀθηναίοις εἰσὶ καὶ νῆες καὶ 30

---

2 ἡμῖν recc. : ὑμῖν codd. [Π¹⁸]   8 ἡμῶν recc. : ὑμῶν codd. [Π¹⁸]
12 μὴ B : om. cett. [Π¹⁸]   13 ἂν om. recc. [Π¹⁸]   17 alt. καὶ
om. B   19 ἢ ὑμῶν (sic) B : ἡμῶν cett. [Π¹⁸]·   22 ἐνθένδε B [Π¹⁸]
23 πλευσουμένους A (-σω-) C E ⟨⏑⟩   ὑμῶν B [Π¹⁸]   29 τε om. B [Π¹⁸]

ἡ ὑπόλοιπος πόλις καὶ τὸ μέγα ὄνομα τῶν Ἀθηνῶν, περὶ
ὧν, εἴ τίς τι ἕτερος ἑτέρου προφέρει ἢ ἐπιστήμῃ ἢ εὐψυχίᾳ,
οὐκ ἂν ἐν ἄλλῳ μᾶλλον καιρῷ ἀποδειξάμενος αὐτός τε
αὑτῷ ὠφέλιμος γένοιτο καὶ τοῖς ξύμπασι σωτήριος.'

5 Ὁ μὲν Νικίας τοσαῦτα παρακελευσάμενος εὐθὺς ἐκέλευε 65
πληροῦν τὰς ναῦς. τῷ δὲ Γυλίππῳ καὶ τοῖς Συρακοσίοις
παρῆν μὲν αἰσθάνεσθαι, ὁρῶσι καὶ αὐτὴν τὴν παρασκευήν,
ὅτι ναυμαχήσουσιν οἱ Ἀθηναῖοι, προηγγέλθη δ' αὐτοῖς
καὶ ἡ ἐπιβολὴ τῶν σιδηρῶν χειρῶν, καὶ πρός τε τἆλλα 2
10 ἐξηρτύσαντο ὡς ἕκαστα καὶ πρὸς τοῦτο· τὰς γὰρ πρῴρας
καὶ τῆς νεὼς ἄνω ἐπὶ πολὺ κατεβύρσωσαν, ὅπως ἂν ἀπολισθάνοι καὶ μὴ ἔχοι ἀντιλαβὴν ἡ χεὶρ ἐπιβαλλομένη.
καὶ ἐπειδὴ πάντα ἑτοῖμα ἦν, παρεκελεύσαντο ἐκείνοις οἵ τε 3
στρατηγοὶ καὶ Γύλιππος καὶ ἔλεξαν τοιάδε.

15 '"Ὅτι μὲν καλὰ τὰ προειργασμένα καὶ ὑπὲρ καλῶν τῶν 66
μελλόντων ὁ ἀγὼν ἔσται, ὦ Συρακόσιοι καὶ ξύμμαχοι, οἵ
τε πολλοὶ δοκεῖτε ἡμῖν εἰδέναι (οὐδὲ γὰρ ἂν οὕτως αὐτῶν
προθύμως ἀντελάβεσθε), καὶ εἴ τις μὴ ἐπὶ ὅσον δεῖ ᾔσθηται,
σημανοῦμεν. Ἀθηναίους γὰρ ἐς τὴν χώραν τήνδε ἐλθόντας 2
20 πρῶτον μὲν ἐπὶ τῆς Σικελίας καταδουλώσει, ἔπειτ', εἰ
κατορθώσειαν, καὶ τῆς Πελοποννήσου καὶ τῆς ἄλλης
Ἑλλάδος, καὶ ἀρχὴν τὴν ἤδη μεγίστην τῶν τε πρὶν
Ἑλλήνων καὶ τῶν νῦν κεκτημένους, πρῶτοι ἀνθρώπων
ὑποστάντες τῷ ναυτικῷ, ᾧπερ πάντα κατέσχον, τὰς μὲν
25 νενικήκατε ἤδη ναυμαχίας, τὴν δ' ἐκ τοῦ εἰκότος νῦν
νικήσετε. ἄνδρες γὰρ ἐπειδὰν ᾧ ἀξιοῦσι προύχειν κολου- 3
θῶσι, τό γ' ὑπόλοιπον αὐτῶν τῆς δόξης ἀσθενέστερον αὐτὸ
ἑαυτοῦ ἐστιν ἢ εἰ μηδ' ᾠήθησαν τὸ πρῶτον, καὶ τῷ παρ'
ἐλπίδα τοῦ αὐχήματος σφαλλόμενοι καὶ παρὰ ἰσχὺν τῆς

1 ἢ recc.: om. codd. [Π¹⁸]   Ἀθηναίων suprascr. ὢν Β [Π¹⁸]
5 τοσάδε Β [Π¹⁸]   9 ἐπιβουλὴ recc. Π¹⁸   τἆλλα] πολλὰ C [Π¹⁸]   11
ἂν ! om. Π¹⁸   12 ἔχῃ Β Μ [Π¹⁸]   ἀντιλαβεῖν ! Π¹⁸ m. 1   13 ἑτοῖμα
πάντα Β   17 αὐτῶν οὕτω Β Π¹⁸   20 ἔπειτα δὲ Β [Π¹⁸]   21 Πελοποννήσου τε καὶ Β ! Π¹⁸   22 ἤδη Β Π¹⁸ : om. cett.   26 κολουθῶσι Α :
ἀκολουθῶσι Β : κολοσθῶσι cett. Schol. Patm. [Π¹⁸]   27 γε λοιπὸν
Β [Π¹⁸]   29 ἀτυχήματος Μ¹ [Π¹⁸]

δυνάμεως ἐνδιδόασιν· ὁ νῦν Ἀθηναίους εἰκὸς πεπονθέναι.

67 ἡμῶν δὲ τό τε ὑπάρχον πρότερον, ᾧπερ καὶ ἀνεπιστήμονες
ἔτι ὄντες ἀπετολμήσαμεν, βεβαιότερον νῦν, καὶ τῆς δοκήσεως προσγεγενημένης αὐτῷ, τὸ κρατίστους εἶναι εἰ τοὺς
κρατίστους ἐνικήσαμεν, διπλασία ἑκάστου ἡ ἐλπίς· τὰ δὲ 5
πολλὰ πρὸς τὰς ἐπιχειρήσεις ἡ μεγίστη ἐλπὶς μεγίστην καὶ
τὴν προθυμίαν παρέχεται.

2 'Τά τε τῆς ἀντιμιμήσεως αὐτῶν τῆς παρασκευῆς ἡμῶν
τῷ μὲν ἡμετέρῳ τρόπῳ ξυνήθη τέ ἐστι καὶ οὐκ ἀνάρμοστοι
πρὸς ἕκαστον αὐτῶν ἐσόμεθα· οἱ δ', ἐπειδὰν πολλοὶ μὲν 10
ὁπλῖται ἐπὶ τῶν καταστρωμάτων παρὰ τὸ καθεστηκὸς ὦσι,
πολλοὶ δὲ καὶ ἀκοντισταὶ χερσαῖοι ὡς εἰπεῖν Ἀκαρνᾶνές
τε καὶ ἄλλοι ἐπὶ ναῦς ἀναβάντες, οἳ οὐδ' ὅπως καθεζομένους
χρὴ τὸ βέλος ἀφεῖναι εὑρήσουσι, πῶς οὐ σφαλοῦσί τε τὰς
ναῦς καὶ ἐν σφίσιν αὐτοῖς πάντες οὐκ ἐν τῷ ἑαυτῶν τρόπῳ 15
3 κινούμενοι ταράξονται; ἐπεὶ καὶ τῷ πλήθει τῶν νεῶν οὐκ
ὠφελήσονται, εἴ τις καὶ τόδε ὑμῶν, ὅτι οὐκ ἴσαις ναυ-
μαχήσει, πεφόβηται· ἐν ὀλίγῳ γὰρ πολλαὶ ἀργότεραι μὲν
ἐς τὸ δρᾶν τι ὧν βούλονται ἔσονται, ῥᾷσται δὲ ἐς τὸ βλά-
4 πτεσθαι ἀφ' ὧν ἡμῖν παρεσκεύασται. τὸ δ' ἀληθέστατον 20
γνῶτε ἐξ ὧν ἡμεῖς οἰόμεθα σαφῶς πεπύσθαι· ὑπερβαλ-
λόντων γὰρ αὐτοῖς τῶν κακῶν καὶ βιαζόμενοι ὑπὸ τῆς
παρούσης ἀπορίας ἐς ἀπόνοιαν καθεστήκασιν οὐ παρασκευῆς
πίστει μᾶλλον ἢ τύχης ἀποκινδυνεῦσαι οὕτως ὅπως δύνανται,
ἵν' ἢ βιασάμενοι ἐκπλεύσωσιν ἢ κατὰ γῆν μετὰ τοῦτο τὴν 25
ἀποχώρησιν ποιῶνται, ὡς τῶν γε παρόντων οὐκ ἂν πράξαντες
68 χεῖρον. πρὸς οὖν ἀταξίαν τε τοιαύτην καὶ τύχην ἀνδρῶν
ἑαυτὴν παραδεδωκυῖαν πολεμιωτάτων ὀργῇ προσμείξωμεν,
καὶ νομίσωμεν ἅμα μὲν νομιμώτατον εἶναι πρὸς τοὺς

2 ἡμῶν Stephanus : ὑμῶν codd. [Π¹⁸]   3 καὶ in G erasum, om.
Λ F M [Π¹⁸]   4 τὸ secl. Reiske : τοῦ Krüger [Π¹⁸]   5 τὰ δὲ . . .
ἐλπὶς Β Π¹⁸ : om. cett.   10 ἕκαστον Β Π¹⁸ : τὴν ἐκάστην cett.   12 καὶ
om. C E ? Π¹⁸   15 ἑαυτῶν B : αὐτῶν A C F Π¹⁸ : οὑτῷ cett.   24 ἀποκινδυνεῦσαι Duker : ἀποκινδυνεύσει codd. [Π¹⁸]   25 βιαζόμενοι M [Π¹⁸]
26 ποιοῦνται C E F M [Π¹⁸]   πράξαντες A F : πράξοντες cett. [Π¹⁸]
28 αὐτὴν B [Π¹⁸]

ἐναντίους οἳ ἂν ὡς ἐπὶ τιμωρίᾳ τοῦ προσπεσόντος δικαιώσωσιν ἀποπλῆσαι τῆς γνώμης τὸ θυμούμενον, ἅμα δὲ ἐχθροὺς ἀμύνασθαι ἐκγενησόμενον ἡμῖν καὶ τὸ λεγόμενόν που ἥδιστον εἶναι. ὡς δὲ ἐχθροὶ καὶ ἔχθιστοι, πάντες 2
5 ἴστε, οἵ γε ἐπὶ τὴν ἡμετέραν ἦλθον δουλωσόμενοι, ἐν ᾧ, εἰ κατώρθωσαν, ἀνδράσι μὲν ἂν τἄλγιστα προσέθεσαν, παισὶ δὲ καὶ γυναιξὶ τὰ ἀπρεπέστατα, πόλει δὲ τῇ πάσῃ τὴν αἰσχίστην ἐπίκλησιν. ἀνθ᾽ ὧν μὴ μαλακισθῆναί τινα 3
πρέπει μηδὲ τὸ ἀκινδύνως ἀπελθεῖν αὐτοὺς κέρδος νομίσαι.
10 τοῦτο μὲν γὰρ καὶ ἐὰν κρατήσωσιν ὁμοίως δράσουσιν· τὸ
δὲ πραξάντων ἐκ τοῦ εἰκότος ἃ βουλόμεθα τούσδε τε κολασθῆναι καὶ τῇ πάσῃ Σικελίᾳ καρπουμένῃ καὶ πρὶν ἐλευθερίαν
βεβαιοτέραν παραδοῦναι, καλὸς ὁ ἀγών. καὶ κινδύνων
οὗτοι σπανιώτατοι οἳ ἂν ἐλάχιστα ἐκ τοῦ σφαλῆναι
15 βλάπτοντες πλεῖστα διὰ τὸ εὐτυχῆσαι ὠφελῶσιν.᾽

Καὶ οἱ μὲν τῶν Συρακοσίων στρατηγοὶ καὶ Γύλιππος 69
τοιαῦτα καὶ αὐτοὶ τοῖς σφετέροις στρατιώταις παρακελευσάμενοι ἀντεπλήρουν τὰς ναῦς εὐθὺς ἐπειδὴ καὶ τοὺς Ἀθηναίους
ᾐσθάνοντο. ὁ δὲ Νικίας ὑπὸ τῶν παρόντων ἐκπεπληγμένος 2
20 καὶ ὁρῶν οἷος ὁ κίνδυνος καὶ ὡς ἐγγὺς ἤδη [ἦν], ἐπειδὴ καὶ
ὅσον οὐκ ἔμελλον ἀνάγεσθαι, καὶ νομίσας, ὅπερ πάσχουσιν
ἐν τοῖς μεγάλοις ἀγῶσι, πάντα τε ἔργῳ ἔτι σφίσιν ἐνδεᾶ
εἶναι καὶ λόγῳ αὐτοῖς οὔπω ἱκανὰ εἰρῆσθαι, αὖθις τῶν
τριηράρχων ἕνα ἕκαστον ἀνεκάλει, πατρόθεν τε ἐπονομάζων
25 καὶ αὐτοὺς ὀνομαστὶ καὶ φυλήν, ἀξιῶν τό τε καθ᾽ ἑαυτόν,
ᾧ ὑπῆρχε λαμπρότητός τι, μὴ προδιδόναι τινὰ καὶ τὰς
πατρικὰς ἀρετάς, ὧν ἐπιφανεῖς ἦσαν οἱ πρόγονοι, μὴ ἀφανίζειν, πατρίδος τε τῆς ἐλευθερωτάτης ὑπομιμνῄσκων καὶ
τῆς ἐν αὐτῇ ἀνεπιτάκτου πᾶσιν ἐς τὴν δίαιταν ἐξουσίας,
30 ἄλλα τε λέγων ὅσα ἐν τῷ τοιούτῳ ἤδη τοῦ καιροῦ ὄντες

---

1 [δικαίως] ἴωσι Π¹⁸   3 ἐκγενησόμενον B : ἐγγενησόμενον cett.
[Π¹⁸] καὶ om. recc.   4 ᾧ[ς desinit Π¹⁸   11 post πραξάντων add.
ἡμῶν B   12 καρπουμένῃ B   15 ὠφελῶσι B : ὠφελοῦσι cett.
20 ἦν om. B (habet γρ. B)   22 ἔτι om. A E F M   27 ἀφανίζειν]
ἀτιμάζειν M suprascr. G¹   30 ὄντες B : ὄντος cett.

ἄνθρωποι οὐ πρὸς τὸ δοκεῖν τινὶ ἀρχαιολογεῖν· φυλαξάμενοι
εἴποιεν ἄν, καὶ ὑπὲρ ἁπάντων παραπλήσια ἔς τε γυναῖκας
καὶ παῖδας καὶ θεοὺς πατρῴους προφερόμενα, ἀλλ' ἐπὶ τῇ
παρούσῃ ἐκπλήξει ὠφέλιμα νομίζοντες ἐπιβοῶνται.

3   Καὶ ὁ μὲν οὐχ ἱκανὰ μᾶλλον ἢ καὶ ἀναγκαῖα νομίσας 5
παρῃνῆσθαι, ἀποχωρήσας ἦγε τὸν πεζὸν πρὸς τὴν θάλασσαν
καὶ παρέταξεν ὡς ἐπὶ πλεῖστον ἐδύνατο, ὅπως ὅτι μεγίστη
4 τοῖς ἐν ταῖς ναυσὶν ὠφελία ἐς τὸ θαρσεῖν γίγνοιτο· ὁ δὲ
Δημοσθένης καὶ Μένανδρος καὶ Εὐθύδημος (οὗτοι γὰρ ἐπὶ
τὰς ναῦς τῶν Ἀθηναίων στρατηγοὶ ἐπέβησαν) ἄραντες ἀπὸ 10
τοῦ ἑαυτῶν στρατοπέδου εὐθὺς ἔπλεον πρὸς τὸ ζεῦγμα
τοῦ λιμένος καὶ τὸν παραλειφθέντα διέκπλουν, βουλόμενοι
70 βιάσασθαι ἐς τὸ ἔξω.   προεξαγαγόμενοι δὲ οἱ Συρακόσιοι
καὶ οἱ ξύμμαχοι ναυσὶ παραπλησίαις τὸν ἀριθμὸν καὶ
πρότερον, κατά τε τὸν ἔκπλουν μέρει αὐτῶν ἐφύλασσον 15
καὶ κατὰ τὸν ἄλλον κύκλῳ λιμένα, ὅπως πανταχόθεν ἅμα
προσπίπτοιεν τοῖς Ἀθηναίοις, καὶ ὁ πεζὸς ἅμα αὐτοῖς παρεβοήθει ᾗπερ καὶ αἱ νῆες κατίσχοιεν.   ἦρχον δὲ τοῦ ναυτικοῦ
τοῖς Συρακοσίοις Σικανὸς μὲν καὶ Ἀγάθαρχος, κέρας ἑκάτερος
τοῦ παντὸς ἔχων, Πυθὴν δὲ καὶ οἱ Κορίνθιοι τὸ μέσον. 20
2 ἐπειδὴ δὲ οἱ ἄλλοι Ἀθηναῖοι προσέμισγον τῷ ζεύγματι, τῇ
μὲν πρώτῃ ῥύμῃ ἐπιπλέοντες ἐκράτουν τῶν τεταγμένων νεῶν
πρὸς αὐτῷ καὶ ἐπειρῶντο λύειν τὰς κλῄσεις· μετὰ δὲ τοῦτο
πανταχόθεν σφίσι τῶν Συρακοσίων καὶ ξυμμάχων ἐπιφερομένων οὐ πρὸς τῷ ζεύγματι ἔτι μόνον ἡ ναυμαχία, ἀλλὰ 25
καὶ κατὰ τὸν λιμένα ἐγίγνετο, καὶ ἦν καρτερὰ καὶ οἷα οὐχ
3 ἑτέρα τῶν προτέρων.   πολλὴ μὲν γὰρ ἑκατέροις προθυμία
ἀπὸ τῶν ναυτῶν ἐς τὸ ἐπιπλεῖν ὁπότε κελευσθείη ἐγίγνετο,

3 προσφερόμενα B   5 ἢ B : om. cett.   καὶ om. B   9 Εὐθύδημος B : Εὔδημος cett.   12 παραλειφθέντα A C E F M γρ. B Schol.,
Dion. Hal. : παραληφθέντα G : καταλειφθέντα B   13 προεξαναγό-
μενοι Dion. Hal.   17 αὐτοῖς ἅμα A C E F ⟨G⟩ M Dion. Hal.   παρεβοήθει Dion. Hal. : παραβοηθῇ A B F : παραβοηθεῖ cett.   21 δὲ] δὲ
καὶ E Dion. Hal.   οἱ ἄλλοι om. B, habet Dion. Hal.   25 post
μόνον add. ἦν B

8 ἐπαυξῆσαι. καὶ οἱ στρατηγοὶ προσέτι · ἑκατέρων, εἴ τινά
που ὁρῷεν μὴ κατ᾽ ἀνάγκην πρύμναν κρουόμενον, ἀνακα-
λοῦντες ὀνομαστὶ τὸν τριήραρχον ἠρώτων, οἱ μὲν Ἀθηναῖοι
εἰ τὴν πολεμιωτάτην γῆν οἰκειοτέραν ἤδη τῆς οὐ δι᾽ ὀλίγου
πόνου κεκτημένης θαλάσσης ἡγούμενοι ὑποχωροῦσιν, οἱ δὲ 5
Συρακόσιοι εἰ οὓς σαφῶς ἴσασι προθυμουμένους Ἀθηναίους
παντὶ τρόπῳ διαφυγεῖν, τούτους αὐτοὶ φεύγοντας φεύγουσιν.

71 ὅ τε ἐκ τῆς γῆς πεζὸς ἀμφοτέρων ἰσορρόπου τῆς ναυμαχίας
καθεστηκυίας πολὺν τὸν ἀγῶνα καὶ ξύστασιν τῆς γνώμης
εἶχε, φιλονικῶν μὲν ὁ αὐτόθεν περὶ τοῦ πλέονος ἤδη καλοῦ, 10
δεδιότες δὲ οἱ ἐπελθόντες μὴ τῶν παρόντων ἔτι χείρω
2 πράξωσιν. πάντων γὰρ δὴ ἀνακειμένων τοῖς Ἀθηναίοις
ἐς τὰς ναῦς ὅ τε φόβος ἦν ὑπὲρ τοῦ μέλλοντος οὐδενὶ
ἐοικώς, καὶ διὰ τὸ (ἀνώμαλον) τῆς ναυμαχίας ἀνώμαλον
3 καὶ τὴν ἔποψιν ἐκ τῆς γῆς ἠναγκάζοντο ἔχειν. δι᾽ ὀλίγου 15
γὰρ οὔσης τῆς θέας καὶ οὐ πάντων ἅμα ἐς τὸ αὐτὸ σκο-
πούντων, εἰ μέν τινες ἴδοιέν πῃ τοὺς σφετέρους ἐπικρα-
τοῦντας, ἀνεθάρσησάν τε ἂν καὶ πρὸς ἀνάκλησιν θεῶν μὴ
στερῆσαι σφᾶς τῆς σωτηρίας ἐτρέποντο, οἱ δ᾽ ἐπὶ τὸ ἡσσώ-
μενον βλέψαντες ὀλοφυρμῷ τε ἅμα μετὰ βοῆς ἐχρῶντο 20
καὶ ἀπὸ τῶν δρωμένων τῆς ὄψεως καὶ τὴν γνώμην μᾶλλον
τῶν ἐν τῷ ἔργῳ ἐδουλοῦντο· ἄλλοι δὲ καὶ πρὸς ἀντίπαλόν
τι τῆς ναυμαχίας ἀπιδόντες, διὰ τὸ ἀκρίτως ξυνεχὲς τῆς
ἁμίλλης καὶ τοῖς σώμασιν αὐτοῖς ἴσα τῇ δόξῃ περιδεῶς
ξυναπονεύοντες ἐν τοῖς χαλεπώτατα διῆγον· αἰεὶ γὰρ παρ᾽ 25
4 ὀλίγον ἢ διέφευγον ἢ ἀπώλλυντο. ἦν τε ἐν τῷ αὐτῷ
στρατεύματι τῶν Ἀθηναίων, ἕως ἀγχώμαλα ἐναυμάχουν,
πάντα ὁμοῦ ἀκοῦσαι, ὀλοφυρμὸς βοή, νικῶντες κρατούμενοι,
ἄλλα ὅσα ἐν μεγάλῳ κινδύνῳ μέγα στρατόπεδον πολυειδῆ

---

2 κατ᾽] δι᾽ B   5 πόνου B Schol , Dion. Hal. : om. cett.   ὑποχωροῦσιν B : ἀποχωροῦσιν cett.   6 Ἀθηναίους secl. Duker   12 δὴ]
ἤδη suprascr. δὴ B   14 ἀνώμαλον add. Bauer   τῆς ναυμαχίας
post ἔποψιν habent codd., transp. Wölfflin   16 οὐ πάντων] ἀπάντων
B (γρ. οὐ πάντων)   18 ἂν om. B   26 αὐτῷ om. A E F M
Dion Hal.   29 ὅσ᾽ ἂν Herwerden

πολλὴ δὲ ἡ ἀντιτέχνησις τῶν κυβερνητῶν καὶ ἀγωνισμὸς
πρὸς ἀλλήλους· οἵ τε ἐπιβάται ἐθεράπευον, ὁπότε προσπέσοι
ναῦς νηί, μὴ λείπεσθαι τὰ ἀπὸ τοῦ καταστρώματος τῆς
ἄλλης τέχνης· πᾶς τέ τις ἐν ᾧ προσετέτακτο αὐτὸς ἕκαστος
5 ἠπείγετο πρῶτος φαίνεσθαι. ξυμπεσουσῶν δὲ ἐν ὀλίγῳ 4
πολλῶν νεῶν ᾽πλεῖσται γὰρ δὴ αὗται ἐν ἐλαχίστῳ ἐναυ-
μάχησαν· βραχὺ γὰρ ἀπέλιπον ξυναμφότεραι διακόσιαι
γενέσθαι) αἱ μὲν ἐμβολαὶ διὰ τὸ μὴ εἶναι τὰς ἀνακρούσεις
καὶ διέκπλους ὀλίγαι ἐγίγνοντο, αἱ δὲ προσβολαί, ὡς τύχοι
10 ναῦς νηὶ προσπεσοῦσα ἢ διὰ τὸ φεύγειν ἢ ἄλλῃ ἐπιπλέουσα,
πυκνότεραι ἦσαν. καὶ ὅσον μὲν χρόνον προσφέροιτο ναῦς, 5
οἱ ἀπὸ τῶν καταστρωμάτων τοῖς ἀκοντίοις καὶ τοξεύμασι
καὶ λίθοις ἀφθόνως ἐπ᾽ αὐτὴν ἐχρῶντο· ἐπειδὴ δὲ προσμεί-
ξειαν, οἱ ἐπιβάται ἐς χεῖρας ἰόντες ἐπειρῶντο ταῖς ἀλλήλων
15 ναυσὶν ἐπιβαίνειν. ξυνετύγχανέ τε πολλαχοῦ διὰ τὴν 6
στενοχωρίαν τὰ μὲν ἄλλοις ἐμβεβληκέναι, τὰ δὲ αὐτοὺς
ἐμβεβλῆσθαι, δύο τε περὶ μίαν καὶ ἔστιν ᾗ καὶ πλείους
ναῦς κατ᾽ ἀνάγκην ξυνηρτῆσθαι, καὶ τοῖς κυβερνήταις τῶν
μὲν φυλακήν, τῶν δ᾽ ἐπιβουλήν, μὴ καθ᾽ ἓν ἕκαστον, κατὰ
20 πολλὰ δὲ πανταχόθεν, περιεστάναι, καὶ τὸν κτύπον μέγαν
ἀπὸ πολλῶν νεῶν ξυμπιπτουσῶν ἔκπληξίν τε ἅμα καὶ
ἀποστέρησιν τῆς ἀκοῆς ὧν οἱ κελευσταὶ φθέγγοιντο παρέχειν. πολλὴ γὰρ δὴ ἡ παρακέλευσις καὶ βοὴ ἀφ᾽ ἑκατέρων 7
τοῖς κελευσταῖς κατά τε τὴν τέχνην καὶ πρὸς τὴν αὐτίκα
25 φιλονικίαν ἐγίγνετο, τοῖς μὲν Ἀθηναίοις βιάζεσθαί τε τὸν
ἔκπλουν ἐπιβοῶντες καὶ περὶ τῆς ἐς τὴν πατρίδα σωτηρίας
νῦν, εἴ ποτε καὶ αὖθις, προθύμως ἀντιλαβέσθαι, τοῖς δὲ
Συρακοσίοις καὶ ξυμμάχοις καλὸν εἶναι κωλῦσαί τε αὐτοὺς
διαφυγεῖν καὶ τὴν οἰκείαν ἑκάστους πατρίδα νικήσαντας

2 ὁπότε B M : ὅτε cett. Dion. Hal. 7 ἀπέλειπον C 8 ἐμβολαὶ
C E Schol. Patm.: ἐκβολαὶ cett. Dion. Hal 9 ἔτυχον B 10 φυ-
γεῖν A E F M Dion. Hal. 13 ἀφθόνοις Dion. Hal. 21 post
πολλῶν add. τῶν G 22 φθέγγοντο (sic) B : ἐφθέγγοντο Dion Hal.
23 ἤ B : om. cett. 24 τε B Dion. Hal.: om. cett. 27 ἀντιλαμβάνεσθαι Dion. Hal. Hal. 29 ἑκάστου M νικήσαντες suprascr. G¹, v.l.
in Dion. Hal.

F

ἀναγκάζοιτο φθέγγεσθαι. παραπλήσια δὲ καὶ οἱ ἐπὶ τῶν 5
νεῶν αὐτοῖς ἔπασχον, πρίν γε δὴ οἱ Συρακόσιοι καὶ οἱ
ξύμμαχοι ἐπὶ πολὺ ἀντισχούσης τῆς ναυμαχίας ἔτρεψάν
τε τοὺς Ἀθηναίους καὶ ἐπικείμενοι λαμπρῶς, πολλῇ κραυγῇ
5 καὶ διακελευσμῷ χρώμενοι, κατεδίωκον ἐς τὴν γῆν. τότε 6
δὲ ὁ μὲν ναυτικὸς στρατὸς ἄλλος ἄλλῃ, ὅσοι μὴ μετέωροι
ἑάλωσαν, κατενεχθέντες ἐξέπεσον ἐς τὸ στρατόπεδον· ὁ δὲ
πεζὸς οὐκέτι διαφόρως, ἀλλ᾽ ἀπὸ μιᾶς ὁρμῆς οἰμωγῇ τε
καὶ στόνῳ πάντες δυσανασχετοῦντες τὰ γιγνόμενα, οἱ μὲν
10 ἐπὶ τὰς ναῦς παρεβοήθουν, οἱ δὲ πρὸς τὸ λοιπὸν τοῦ τείχους
ἐς φυλακήν, ἄλλοι δὲ καὶ οἱ πλεῖστοι ἤδη περὶ σφᾶς
αὐτοὺς καὶ ὅπη σωθήσοιται διεσκόπουν. ἦν τε ἐν τῷ 7
παραυτίκα οὐδεμιᾶς δὴ τῶν ξυμπασῶν ἐλάσσων ἔκπληξις.
παραπλήσιά τε ἐπεπόνθεσαν καὶ ἔδρασαν αὐτοὶ ἐν Πύλῳ·
15 διαφθαρεισῶν γὰρ τῶν νεῶν τοῖς Λακεδαιμονίοις προσ-
απώλλυντο αὐτοῖς καὶ οἱ ἐν τῇ νήσῳ ἄνδρες διαβεβηκότες,
καὶ τότε τοῖς Ἀθηναίοις ἀνέλπιστον ἦν τὸ κατὰ γῆν
σωθήσεσθαι, ἢν μή τι παρὰ λόγον γίγνηται.

Γενομένης δ᾽ ἰσχυρᾶς τῆς ναυμαχίας καὶ πολλῶν νεῶν 72
20 ἀμφοτέροις καὶ ἀνθρώπων ἀπολομένων οἱ Συρακόσιοι καὶ οἱ
ξύμμαχοι ἐπικρατήσαντες τά τε ναυάγια καὶ τοὺς νεκροὺς
ἀνείλοντο, καὶ ἀποπλεύσαντες πρὸς τὴν πόλιν τροπαῖον
ἔστησαν, οἱ δ᾽ Ἀθηναῖοι ὑπὸ μεγέθους τῶν παρόντων κακῶν 2
νεκρῶν μὲν πέρι ἢ ναυαγίων οὐδὲ ἐπενόουν αἰτῆσαι ἀναίρεσιν,
25 τῆς δὲ νυκτὸς ἐβουλεύοντο εὐθὺς ἀναχωρεῖν. Δημοσθένης 3
δὲ Νικίᾳ προσελθὼν γνώμην ἐποιεῖτο πληρώσαντας ἔτι τὰς
λοιπὰς τῶν νεῶν βιάσασθαι, ἢν δύνωνται, ἅμα ἔῳ τὸν ἔκπλουν, λέγων ὅτι πλείους ἔτι αἱ λοιπαί εἰσι νῆες χρήσιμαι
σφίσιν ἢ τοῖς πολεμίοις· ἦσαν γὰρ τοῖς μὲν Ἀθηναίοις περί-
30 λοιποι ὡς ἑξήκοντα, τοῖς δ᾽ ἐναντίοις ἐλάσσους ἢ πεντήκοντα.
καὶ ξυγχωροῦντος Νικίου τῇ γνώμῃ καὶ βουλομένων πληροῦν 4

8 ὀργῆς M   13 ξυμπασῶν] ξυμφορῶν B   15 τοῖς om. B   16 αὐτοῖς
C G   διαβεβοηκότες B   18 παρὰ λόγον Dion. Hal. : παράλογον codd.
22 ἀπο]πλεύ[σαντες incipit Π¹⁸   25 ἐβούλοντο B   28 ἔτι ! om. Π¹⁸
εἰσι om. B Π¹⁸   30 δ᾽ ἐναντίοις] δὲ πολεμίοις Π¹⁸

αὐτῶν οἱ ναῦται οὐκ ἤθελον ἐσβαίνειν διὰ τὸ καταπεπλῆχθαί
τε τῇ ἥσσῃ καὶ μὴ ἂν ἔτι οἴεσθαι κρατῆσαι.

73   Καὶ οἱ μὲν ὡς κατὰ γῆν ἀναχωρήσοντες ἤδη ξύμπαντες
τὴν γνώμην εἶχον, Ἑρμοκράτης δὲ ὁ Συρακόσιος ὑπονοήσας
αὐτῶν τὴν διάνοιαν καὶ νομίσας δεινὸν εἶναι εἰ τοσαύτη 5
στρατιὰ κατὰ γῆν ὑποχωρήσασα καὶ καθεζομένη ποι τῆς
Σικελίας βουλήσεται αὖθις σφίσι τὸν πόλεμον ποιεῖσθαι,
ἐσηγεῖται ἐλθὼν τοῖς ἐν τέλει οὖσιν ὡς οὐ χρεὼν ἀποχωρῆσαι
τῆς νυκτὸς αὐτοὺς περιιδεῖν, λέγων ταῦτα ἃ καὶ αὐτῷ ἐδόκει,
ἀλλὰ ἐξελθόντας ἤδη πάντας Συρακοσίους καὶ τοὺς ξυμμάχους 10
τάς τε ὁδοὺς ἀποικοδομῆσαι καὶ τὰ στενόπορα τῶν χωρίων
2 προδιαλαβόντας φυλάσσειν. οἱ δὲ ξυνεγίγνωσκον μὲν καὶ
αὐτοὶ οὐχ ἧσσον ταῦτα ἐκείνου, καὶ ἐδόκει ποιητέα εἶναι,
τοὺς δὲ ἀνθρώπους ἄρτι ἀσμένους ἀπὸ ναυμαχίας τε μεγάλης
ἀναπεπαυμένους καὶ ἅμα ἑορτῆς οὔσης (ἔτυχε γὰρ αὐτοῖς 15
Ἡρακλεῖ ταύτην τὴν ἡμέραν θυσία οὖσα) οὐ δοκεῖν ἂν ῥᾳδίως
ἐθελῆσαι ὑπακοῦσαι· ὑπὸ γὰρ τοῦ περιχαροῦς τῆς νίκης πρὸς
πόσιν τετράφθαι τοὺς πολλοὺς ἐν τῇ ἑορτῇ, καὶ πάντα μᾶλλον
ἐλπίζειν ἂν σφῶν πείθεσθαι αὐτοὺς ἢ ὅπλα λαβόντας ἐν τῷ
3 παρόντι ἐξελθεῖν. ὡς δὲ τοῖς ἄρχουσι ταῦτα λογιζομένοις 20
ἐφαίνετο ἄπορα καὶ οὐκέτι ἔπειθεν αὐτοὺς ὁ Ἑρμοκράτης,
αὐτὸς ἐπὶ τούτοις τάδε μηχανᾶται, δεδιὼς μὴ οἱ Ἀθηναῖοι
καθ᾽ ἡσυχίαν προφθάσωσιν ἐν τῇ νυκτὶ διελθόντες τὰ χαλεπώτατα τῶν χωρίων. πέμπει τῶν ἑταίρων τινὰς τῶν ἑαυτοῦ
μετὰ ἱππέων πρὸς τὸ τῶν Ἀθηναίων στρατόπεδον, ἡνίκα 25
ξυνεσκόταζεν· οἳ προσελάσαντες ἐξ ὅσου τις ἔμελλεν ἀκού-
σεσθαι καὶ ἀνακαλεσάμενοί τινας ὡς ὄντες τῶν Ἀθηναίων
ἐπιτήδειοι (ἦσαν γάρ τινες τῷ Νικίᾳ διάγγελοι τῶν ἔνδοθεν)
ἐκέλευον φράζειν Νικίᾳ μὴ ἀπάγειν τῆς νυκτὸς τὸ στράτευμα

1 αὐτὸν A C F G   2 τε B Π¹⁸ : om. cett.   3 ἀναχωρήσαντες
C M Π¹⁸ m. 1   6 ἀποχωρήσασα C E Π¹⁸   ποι Π¹⁸ recc.   9 ἃ καὶ]
καὶ ἃ E M : καὶ ἃ καὶ A F   12 προδιαλαβόντας Jones : διαλαβόντας B :
προφθάσαντας cett. Π¹⁸ γρ. B   13 ἃ καὶ Π¹⁸   14 τε ναυμαχίας Π¹⁸
15 πεπαυμένους B Π¹⁸   αὐτοῖς Ἡρακλεῖ] Ἡράκλεια B (αὐτοῖς Ἡρακλεῖ γρ.
B)   21 οὐκέτι] οὐκ Π¹⁸ recc.   23 φθάσωσι Π¹⁸

ὡς Συρακοσίων τὰς ὁδοὺς φυλασσόντων, ἀλλὰ καθ' ἡσυχίαν
τῆς ἡμέρας παρασκευασάμενον ἀποχωρεῖν. καὶ οἱ μὲν 4
εἰπόντες ἀπῆλθον, καὶ οἱ ἀκούσαντες διήγγειλαν τοῖς στρα-
τηγοῖς τῶν Ἀθηναίων· οἱ δὲ πρὸς τὸ ἄγγελμα ἐπέσχον τὴν 74
5 νύκτα, νομίσαντες οὐκ ἀπάτην εἶναι. καὶ ἐπειδὴ καὶ ὡς
οὐκ εὐθὺς ὥρμησαν, ἔδοξεν αὐτοῖς καὶ τὴν ἐπιοῦσαν ἡμέραν
περιμεῖναι, ὅπως ξυσκευάσαιντο ὡς ἐκ τῶν δυνατῶν οἱ στρατιῶται ὅτι χρησιμώτατα, καὶ τὰ μὲν ἄλλα πάντα καταλιπεῖν,
ἀναλαβόντες δὲ αὐτὰ ὅσα περὶ τὸ σῶμα ἐς δίαιταν ὑπῆρχεν
10 ἐπιτήδεια ἀφορμᾶσθαι. Συρακόσιοι δὲ καὶ Γύλιππος τῷ 2
μὲν πεζῷ προεξελθόντες τάς τε ὁδοὺς τὰς κατὰ τὴν χώραν,
ᾗ εἰκὸς ἦν τοὺς Ἀθηναίους ἰέναι, ἀπεφάργνυσαν καὶ τῶν
ῥείθρων καὶ [τῶν] ποταμῶν τὰς διαβάσεις ἐφύλασσον καὶ
ἐς ὑποδοχὴν τοῦ στρατεύματος ὡς κωλύσοντες ᾗ ἐδόκει
15 ἐτάσσοντο· ταῖς δὲ ναυσὶ προσπλεύσαντες τὰς ναῦς τῶν
Ἀθηναίων ἀπὸ τοῦ αἰγιαλοῦ ἀφεῖλκον (ἐνέπρησαν δέ τινας
ὀλίγας, ὥσπερ διενοήθησαν, αὐτοὶ οἱ Ἀθηναῖοι) τὰς δ' ἄλλας
καθ' ἡσυχίαν οὐδενὸς κωλύοντος ὡς ἑκάστην ποι ἐκπεπτωκυῖαν ἀναδησάμενοι ἐκόμιζον ἐς τὴν πόλιν.

20 Μετὰ δὲ τοῦτο, ἐπειδὴ ἐδόκει τῷ Νικίᾳ καὶ τῷ Δημοσθένει 75
ἱκανῶς παρεσκευάσθαι, καὶ ἡ ἀνάστασις ἤδη τοῦ στρατεύματος
τρίτῃ ἡμέρᾳ ἀπὸ τῆς ναυμαχίας ἐγίγνετο. δεινὸν οὖν ἦν οὐ 2
καθ' ἓν μόνον τῶν πραγμάτων, ὅτι τάς τε ναῦς ἀπολωλεκότες
πάσας ἀπεχώρουν καὶ ἀντὶ μεγάλης ἐλπίδος καὶ αὐτοὶ καὶ ἡ
25 πόλις κινδυνεύοντες, ἀλλὰ καὶ ἐν τῇ ἀπολείψει τοῦ στρατοπέδου ξυνέβαινε τῇ τε ὄψει ἑκάστῳ ἀλγεινὰ καὶ τῇ γνώμῃ
αἰσθέσθαι. τῶν τε γὰρ νεκρῶν ἀτάφων ὄντων, ὁπότε τις 3
ἴδοι τινὰ τῶν ἐπιτηδείων κείμενον, ἐς λύπην μετὰ φόβου
καθίστατο, καὶ οἱ ζῶντες καταλειπόμενοι τραυματίαι τε καὶ
30 ἀσθενεῖς πολὺ τῶν τεθνεώτων τοῖς ζῶσι λυπηρότεροι ἦσαν
καὶ τῶν ἀπολωλότων ἀθλιώτεροι. πρὸς γὰρ ἀντιβολίαν καὶ 4

1 φυλασ[σόντων desinit Π¹⁸   7 συσκευάσωνται Μ   11 προεξελθόντες Β : προσεξελθόντες cett.   13 τῶν om. Β   16 ἀφεῖλον Μ
20 alterum τῷ om. Β

ὀλοφυρμὸν τραπόμενοι ἐς ἀπορίαν καθίστασαν, ἄγειν τε σφᾶς
ἀξιοῦντες καὶ ἕνα ἕκαστον ἐπιβοώμενοι, εἴ τινά πού τις ἴδοι
ἢ ἑταίρων ἢ οἰκείων, τῶν τε ξυσκήνων ἤδη ἀπιόντων ἐκκρε-
μαννύμενοι καὶ ἐπακολουθοῦντες ἐς ὅσον δύναιντο, εἴ τῳ δὲ
προλίποι ἡ ῥώμη καὶ τὸ σῶμα, οὐκ ἄνευ ὀλίγων ἐπιθειασμῶν 5
καὶ οἰμωγῆς ὑπολειπόμενοι, ὥστε δάκρυσι πᾶν τὸ στράτευμα
πλησθὲν καὶ ἀπορίᾳ τοιαύτῃ μὴ ῥᾳδίως ἀφορμᾶσθαι, καίπερ
ἐκ πολεμίας τε καὶ μείζω ἢ κατὰ δάκρυα τὰ μὲν πεπονθότας
ἤδη, τὰ δὲ περὶ τῶν ἐν ἀφανεῖ δεδιότας μὴ πάθωσιν.
5 κατήφειά τέ τις ἅμα καὶ κατάμεμψις σφῶν αὐτῶν πολλὴ 10
ἦν. οὐδὲν γὰρ ἄλλο ἢ πόλει ἐκπεπολιορκημένῃ ἐῴκεσαν
ὑποφευγούσῃ, καὶ ταύτῃ οὐ σμικρᾷ· μυριάδες γὰρ τοῦ
ξύμπαντος ὄχλου οὐκ ἐλάσσους τεσσάρων ἅμα ἐπορεύοντο.
καὶ τούτων οἵ τε ἄλλοι πάντες ἔφερον ὅτι τις ἐδύνατο
ἕκαστος χρήσιμον, καὶ οἱ ὁπλῖται καὶ οἱ ἱππῆς παρὰ τὸ 15
εἰωθὸς αὐτοὶ τὰ σφέτερα αὐτῶν σιτία ὑπὸ τοῖς ὅπλοις, οἱ
μὲν ἀπορίᾳ ἀκολούθων, οἱ δὲ ἀπιστίᾳ· ἀπηυτομολήκεσαν γὰρ
πάλαι τε καὶ οἱ πλεῖστοι παραχρῆμα. ἔφερον δὲ οὐδὲ ταῦτα
6 ἱκανά· σῖτος γὰρ οὐκέτι ἦν ἐν τῷ στρατοπέδῳ. καὶ μὴν ἡ
ἄλλη αἰκία καὶ ἡ ἰσομοιρία τῶν κακῶν, ἔχουσά τινα ὅμως 20
τὸ μετὰ πολλῶν κούφισιν, οὐδ᾽ ὡς ῥᾳδία ἐν τῷ παρόντι
ἐδοξάζετο, ἄλλως τε καὶ ἀπὸ οἵας λαμπρότητος καὶ αὐχήματος τοῦ πρώτου ἐς οἵαν τελευτὴν καὶ ταπεινότητα ἀφῖκτο.
7 μέγιστον γὰρ δὴ τὸ διάφορον τοῦτο [τῷ] Ἑλληνικῷ στρατεύματι ἐγένετο, οἷς ἀντὶ μὲν τοῦ ἄλλους δουλωσομένους 25
ἥκειν αὐτοὺς τοῦτο μᾶλλον δεδιότας μὴ πάθωσι ξυνέβη
ἀπιέναι, ἀντὶ δ᾽ εὐχῆς τε καὶ παιάνων, μεθ᾽ ὧν ἐξέπλεον,
πάλιν τούτων τοῖς ἐναντίοις ἐπιφημίσμασιν ἀφορμᾶσθαι,

4 ἐς B : om. cett.　　5 προλίποι B : προλείπει G : προλείποι cett.
ὀλίγων secl. Krüger　　6 ὑπολειπόμενοι B : ἀπολειπόμενοι cett.
9 post ἐν add. τῷ B　　post μὴ add. τι A C E F G M　　14 ἔφερον
πάντες B　　15 ἕκαστος B : κατὰ τὸ cett. γρ. B·　　16 post αὐτοὶ
add. τε καὶ C, τε A E F G M　　ὑπὸ τοῖς ὅπλοις om. C　　ὑπὸ] ἐπὶ
Pluygers　　23 post οἵαν add. τε A E F　　ἀφίκατο Badham
24 τῷ secl. Schol.　　27 παιώνων A C E F M

πεζούς τε ἀντὶ ναυβατῶν πορευομένους καὶ ὁπλιτικῷ προσ-
έχοντας μᾶλλον ἢ ναυτικῷ. ὅμως δὲ ὑπὸ μεγέθους τοῦ
ἐπικρεμαμένου ἔτι κινδύνου πάντα ταῦτα αὐτοῖς οἰστὰ
ἐφαίνετο.

5 Ὁρῶν δὲ ὁ Νικίας τὸ στράτευμα ἀθυμοῦν καὶ ἐν μεγάλῃ **76**
μεταβολῇ ὄν, ἐπιπαριὼν ὡς ἐκ τῶν ὑπαρχόντων ἐθάρσυνέ
τε καὶ παρεμυθεῖτο, βοῇ τε χρώμενος ἔτι μᾶλλον ἑκάστοις
καθ' οὓς γίγνοιτο ὑπὸ προθυμίας καὶ βουλόμενος ὡς ἐπὶ
πλεῖστον γεγωνίσκων ὠφελεῖν τι.

10 ' Καὶ ἐκ τῶν παρόντων, ὦ Ἀθηναῖοι καὶ ξύμμαχοι, ἐλπίδα **77**
χρὴ ἔχειν (ἤδη τινὲς καὶ ἐκ δεινοτέρων ἢ τοιῶνδε ἐσώθησαν),
μηδὲ καταμέμφεσθαι ὑμᾶς ἄγαν αὐτοὺς μήτε ταῖς ξυμφοραῖς
μήτε ταῖς παρὰ τὴν ἀξίαν νῦν κακοπαθίαις. κἀγώ τοι **2**
οὐδενὸς ὑμῶν οὔτε ῥώμῃ προφέρων (ἀλλ' ὁρᾶτε δὴ ὡς
15 διάκειμαι ὑπὸ τῆς νόσου) οὔτ' εὐτυχίᾳ δοκῶν που ὕστερός
του εἶναι κατά τε τὸν ἴδιον βίον καὶ ἐς τὰ ἄλλα, νῦν ἐν τῷ
αὐτῷ κινδύνῳ τοῖς φαυλοτάτοις αἰωροῦμαι· καίτοι πολλὰ
μὲν ἐς θεοὺς νόμιμα δεδιῄτημαι, πολλὰ δὲ ἐς ἀνθρώπους
οἴκαια καὶ ἀνεπίφθονα. ἀνθ' ὧν ἡ μὲν ἐλπὶς ὅμως θρασεῖα **3**
20 τοῦ μέλλοντος, αἱ δὲ ξυμφοραὶ οὐ κατ' ἀξίαν δὴ φοβοῦσιν.
τάχα δὲ ἂν καὶ λωφήσειαν· ἱκανὰ γὰρ τοῖς τε πολεμίοις
ηὐτύχηται, καὶ εἴ τῳ θεῶν ἐπίφθονοι ἐστρατεύσαμεν, ἀπο-
χρώντως ἤδη τετιμωρήμεθα. ἦλθον γάρ που καὶ ἄλλοι **4**
τινὲς ἤδη ἐφ' ἑτέρους, καὶ ἀνθρώπεια δράσαντες ἀνεκτὰ
25 ἔπαθον. καὶ ἡμᾶς εἰκὸς νῦν τά τε ἀπὸ τοῦ θεοῦ ἐλπίζειν
ἠπιώτερα ἕξειν (οἴκτου γὰρ ἀπ' αὐτῶν ἀξιώτεροι ἤδη ἐσμὲν
ἢ φθόνου), καὶ ὁρῶντες ὑμᾶς αὐτοὺς οἷοι ὁπλῖται ἅμα καὶ ὅσοι
ξυντεταγμένοι χωρεῖτε μὴ καταπέπληχθε ἄγαν, λογίζεσθε δὲ
ὅτι αὐτοί τε πόλις εὐθύς ἐστε ὅποι ἂν καθέζησθε καὶ ἄλλη

---

1 τε (in rasura` B¹ : δὲ cett.   προσέχοντας B : προσχόντας
cett. (ex -ωντας c`    9 τι B : ἔτι (cum sequentibus iunctum` cett.
12 καταμέμφεσθαι B : καταμέυψασθαι cett.   16 τε B Schol. : om.
cett.   20 δὴ] ἤδη suprascr. δὴ B   φοβοῦσαι suprascr. ι M
25 θεῖον Krüger   27 οἴοι C : οἶ οἴ (sic` B : οἱ cett.   28 κατα-
πεπλῆχθαι B

οὐδεμία ὑμᾶς τῶν ἐν Σικελίᾳ οὔτ' ἂν ἐπιόντας δέξαιτο ῥᾳδίως
5 οὔτ' ἂν ἱδρυθέντας που ἐξαναστήσειεν. τὴν δὲ πορείαν ὥστ'
ἀσφαλῆ καὶ εὔτακτον εἶναι αὐτοὶ φυλάξατε, μὴ ἄλλο τι
ἡγησάμενος ἕκαστος ἢ ἐν ᾧ ἂν ἀναγκασθῇ χωρίῳ μάχεσθαι,
6 τοῦτο καὶ πατρίδα καὶ τεῖχος κρατήσας ἕξειν. σπουδῇ δὲ 5
ὁμοίως καὶ νύκτα καὶ ἡμέραν ἔσται τῆς ὁδοῦ· τὰ γὰρ ἐπιτήδεια
βραχέα ἔχομεν, καὶ ἢν ἀντιλαβώμεθά του φιλίου χωρίου τῶν
Σικελῶν (οὗτοι γὰρ ἡμῖν διὰ τὸ Συρακοσίων δέος ἔτι βέβαιοι
εἰσίν), ἤδη νομίζετε ἐν τῷ ἐχυρῷ εἶναι. προπέπεμπται δ'
ὡς αὐτούς, καὶ ἀπαντᾶν εἰρημένον καὶ σιτία ἄλλα κομίζειν. 10
7 ‘ Τό τε ξύμπαν γνῶτε, ὦ ἄνδρες στρατιῶται, ἀναγκαῖόν τε
ὂν ὑμῖν ἀνδράσιν ἀγαθοῖς γίγνεσθαι ὡς μὴ ὄντος χωρίου
ἐγγὺς ὅποι ἂν μαλακισθέντες σωθείητε καί, ἢν νῦν διαφύγητε
τοὺς πολεμίους, οἵ τε ἄλλοι τευξόμενοι ὧν ἐπιθυμεῖτέ που
ἐπιδεῖν καὶ οἱ Ἀθηναῖοι τὴν μεγάλην δύναμιν τῆς πόλεως 15
καίπερ πεπτωκυῖαν ἐπανορθώσοντες· ἄνδρες γὰρ πόλις, καὶ
οὐ τείχη οὐδὲ νῆες ἀνδρῶν κεναί.’
78 Ὁ μὲν Νικίας τοιάδε παρακελευόμενος ἅμα ἐπήει τὸ
στράτευμα, καὶ εἴ πῃ ὁρῴη διεσπασμένον καὶ μὴ ἐν τάξει
χωροῦν ξυνάγων καὶ καθιστάς, καὶ ὁ Δημοσθένης οὐδὲν 20
ἧσσον τοῖς καθ' ἑαυτὸν τοιαῦτά τε καὶ παραπλήσια λέγων.
2 τὸ δὲ ἐχώρει ἐν πλαισίῳ τεταγμένον, πρῶτον μὲν ἡγούμενον τὸ Νικίου, ἐφεπόμενον δὲ τὸ Δημοσθένους· τοὺς δὲ
σκευοφόρους καὶ τὸν πλεῖστον ὄχλον ἐντὸς εἶχον οἱ ὁπλῖται.
3 καὶ ἐπειδὴ [τε] ἐγένοντο ἐπὶ τῇ διαβάσει τοῦ Ἀνάπου ποτα- 25
μοῦ, ηὗρον ἐπ' αὐτῷ παρατεταγμένους τῶν Συρακοσίων καὶ
ξυμμάχων, καὶ τρεψάμενοι αὐτοὺς καὶ κρατήσαντες τοῦ
πόρου ἐχώρουν ἐς τὸ πρόσθεν· οἱ δὲ Συρακόσιοι παριπ-
πεύοντές τε προσέκειτο καὶ ἐσακοντίζοντες οἱ ψιλοί.

---

4 ἂν B: om. cett.   7 του f: τοῦ codd.   9 ἐχυρῷ B:
ὀχυρῷ cett.   προπέπεμπται B: προπέμπετε cett.   10 ἄλλα] ἅμα
Reiske (pariter Valla)   11 τε B: δὲ cett.   13 διασωθείητε B
22 πλαισίῳ B: διπλασίῳ cett.: διπλασίῳ Heitland   πρῶτον μὲν
ἡγούμενον B: om. cett.   23 ἐπόμενον B   25 τε secl. Krüger
ἐπὶ] ἐν B   26 post καὶ add. τῶν B

Καὶ ταύτῃ μὲν τῇ ἡμέρᾳ προελθόντες σταδίους ὡς 4
τεσσαράκοντα ηὐλίσαντο πρὸς λόφῳ τινὶ οἱ Ἀθηναῖοι· τῇ
δ' ὑστεραίᾳ πρῲ ἐπορεύοντο καὶ προῆλθον ὡς εἴκοσι σταδίους,
καὶ κατέβησαν ἐς χωρίον ἄπεδόν τι καὶ αὐτοῦ ἐστρατοπε-
5 δεύσαντο, βουλόμενοι ἔκ τε τῶν οἰκιῶν λαβεῖν τι ἐδώδιμον
(ᾠκεῖτο γὰρ ὁ χῶρος) καὶ ὕδωρ μετὰ σφῶν αὐτῶν φέρεσθαι
αὐτόθεν· ἐν γὰρ τῷ πρόσθεν ἐπὶ πολλὰ στάδια, ᾗ ἔμελλον
ἰέναι, οὐκ ἄφθονον ἦν. οἱ δὲ Συρακόσιοι ἐν τούτῳ προελ- 5
θόντες τὴν δίοδον τὴν ἐν τῷ πρόσθεν ἀπετείχιζον· ἦν δὲ
10 λόφος καρτερὸς καὶ ἑκατέρωθεν αὐτοῦ χαράδρα κρημνώδης,
ἐκαλεῖτο δὲ Ἀκραῖον λέπας.

Τῇ δ' ὑστεραίᾳ οἱ Ἀθηναῖοι προῇσαν, καὶ οἱ τῶν 6
Συρακοσίων καὶ ξυμμάχων αὐτοὺς ἱππῆς καὶ ἀκοντισταὶ
ὄντες πολλοὶ ἑκατέρωθεν ἐκώλυον καὶ ἐσηκόντιζόν τε καὶ
15 παρίππευον. καὶ χρόνον μὲν πολὺν ἐμάχοντο οἱ Ἀθηναῖοι,
ἔπειτα ἀνεχώρησαν πάλιν ἐς τὸ αὐτὸ στρατόπεδον. καὶ τὰ
ἐπιτήδεια οὐκέτι ὁμοίως εἶχον· οὐ γὰρ ἔτι ἀποχωρεῖν οἷόν
τ' ἦν ὑπὸ τῶν ἱππέων.

Πρῲ δὲ ἄραντες ἐπορεύοντο αὖθις, καὶ ἐβιάσαντο πρὸς 79
20 τὸν λόφον ἐλθεῖν τὸν ἀποτετειχισμένον, καὶ ηὗρον πρὸ
ἑαυτῶν ὑπὲρ τοῦ ἀποτειχίσματος τὴν πεζὴν στρατιὰν
παρατεταγμένην οὐκ ἐπ' ὀλίγων ἀσπίδων· στενὸν γὰρ ἦν
τὸ χωρίον. καὶ προσβαλόντες οἱ Ἀθηναῖοι ἐτειχομάχουν, 2
καὶ βαλλόμενοι ὑπὸ πολλῶν ἀπὸ τοῦ λόφου ἐπάντους ὄντος
25 (διικνοῦντο γὰρ ῥᾷον οἱ ἄνωθεν) καὶ οὐ δυνάμενοι βιάσασθαι ἀνεχώρουν πάλιν καὶ ἀνεπαύοντο. ἔτυχον δὲ 3
καὶ βρονταί τινες ἅμα γενόμεναι καὶ ὕδωρ, οἷα τοῦ ἔτους
πρὸς μετόπωρον ἤδη ὄντος φιλεῖ γίγνεσθαι· ἀφ' ὧν οἱ
Ἀθηναῖοι μᾶλλον ἔτι ἠθύμουν καὶ ἐνόμιζον ἐπὶ τῷ σφετέρῳ
30 ὀλέθρῳ καὶ ταῦτα πάντα γίγνεσθαι. ἀναπαυομένων δ' 4

1 προελθόντες G (ex προσ. rasura factum) : προσελθόντες cett.
5 οἰκιῶν G M : οἰκείων cett.   7 ᾗ om. B   8 τ]ούτ[ῳ incipit Π¹⁸
14 ἑκατέρωθεν B : ἑκάτεροι cett. Π¹⁸   20 ἐλθεῖν secl. Krüger [Π¹⁸]
26 ἀπεχώρουν B [Π¹⁸]   δὲ] γὰρ B [Π¹⁸]   29 post μᾶλλον add. γὰρ B
[Π¹⁸]

αὐτῶν ὁ Γύλιππος καὶ οἱ Συρακόσιοι πέμπουσι μέρος τι τῆς
στρατιᾶς ἀποτειχιοῦντας αὖ ἐκ τοῦ ὄπισθεν αὐτοὺς ᾗ προε-
ληλύθεσαν· ἀντιπέμψαντες δὲ κἀκεῖνοι σφῶν αὐτῶν τινὰς
5 διεκώλυσαν. καὶ μετὰ ταῦτα πάσῃ τῇ στρατιᾷ ἀναχωρήσαντες πρὸς τὸ πεδίον μᾶλλον οἱ Ἀθηναῖοι ηὐλίσαντο.   5
Τῇ δ' ὑστεραίᾳ προυχώρουν, καὶ οἱ Συρακόσιοι προσ-
έβαλλόν τε πανταχῇ αὐτοῖς κύκλῳ καὶ πολλοὺς κατετραυ-
μάτιζον, καὶ εἰ μὲν ἐπίοιεν οἱ Ἀθηναῖοι, ὑπεχώρουν, εἰ
δ' ἀναχωροῖεν, ἐπέκειντο, καὶ μάλιστα τοῖς ὑστάτοις προσ-
πίπτοντες, εἴ πως κατὰ βραχὺ τρεψάμενοι πᾶν τὸ στράτευμα 10
6 φοβήσειαν. καὶ ἐπὶ πολὺ μὲν τοιούτῳ τρόπῳ ἀντεῖχον οἱ
Ἀθηναῖοι, ἔπειτα προελθόντες πέντε ἢ ἐξ σταδίους ἀνεπαύοντο ἐν τῷ πεδίῳ· ἀνεχώρησαν δὲ καὶ οἱ Συρακόσιοι
ἀπ' αὐτῶν ἐς τὸ ἑαυτῶν στρατόπεδον.
80   Τῆς δὲ νυκτὸς τῷ Νικίᾳ καὶ Δημοσθένει ἐδόκει, ἐπειδὴ 15
κακῶς σφίσι τὸ στράτευμα εἶχε τῶν τε ἐπιτηδείων πάντων
ἀπορίᾳ ἤδη, καὶ κατατετραυματισμένοι ἦσαν πολλοὶ ἐν
πολλαῖς προσβολαῖς τῶν πολεμίων γεγενημέναις, πυρὰ
καύσαντας ὡς πλεῖστα ἀπάγειν τὴν στρατιάν, μηκέτι τὴν
αὐτὴν ὁδὸν ᾗ διενοήθησαν, ἀλλὰ τοὐναντίον ἢ οἱ Συρακόσιοι 20
2 ἐτήρουν, πρὸς τὴν θάλασσαν. ἦν δὲ ἡ ξύμπασα ὁδὸς αὕτη
οὐκ ἐπὶ Κατάνης τῷ στρατεύματι, ἀλλὰ κατὰ τὸ ἕτερον
μέρος τῆς Σικελίας τὸ πρὸς Καμάρωαν καὶ Γέλαν καὶ τὰς
3 ταύτῃ πόλεις καὶ Ἑλληνίδας καὶ βαρβάρους. καύσαντες
οὖν πυρὰ πολλὰ ἐχώρουν ἐν τῇ νυκτί. καὶ αὐτοῖς, οἷον 25
φιλεῖ καὶ πᾶσι στρατοπέδοις, μάλιστα δὲ τοῖς μεγίστοις,
φόβοι καὶ δείματα ἐγγίγνεσθαι, ἄλλως τε καὶ ἐν νυκτί τε
καὶ διὰ πολεμίας καὶ ἀπὸ πολεμίων οὐ πολὺ ἀπεχόντων
4 ἰοῦσιν, ἐμπίπτει ταραχή· καὶ τὸ μὲν Νικίου στράτευμα,

1 post αὐτῶν add. καὶ B [Π¹⁸]   2 αὖ B : om. cett. [Π¹⁸]   4 τοῦτο
B [Π¹⁸]   6 προσέβαλόν G M [Π¹⁸]   10 τρεψόμενοι B [Π¹⁸]   15 post
καὶ add. τῷ M [Π¹⁸]   16 τε om. B [Π¹⁸]   19 καύσαντες C G [Π¹⁸]
20 ἢ c f G : ᾗ vel ἢ cett. [Π¹⁸]   23 μέρος om. B   28 ἀπὸ secl.
Reiske [Π¹⁸]

ὥσπερ ἡγεῖτο, ξυνέμενέ τε καὶ προύλαβε πολλῷ, τὸ δὲ
Δημοσθένους, τὸ ἥμισυ μάλιστα καὶ πλέον, ἀπεσπάσθη τε
καὶ ἀτακτότερον ἐχώρει. ἅμα δὲ τῇ ἕῳ ἀφικνοῦνται ὅμως 5
πρὸς τὴν θάλασσαν, καὶ ἐσβάντες ἐς τὴν ὁδὸν τὴν Ἑλωρίνην
5 καλουμένην ἐπορεύοντο, ὅπως, ἐπειδὴ γένοιντο ἐπὶ τῷ
ποταμῷ τῷ Κακυπάρει, παρὰ τὸν ποταμὸν ἴοιεν ἄνω διὰ
μεσογείας· ἤλπιζον γὰρ καὶ τοὺς Σικελοὺς ταύτῃ οὓς μετε-
πέμψαντο ἀπαντήσεσθαι. ἐπειδὴ δ' ἐγένοντο ἐπὶ τῷ 6
ποταμῷ, ηὗρον καὶ ἐνταῦθα φυλακήν τινα τῶν Συρακοσίων
10 ἀποτειχίζουσάν τε καὶ ἀποσταυροῦσαν τὸν πόρον. καὶ
βιασάμενοι αὐτὴν διέβησάν τε τὸν ποταμὸν καὶ ἐχώρουν
αὖθις πρὸς ἄλλον ποταμὸν τὸν Ἐρινεόν· ταύτῃ γὰρ οἱ
ἡγεμόνες ἐκέλευον.

Ἐν τούτῳ δ' οἱ Συρακόσιοι καὶ οἱ ξύμμαχοι, ὡς ἥ τε 81
15 ἡμέρα ἐγένετο καὶ ἔγνωσαν τοὺς Ἀθηναίους ἀπεληλυθότας,
ἐν αἰτίᾳ τε οἱ πολλοὶ τὸν Γύλιππον εἶχον ἑκόντα ἀφεῖναι
τοὺς Ἀθηναίους, καὶ κατὰ τάχος διώκοντες, ᾗ οὐ χαλεπῶς
ᾐσθάνοντο κεχωρηκότας, καταλαμβάνουσι περὶ ἀρίστου
ὥραν. καὶ ὡς προσέμειξαν τοῖς μετὰ τοῦ Δημοσθένους 2
20 ὑστέροις τ' οὖσι καὶ σχολαίτερον καὶ ἀτακτότερον χωροῦσιν,
ὡς τῆς νυκτὸς τότε ξυνεταράχθησαν, εὐθὺς προσπεσόντες
ἐμάχοντο, καὶ οἱ ἱππῆς τῶν Συρακοσίων ἐκυκλοῦντό τε
ῥᾷον αὐτοὺς δίχα δὴ ὄντας καὶ ξυνῆγον ἐς ταὐτό. τὸ δὲ 3
Νικίου στράτευμα ἀπεῖχεν ἐν τῷ πρόσθεν καὶ πεντήκοντα
25 σταδίους· θᾶσσόν τε γὰρ ὁ Νικίας ἦγε, νομίζων οὐ τὸ
ὑπομένειν ἐν τῷ τοιούτῳ ἑκόντας εἶναι καὶ μάχεσθαι
σωτηρίαν, ἀλλὰ τὸ ὡς τάχιστα ὑποχωρεῖν, τοσαῦτα μαχο-
μένους ὅσα ἀναγκάζονται. ὁ δὲ Δημοσθένης ἐτύγχανέ τε 4

1 ὅσπερ Dobree [Π¹⁸]   2 post καὶ add. τὸ A C E F G M [Π¹⁸]
5 ἐπὶ Β Π¹⁸: παρὰ cett.   6 post διὰ add. τῆς Β ؟ Π¹⁸   7 μετεπέμ-
ψαντο Β: μετέπεμψαν cett. suprascr. Β [Π¹⁸]   8 ἐπεὶ C G [Π¹⁸]
10 τε Β: om. cett. [Π¹⁸]   16 τε om. Π¹⁸   19 ὡς Β: ὥσπερ cett.
[Π¹⁸]   20 ἰοῦσι Krüger [Π¹⁸]   21 τότε] τε (post rasuram) Β
22 ἐν[εκυκ]λοῦν[το Π¹⁸   23 δὴ] ἤδη Β (δὴ suprascr.) ؟ Π¹⁸   24
post πρόσθεν add. ἑκατὸν Β   27 σωτηρίαν A C E F G M Π¹⁸ m. 1
suprascr. Β: σωτήριον Β Π¹⁸ m. 2   28 δσ' ἂν Dobree ἀναγκάζωνται C

τὰ πλείω ἐν πόνῳ ξυνεχεστέρῳ ὧν διὰ τὸ ὑστέρῳ ἀναχω-
ροῦντι αὐτῷ πρώτῳ ἐπικεῖσθαι τοὺς πολεμίους καὶ τότε
γνοὺς τοὺς Συρακοσίους διώκοντας οὐ προυχώρει μᾶλλον
ἢ ἐς μάχην ξυνετάσσετο, ἕως ἐνδιατρίβων κυκλοῦταί τε ὑπ'
αὐτῶν καὶ ἐν πολλῷ θορύβῳ αὐτός τε καὶ οἱ μετ' αὐτοῦ 5
Ἀθηναῖοι ἦσαν· ἀνειληθέντες γὰρ ἔς τι χωρίον ᾧ κύκλῳ
μὲν τειχίον περιῆν, ὁδὸς δὲ ἔνθεν [τε] καὶ ἔνθεν, ἐλάας δὲ
5 οὐκ ὀλίγας εἶχεν, ἐβάλλοντο περισταδὸν·. τοιαύταις δὲ
προσβολαῖς καὶ οὐ ξυσταδὸν μάχαις οἱ Συρακόσιοι εἰκότως
ἐχρῶντο· τὸ γὰρ ἀποκινδυνεύειν πρὸς ἀνθρώπους ἀπο- 10
νενοημένους οὐ πρὸς ἐκείνων μᾶλλον ἦν ἔτι ἢ πρὸς τῶν
Ἀθηναίων, καὶ ἅμα φειδώ τέ τις ἐγίγνετο ἐπ' εὐπραγίᾳ
ἤδη σαφεῖ μὴ προαναλωθῆναί τῳ, καὶ ἐνόμιζον καὶ ὣς ταύτῃ
82 τῇ ἰδέᾳ καταδαμασάμενοι λήψεσθαι αὐτούς. ἐπειδὴ δ' οὖν
δι' ἡμέρας βάλλοντες πανταχόθεν τοὺς Ἀθηναίους καὶ 15
ξυμμάχους ἑώρων ἤδη τεταλαιπωρημένους τοῖς τε τραύμασι
καὶ τῇ ἄλλῃ κακώσει, κήρυγμα ποιοῦνται Γύλιππος καὶ
Συρακόσιοι καὶ οἱ ξύμμαχοι πρῶτον μὲν τῶν νησιωτῶν
εἴ τις βούλεται ἐπ' ἐλευθερίᾳ ὡς σφᾶς ἀπιέναι· καὶ ἀπε-
2 χώρησάν τινες πόλεις οὐ πολλαί. ἔπειτα δ' ὕστερον καὶ 20
πρὸς τοὺς ἄλλους ἅπαντας τοὺς μετὰ Δημοσθένους ὁμολογίᾳ
γίγνεται ὥστε ὅπλα τε παραδοῦναι καὶ μὴ ἀποθανεῖν μηδένα
μήτε βιαίως μήτε δεσμοῖς μήτε τῆς ἀναγκαιοτάτης ἐνδείᾳ
3 διαίτης. καὶ παρέδοσαν οἱ πάντες σφᾶς αὐτοὺς ἑξακισχίλιοι,
καὶ τὸ ἀργύριον ὃ εἶχον ἅπαν κατέθεσαν ἐσβαλόντες ἐς 25
ἀσπίδας ὑπτίας, καὶ ἐνέπλησαν ἀσπίδας τέσσαρας. καὶ
τούτους μὲν εὐθὺς ἀπεκόμιζον ἐς τὴν πόλιν· Νικίας δὲ καὶ
οἱ μετ' αὐτοῦ ταύτῃ τῇ ἡμέρᾳ ἀφικνοῦνται ἐπὶ τὸν ποταμὸν

---

1 post πόνῳ add. τε A C E F G M   2 πρώτῳ om. C G   5 ἐν B :
om. cett. [Π¹⁸]   6 Ἀθηναῖοι secl. Krüger [Π¹⁸]   7 τε om. C M [Π¹⁸]
8 ἐβάλλοντο B : ἔβαλλον τότε C : ἐβάλλοντό (-βάλ- M) τε cett. [Π¹⁸]
11 post alt. πρὸς add. τὸ A E F M [Π¹⁸]   12 ἐγίγνετο B : ἐγένετο
cett. [Π¹⁸]   13 τῷ A B C E F M   14 δ' οὖν Dobree : γοῦν codd. Π¹⁸
18 οἱ Συρακόσιοι Π¹⁸ recc.   οἱ om. ? Π¹⁸   21 post μετὰ add. τοῦ M
[Π¹⁸]   25 κατέ]θεσα[ν desinit Π¹⁸   ἐσβαλλόντες (sic) B   28
αὐτὸν A E F M   ταύτῃ B : αὐτῇ cett. γρ. B   τῇ αὐτῇ Herwerden   ἀφικνοῦνται post αὐτοῦ habent A C E F G M γρ. B

τὸν Ἐρινεόν, καὶ διαβὰς πρὸς μετέωρόν τι καθῖσε τὴν
στρατιάν.

Οἱ δὲ Συρακόσιοι τῇ ὑστεραίᾳ καταλαβόντες αὐτὸν 83
ἔλεγον ὅτι οἱ μετὰ Δημοσθένους παραδεδώκοιεν σφᾶς
5 αὑτούς, κελεύοντες κἀκεῖνον τὸ αὐτὸ δρᾶν· ὁ δ' ἀπιστῶν
σπένδεται ἱππέα πέμψαι σκεψόμενον. ὡς δ' οἰχόμενος 2
ἀπήγγειλε πάλιν παραδεδωκότας, ἐπικηρυκεύεται Γυλίππῳ
καὶ Συρακοσίοις εἶναι ἕτοιμος ὑπὲρ Ἀθηναίων ξυμβῆναι,
ὅσα ἀνήλωσαν χρήματα Συρακόσιοι ἐς τὸν πόλεμον, ταῦτα
10 ἀποδοῦναι, ὥστε τὴν μετ' αὐτοῦ στρατιὰν ἀφεῖναι αὐτούς·
μέχρι οὗ δ' ἂν τὰ χρήματα ἀποδοθῇ, ἄνδρας δώσειν Ἀθηναίων ὁμήρους, ἕνα κατὰ τάλαντον. οἱ δὲ Συρακόσιοι καὶ 3
Γύλιππος οὐ προσεδέχοντο τοὺς λόγους, ἀλλὰ προσπεσόντες
καὶ περιστάντες πανταχόθεν ἔβαλλον καὶ τούτους μέχρι
15 ὀψέ. εἶχον δὲ καὶ οὗτοι πονήρως σίτου τε καὶ τῶν ἐπιτη- 4
δείων ἀπορίᾳ. ὅμως δὲ τῆς νυκτὸς φυλάξαντες τὸ ἡσυχάζον
ἔμελλον πορεύσεσθαι. καὶ ἀναλαμβάνουσί τε τὰ ὅπλα καὶ
οἱ Συρακύσιοι αἰσθάνονται καὶ ἐπαιάνισαν. γνόντες δὲ 5
οἱ Ἀθηναῖοι ὅτι οὐ λανθάνουσι, κατέθεντο πάλιν πλὴν
20 τριακοσίων μάλιστα ἀνδρῶν· οὗτοι δὲ διὰ τῶν φυλάκων
βιασάμενοι ἐχώρουν τῆς νυκτὸς ᾗ ἐδύναντο.

Νικίας δ' ἐπειδὴ ἡμέρα ἐγένετο ἦγε τὴν στρατιάν· οἱ δὲ 84
Συρακόσιοι καὶ οἱ ξύμμαχοι προσέκειντο τὸν αὐτὸν τρόπον
πανταχόθεν βάλλοντές τε καὶ κατακοντίζοντες. καὶ οἱ 2
25 Ἀθηναῖοι ἠπείγοντο πρὸς τὸν Ἀσσίναρον ποταμόν, ἅμα
μὲν βιαζόμενοι ὑπὸ τῆς πανταχόθεν προσβολῆς ἱππέων τε
πολλῶν καὶ τοῦ ἄλλου ὄχλου, οἰόμενοι ῥᾷόν τι σφίσιν
ἔσεσθαι, ἢν διαβῶσι τὸν ποταμόν, ἅμα δ' ὑπὸ τῆς ταλαι-
πωρίας καὶ τοῦ πιεῖν ἐπιθυμίᾳ. ὡς δὲ γίγνονται ἐπ' αὐτῷ, 3
30 ἐσπίπτουσιν οὐδενὶ κόσμῳ ἔτι, ἀλλὰ πᾶς τέ τις διαβῆναι
αὐτὸς πρῶτος βουλόμενος καὶ οἱ πολέμιοι ἐπικείμενοι χαλε-

4 post μετὰ add. τοῦ M   5 καὶ ἐκεῖνον B (κἀκεῖνον γο. B)
11 δ' οὗ B   17 πορεύεσθαι A B   18 ἐπαιάνισαν c f : ἐπαιώνισαν
codd.

πὴν ἤδη τὴν διάβασιν ἐποίουν· ἀθρόοι γὰρ ἀναγκαζόμενοι
χωρεῖν ἐπέπιπτόν τε ἀλλήλοις καὶ κατεπάτουν, περί τε τοῖς
δορατίοις καὶ σκεύεσιν οἱ μὲν εὐθὺς διεφθείροντο, οἱ δὲ
4 ἐμπαλασσόμενοι κατέρρεον. ἐς τὰ ἐπὶ θάτερά τε τοῦ ποταμοῦ παραστάντες οἱ Συρακόσιοι (ἦν δὲ κρημνώδες) ἔβαλλον 5
ἄνωθεν τοὺς Ἀθηναίους, πίνοντάς τε τοὺς πολλοὺς ἀσμένους καὶ ἐν κοίλῳ ὄντι τῷ ποταμῷ ἐν σφίσιν αὐτοῖς ταρασ-
5 σομένους. οἵ τε Πελοποννήσιοι ἐπικαταβάντες τοὺς ἐν τῷ
ποταμῷ μάλιστα ἔσφαζον. καὶ τὸ ὕδωρ εὐθὺς διέφθαρτο,
ἀλλ' οὐδὲν ἧσσον ἐπίνετό τε ὁμοῦ τῷ πηλῷ ᾑματωμένον καὶ 10
85 περιμάχητον ἦν τοῖς πολλοῖς. τέλος δὲ νεκρῶν τε πολλῶν
ἐπ' ἀλλήλοις ἤδη κειμένων ἐν τῷ ποταμῷ καὶ διεφθαρμένου
τοῦ στρατεύματος τοῦ μὲν κατὰ τὸν ποταμόν, τοῦ δὲ καί, εἴ
τι διαφύγοι, ὑπὸ τῶν ἱππέων, Νικίας Γυλίππῳ ἑαυτὸν παρα-
δίδωσι, πιστεύσας μᾶλλον αὐτῷ ἢ τοῖς Συρακοσίοις· καὶ 15
ἑαυτῷ μὲν χρήσασθαι ἐκέλευεν ἐκεῖνόν τε καὶ Λακεδαι-
μονίους ὅτι βούλονται, τοὺς δὲ ἄλλους στρατιώτας παύ-
2 σασθαι φονεύοντας. καὶ ὁ Γύλιππος μετὰ τοῦτο ζωγρεῖν
ἤδη ἐκέλευεν· καὶ τούς τε λοιποὺς ὅσους μὴ ἀπεκρύψαντο
(πολλοὶ δὲ οὗτοι ἐγένοντο) ξυνεκόμισαν ζῶντας, καὶ ἐπὶ 20
τοὺς τριακοσίους, οἳ τὴν φυλακὴν διεξῆλθον τῆς νυκτός,
3 πέμψαντες τοὺς διωξομένους ξυνέλαβον. τὸ μὲν οὖν
ἀθροισθὲν τοῦ στρατεύματος ἐς τὸ κοινὸν οὐ πολὺ ἐγένετο,
τὸ δὲ διακλαπὲν πολύ, καὶ διεπλήσθη πᾶσα Σικελία αὐτῶν,
ἅτε οὐκ ἀπὸ ξυμβάσεως ὥσπερ τῶν μετὰ Δημοσθένους 25
4 ληφθέντων. μέρος δέ τι οὐκ ὀλίγον καὶ ἀπέθανεν· πλεῖ-
στος γὰρ δὴ φόνος οὗτος καὶ οὐδενὸς ἐλάσσων τῶν ἐν τῷ
[Σικελικῷ] πολέμῳ τούτῳ ἐγένετο. καὶ ἐν ταῖς ἄλλαις
προσβολαῖς ταῖς κατὰ τὴν πορείαν συχναῖς γενομέναις οὐκ
ὀλίγοι ἐτεθνήκεσαν. πολλοὶ δὲ ὅμως καὶ διέφυγον, οἱ μὲν 30

---

6 ἀσμένως B   10 τε om. C   16 χρήσασθαι B : χρῆσθαι
cett.   20 ξυνεκόμισαν B : συγκομίσας cett.   25 post μετὰ add.
τοῦ M   8 Σικελικῷ secl. Dobree   29 προσβολαῖς B : om.
cett.

καὶ παραυτίκα, οἱ δὲ καὶ δουλεύσαντες καὶ διαδιδράσκοντες
ὕστερον· τούτοις δ' ἦν ἀναχώρησις ἐς Κατάνην.

Ξυναθροισθέντες δὲ οἱ Συρακόσιοι καὶ οἱ ξύμμαχοι, τῶν **86**
τε αἰχμαλώτων ὅσους ἐδύναντο πλείστους καὶ τὰ σκῦλα
5 ἀναλαβόντες, ἀνεχώρησαν ἐς τὴν πόλιν. καὶ τοὺς μὲν **2**
ἄλλους Ἀθηναίων καὶ τῶν ξυμμάχων ὁπόσους ἔλαβον κατε-
βίβασαν ἐς τὰς λιθοτομίας, ἀσφαλεστάτην εἶναι νομίσαντες
τήρησιν, Νικίαν δὲ καὶ Δημοσθένη ἄκοντος τοῦ Γυλίππου
ἀπέσφαξαν. ὁ γὰρ Γύλιππος καλὸν τὸ ἀγώνισμα ἐνόμιζέν
10 οἱ εἶναι ἐπὶ τοῖς ἄλλοις καὶ τοὺς ἀντιστρατήγους κομίσαι
Λακεδαιμονίοις. ξυνέβαινε δὲ τὸν μὲν πολεμιώτατον αὐ- **3**
τοῖς εἶναι, Δημοσθένη, διὰ τὰ ἐν τῇ νήσῳ καὶ Πύλῳ, τὸν
δὲ διὰ τὰ αὐτὰ ἐπιτηδειότατον· τοὺς γὰρ ἐκ τῆς νήσου
ἄνδρας τῶν Λακεδαιμονίων ὁ Νικίας προυθυμήθη, σπονδὰς
15 πείσας τοὺς Ἀθηναίους ποιήσασθαι, ὥστε ἀφεθῆναι. ἀνθ' **4**
ὧν οἵ τε Λακεδαιμόνιοι ἦσαν αὐτῷ προσφιλεῖς κἀκεῖνος οὐχ
ἥκιστα διὰ τοῦτο πιστεύσας ἑαυτὸν τῷ Γυλίππῳ παρέδωκεν.
ἀλλὰ τῶν Συρακοσίων τινές, ὡς ἐλέγετο, οἱ μὲν δείσαντες,
ὅτι πρὸς αὐτὸν ἐκεκοινολόγηντο, μὴ βασανιζόμενος διὰ τὸ
20 τοιοῦτο ταραχὴν σφίσιν ἐν εὐπραγίᾳ ποιήσῃ, ἄλλοι δέ, καὶ
οὐχ ἥκιστα οἱ Κορίνθιοι, μὴ χρήμασι δὴ πείσας τινάς, ὅτι
πλούσιος ἦν, ἀποδρᾷ καὶ αὖθις σφίσι νεώτερόν τι ἀπ' αὐτοῦ
γένηται, πείσαντες τοὺς ξυμμάχους ἀπέκτειναν αὐτόν. καὶ **5**
ὁ μὲν τοιαύτῃ ἢ ὅτι ἐγγύτατα τούτων αἰτίᾳ ἐτεθνήκει,
25 ἥκιστα δὴ ἄξιος ὢν τῶν γε ἐπ' ἐμοῦ Ἑλλήνων ἐς τοῦτο
δυστυχίας ἀφικέσθαι διὰ τὴν πᾶσαν ἐς ἀρετὴν νενομισμένην
ἐπιτήδευσιν.

Τοὺς δ' ἐν ταῖς λιθοτομίαις οἱ Συρακόσιοι χαλεπῶς τοὺς **87**
πρώτους χρόνους μετεχείρισαν. ἐν γὰρ κοίλῳ χωρίῳ ὄντας
30 καὶ ὀλίγῳ πολλοὺς οἵ τε ἥλιοι τὸ πρῶτον καὶ τὸ πνῖγος ἔτι

5 λαβόντες A E F M   8 τοῦ B : om. cett.   17 διὰ τοῦτο
B : om. cett.   21 δὴ B : om. cett.   23 post πείσαντες add. τε
A C E F G M   26 πᾶσαν ἐς ἀρετὴν B γρ. M : om. cett.   30 καὶ
ὀλίγῳ B : om. cett.

ἐλύπει διὰ τὸ ἀστέγαστον καὶ αἱ νύκτες ἐπιγιγνόμεναι τοὐναντίον μετοπωριναὶ καὶ ψυχραὶ τῇ μεταβολῇ ἐς ἀσθένειαν
2 ἐνεωτέριζον, πάντα τε ποιούντων αὐτῶν διὰ στενοχωρίαν
ἐν τῷ αὐτῷ καὶ προσέτι τῶν νεκρῶν ὁμοῦ ἐπ' ἀλλήλοις
ξυννενηημένων, οἳ ἔκ τε τῶν τραυμάτων καὶ διὰ τὴν μετα- 5
βολὴν καὶ τὸ τοιοῦτον ἀπέθνῃσκον, καὶ ὀσμαὶ ἦσαν οὐκ
ἀνεκτοί, καὶ λιμῷ ἅμα καὶ δίψῃ ἐπιέζοντο (ἐδίδοσαν γὰρ
αὐτῶν ἑκίστῳ ἐπὶ ὀκτὼ μῆνας κοτύλην ὕδατος καὶ δύο
κοτύλας σίτου), ἄλλα τε ὅσα εἰκὸς ἐν τῷ τοιούτῳ χωρίῳ
ἐμπεπτωκότας κακοπαθῆσαι, οὐδὲν ὅτι οὐκ ἐπεγένετο αὐτοῖς· 10
3 καὶ ἡμέρας μὲν ἑβδομήκοντά τινας οὕτω διῃτήθησαν ἀθρόοι·
ἔπειτα πλὴν Ἀθηναίων καὶ εἴ τινες Σικελιωτῶν ἢ Ἰταλιω-
4 τῶν ξυνεστράτευσαν, τοὺς ἄλλους ἀπέδοντο. ἐλήφθησαν
δὲ οἱ ξύμπαντες, ἀκριβείᾳ μὲν χαλεπὸν ἐξειπεῖν, ὅμως δὲ
5 οὐκ ἐλάσσους ἑπτακισχιλίων. ξυνέβη τε ἔργον τοῦτο 15
[Ἑλληνικὸν] τῶν κατὰ τὸν πόλεμον τόνδε μέγιστον γενέσθαι, δοκεῖν δ' ἔμοιγε καὶ ὧν ἀκοῇ Ἑλληνικῶν ἴσμεν, καὶ
τοῖς τε κρατήσασι λαμπρότατον καὶ τοῖς διαφθαρεῖσι δυστυ-
6 χέστατον· κατὰ πάντα γὰρ πάντως νικηθέντες καὶ οὐδὲν
ὀλίγον ἐς οὐδὲν κακοπαθήσαντες πανωλεθρίᾳ δὴ τὸ λεγό- 20
μενον καὶ πεζὸς καὶ νῆες καὶ οὐδὲν ὅτι οὐκ ἀπώλετο, καὶ
ὀλίγοι ἀπὸ πολλῶν ἐπ' οἴκου ἀπενόστησαν. ταῦτα μὲν τὰ
περὶ Σικελίαν γενόμενα.

2 ἐπ' ἀσθενείᾳ B   5 ξυννενηνεγμένων B M   7 δίψῃ recc. :
δίψει codd.   9 τῷ B : om. cett.   14 post δὲ add. καὶ B
εἰπεῖν B   16 Ἑλληνικὸν secl. Krüger

COMMENTARY

JULY–SEPTEMBER 414

1–3. Arrival of Gylippos

AT the end of Book VI Gylippos the Spartan and Pythen the Corinthian, on their way to Syracuse with four ships, are at Taras, repairing their ships after the storm which thwarted their first attempt to reach Sicily.

1. 1. ἐς Λοκροὺς τοὺς Ἐπιζεφυρίους: Lokroi, like Taras, was consistently hostile to the Athenians.

κατὰ τὰς Ἐπιπολάς: The plateau overlooking Syracuse from the north and north-west.

αὐτούς τε ἐκείνους: 'Himera itself.'

2. καὶ τῶν Ἀττικῶν . . . ἀπέστειλεν: Nikias did not attach any importance to the presence of Gylippos' tiny force at Taras; ὅμως glances back at vi. 104. 3, 'Nikias . . . did not as yet take any precautions'. (The division of the story of the Sicilian Expedition into two at vi. 105. 3 / vii. 1. 1 does not go back to Thucydides himself and is not even the only division current in Hellenistic times.)

διὰ τοῦ πορθμοῦ: The Straits of Messina.

ἐς Ἱμέραν: Himera had rebuffed Athenian overtures in 415.

3. τούς τε Ἱμεραίους: This τε is co-ordinated with καὶ τοὺς Σελινουντίους at the end of the section.

καὶ τοῖς ἐκ τῶν νεῶν . . . παρασχεῖν: Since their four ships would have a total of crew of c. 800, and we find (in § 5) 700 of these serving as infantry, it seems that the advice which Alkibiades gave the Spartans, to send 'men who would row themselves and serve as hoplites immediately on arrival' (vi. 91. 4), had been carried out.

πανστρατιᾷ: If this request was made, it was certainly not granted, for Selinus sent 'some light-armed troops and cavalry' (§ 5); the alternative reading στρατιᾷ is therefore preferable.

4. Ἀρχωνίδου: This man was the ruler of Herbita, c. 70 km. east-south-east of Himera. In the 440's he had collaborated with Duketios, the champion of the Sikels against Syracuse, and was thus predisposed to friendship with Athens.

5. καὶ ἐπιβατῶν: The complement of a trireme normally included

a small number of men armed as hoplites. 'Those of his sailors and
ἐπιβάται who were armed' means 'His ἐπιβάται and those of his sailors
(cf. § 3) who were armed'.

2. 1. οἱ δ' ἐκ τῆς Λευκάδος Κορίνθιοι: Thirteen ships in all.

περὶ ἀπαλλαγῆς . . . ἐκκλησιάσειν: After the capture and destruction
of both the counterwalls which they had built earlier in the summer
the Syracusans had abandoned hope of preventing the Athenians
from completing a siege-wall (vi. 103. 3 f.).

2. ἐξῆλθον: To the north of the Athenian 'Circle', across the line
which the northward Athenian wall was intended to follow; but they
are not likely to have taken the risk of leaving the plateau and finding
on their return that the whole Athenian force was drawn up for battle
between them and the city.

3. Ἰέτας: The name is restored from a fragment of Philistos (cf.
Cicero's mention [*Verr.* 3. 103] of the people called *Ietini*); its location
is not known.

κατὰ τὸν Εὐρύηλον: The 'waist' of the plateau, where it can be most
easily ascended from north, south, or west, 6–7 km. from the city.

ᾗπερ . . . τὸ πρῶτον: In the spring of 414 (vi. 97. 2).

ἐχώρει . . . τῶν Ἀθηναίων: From the east or north east, with the
Winter Wall (see map) behind him, as becomes clear from 3. 3; this is
not the only passage in this book which becomes intelligible only in the
light of something which is said later.

4. ἑπτὰ μὲν ἢ ὀκτὼ σταδίων: 'Stade' is a somewhat subjective term in
the Greek historians (rather like 'block' in America), and passages in
which Thucydides states in stades a distance which can be checked
today require values varying between 130 and 170 metres.

ἐς τὸν μέγαν λιμένα: The Athenians began their siege-works in 414
by building the 'Circle' on the plateau; they then started to build
northwards from the Circle, but broke off and built southwards towards the Great Harbour.

διπλοῦν τεῖχος: i.e. two walls a good distance apart, enclosing an
area with the Circle at its top end and the sea at the bottom.

τῷ δὲ ἄλλῳ τοῦ κύκλου: It is clear from vi. 98. 2 and vi. 101. 1 that
the κύκλος (which I translate for ease of reference as 'Circle', though it
was not necessarily circular) was a fortified position, and that the word
does *not* mean the whole of the wall by which the Athenians hoped to
cut off Syracuse from all its landward approaches. This passage is
therefore corrupt, and is best emended by deleting τοῦ κύκλου as an
interpolation, understanding τείχει with τῷ ἄλλῳ. In any case, Thucydides' Greek for 'the rest of the circle' would be τῷ ἄλλῳ κύκλῳ.

πρὸς τὸν Τρωγίλον: Trogilos was the ravine which runs down to the sea at the cove of Santa Panagia.

3. 1. Θέμενος τὰ ὅπλα ἐγγύς: 'Taking up his position' (*not* 'laying down his arms') 'not far from them.'

ἑτοῖμος: Thucydides not infrequently passes from oblique cases into the nominative when the sense justifies it, even if grammatical rules do not (cf. Intr. I. 3. 18); the subject of εἶναι is that of προσπέμπει, namely Gylippos.

3. ἐς τὴν εὐρυχωρίαν μᾶλλον: i.e. northwards and north-westwards, to have more room for manœuvre on his right.

ἐπὶ τὴν ἄκραν . . . καλουμένην: The sanctuary of Apollo Temenites lay on the south edge of the plateau, immediately adjoining the Theatre. ἄκρα Τεμενῖτις was probably the top of the long low spur running south-eastwards from just east of the Theatre.

4. τὸ Λάβδαλον: This lay on the northern edge of the plateau—we do not know exactly where—and the construction of a fort there was one of the first Athenian actions in 414.

5. τῷ λιμένι: In certain passages (e.g. 22. 1 f.) Thucydides distinguishes between 'the Great Harbour', i.e. the bay of which the gap between Ortygia and Plemmyrion is the mouth, and 'the Lesser Harbour', the modern Porto Piccolo, lying between Ortygia and Santa Lucia and facing east. In many passages the context shows that by 'the harbour' he means the Great Harbour. Yet in 4. 4 'the harbour of the Syracusans' must mean the Lesser Harbour, and that is probably the meaning of 'the harbour' here; the variant reading of B, τῷ μεγάλῳ λιμένι, is therefore to be rejected. The Athenian fleet was stationed in the Great Harbour, so that an isolated Athenian ship watching the Lesser Harbour would be far from help if it were cut off by an enterprising Syracusan attack.

4–7. The Third Syracusan Counterwall

Earlier in the summer the Syracusans had built, first, a counterwall just below the southern edge of the plateau, and, second, a palisade and trench further south still, through the marshy area. Both these in turn had been captured and destroyed by the Athenians.

4. 1–4. 3. *The Beginning of the Counterwall*

4. 1. ἄνω: On the plateau, beginning from the northern half of the Winter Wall and heading due west.

πρὸς τὸ ἐγκάρσιον: 'At right angles', sc. to the line of the Athenian wall.

2. ἦν γάρ τι . . . ἀσθενές: Whether on the plateau (south of the Circle) or between the plateau and the sea, we do not know.

3. ἔξω αὐλιζόμενοι: Not all of them—which would be an eccentric way to defend a wall the purpose of which is to defend oneself—but with pickets far enough advanced to give the alarm to the main force.

αὐτοὶ μὲν ταύτῃ ἐφύλασσον: They did not necessarily doubt the loyalty of their allies as a whole, but it does not need many traitors to betray a fortification at night.

4. 4–4. 7. *Nikias Occupies Plemmyrion*

4. 4. πρὸς τῷ λιμένι τῷ τῶν Συρακοσίων: The Lesser Harbour, cf. 3. 5 n.

ἦν τι ναυτικῷ κινῶνται: 'If they (= the Syracusans) made any move', lit., 'with a naval element', i.e. 'at sea'. Cf. X. *Cyr.* i. 4. 20 ἦν ἐπὶ σὲ κινῶνται, 'if they make any move against you'.

ὁρῶν . . . ἀνελπιστότερα ὄντα: The news of Gylippos' approach was enough to sweep away talk of surrender in Syracuse; and his actual arrival seems to have had an equally dramatic effect, but in the opposite sense, upon Nikias. Cf. the pessimistic tone of Nikias' letter, 11 ff.

5. στρατιὰν καὶ τὰς ναῦς: There was now no direct and safe communication by land between the army and the fleet.

6. τῷ τε γὰρ ὕδατι . . . οἱ ναῦται: lit., 'for using the water scarce and not from near, and also whenever the sailors went out to collect firewood . . .', i.e. 'whenever the sailors went out, ⟨as they had to⟩ because their water-supply was inadequate and not close at hand, and also to collect firewood, . . .'.

ἐπὶ τῇ ἐν τῷ 'Ολυμπιείῳ πολίχνῃ: The Olympieion, i.e. the sanctuary of Zeus Olympios, lay on a ridge 1·3 km. inland from the (modern) coastline in the very centre of the Great Harbour. The inhabited locality of which it formed a part was fortified by the Syracusans in the winter of 415/14 (vi. 75. 1).

ἐτετάχατο: The third-person-plural endings -αται and -ατο in the middle/passive perfect fell into disuse after the fifth century and were replaced by periphrastic forms (e.g. τεταγμένοι ἦσαν).

7. καὶ τὰς λοιπάς . . . ναῦς: 2. 1.

5–6. *Continuation of the Counterwall; Defeat of the Athenians*

5. 1. πρὸ τοῦ τειχίσματος: The Syracusans, facing south or south-west, had the Winter Wall on their left and the completed portion of the counterwall behind them.

3. οὐκ ἔφη . . . γενέσθαι: Spartan commanders dealing with allied troops were not always diplomatic—or even bearable—but the best of them had an instinctive awareness of what was needed to attract loyalty.

τῇ τάξει: This goes in sense with τὴν ὠφελίαν; understand αὐτήν (i.e. τὴν τάξιν) as object of ποιήσας.

4. Πελοποννήσιοί τε ὄντες καὶ Δωριῆς: The Dorians traditionally despised all other branches of the Greek race as less martial than themselves. Syracuse, Selinus, Gela, and Kamarina were all Doric-speaking and of Dorian origin, while there was a Dorian element in Himera.

Ἰώνων: 'Ionians' in its most general sense includes the Athenians.

καὶ νησιωτῶν: The Aegean islands constituted a large part of the Athenian Empire, and the part which was most familiar to the Athenians and the mainland Greeks in general.

6. 1. καὶ μετὰ ταῦτα: On the following day, as we are told in 11. 2.

καὶ μηδὲ μάχεσθαι: μηδέ is here 'not . . . at all' rather than 'not even'.

ἀντεπῇσαν οὖν: Unlike English 'therefore', οὖν is not commonly used to introduce a main clause after a subordinate or participial clause; but Thucydides so uses it on several occasions when the subordinate clause is unusually long and complex.

2. ἔξω . . . ἢ πρότερον: i.e. further to the west, so that his right wing did not have the completed portion of the counterwall behind it.

4. εἰ καὶ κρατοῖεν: sc. in a pitched battle in the field; clearly, if they could *capture* the counterwall and destroy it they could proceed with their own siege-wall.

7. 1. *Arrival of the Corinthian Ships*

7. 1. λαθοῦσαι . . . φυλακήν: Failure to prevent the arrival of Gongylos in a single fast ship (2. 1) was forgivable, but failure on the part of twenty Athenian ships (4. 7) to stop the main Corinthian force was less so.

[μέχρι] τοῦ ἐγκαρσίου τείχους: 'As far as the wall at right angles' is senseless; it is the ἐγκάρσιον τεῖχος which they are building. Either (i) Thucydides named a place after μέχρι, but this has been accidentally omitted; or (ii) μέχρι is the remnant of a gloss based on a guess or information from another historical source; or (iii) Thucydides

himself left a blank after μέχρι, intending to fill it in when he knew
the answer. Ignore μέχρι and translate: '. . . and helped the Syracusans
to complete the rest of the wall at right angles.'

7. 2–7. 4. *Syracusan Preparations*

7. 3. τρόπῳ ᾧ ἄν . . . προχωρῇ: As it stands, this clause is not Greek,
and ὅπως ἄν should be deleted as an intrusive variant on τρόπῳ ᾧ ἄν.

ἐν ὁλκάσιν ἢ πλοίοις: Thucydides commonly draws this distinction;
πλοῖον appears to be a much more general word, and ὁλκάς is probably
confined to merchant ships above a certain size. Despite its etymologi-
cal relationship to ἕλκειν, ὁλκάς cannot normally denote a towed barge,
for it is mentioned in estimates of time and distance, e.g. vi. 1. 2: 'it
takes a ὁλκάς not much less than eight days to circumnavigate Sicily.'

8. Nikias Writes a Letter

8. 1. καθ' ἕκαστα τῶν γιγνομένων: 'The details of what happened'; the
phrase καθ' ἕκαστα is sometimes used = ἕκαστα.

2. μνήμης: ACEFM have γνώμης; but the messengers were not required to express any 'judgement' of their own, and although it is
a trivial matter to memorize in the tranquillity of a study all the points
made in Nikias' letter—as presented in 11–15 infra—Nikias was no
doubt aware that nothing is easier than to forget important points
when faced with a critical audience. Moreover, although there is no
reason whatever to doubt that Nikias really did write a letter, he did
not write exactly what Thucydides, in his own unmistakable idiom,
offers us, and the real letter may have contained many more detailed
facts and figures.

τὰ ὄντα: 'The facts', 'the truth'.

ἔγραψεν ἐπιστολήν: Since the letter begins (11. 1) 'You have been
informed of earlier proceedings in many other ἐπιστολαί', it is evident
that ἐπιστολή means 'message' or 'report' (in Hdt. iv. 10. 1 it refers to
verbal instructions) and that the emphasis lies on ἔγραψεν: not 'he
wrote a *letter*', but 'he put a report into *writing*'. It is equally evident
that this was an unusual procedure in 414, though not unprecedented;
Eupolis fr. 308 indicates that Kleon wrote a somewhat arrogant letter
to the Council and Assembly after capturing the Spartiates at Sphakteria.

τὴν αὐτοῦ γνώμην: 'His *personal* opinion', as the position of αὐτοῦ
shows, not simply 'his *opinion*'.

περὶ τῆς ἀληθείας: 'About the true facts of the situation'; cf. Antiphon (*passim*) ἡ ἀλήθεια τῶν πραχθέντων.

3. **φέροντες . . . καὶ ὅσα κτλ.**: 'Bearing the letter and ⟨bearing in mind⟩ what they were to say'—additional data and answers to likely questions and criticisms (cf. 10).

τὰ κατὰ τὸ στρατόπεδον . . . ἐπεμέλετο: In ii. 81. 4 διὰ φυλακῆς ἔχων is intransitive, but phrases of this type are commonly transitive; ἐπιμέλεσθαι normally takes a genitive, but may also take a neuter plural as internal accusative; thus τὰ κατὰ τὸ στρατόπεδον may well be regarded as the object both of ἔχων and of ἐπεμέλετο.

SEPTEMBER–OCTOBER 414

9. Operations in Thrace

9. Εὐετίων: Nothing else is known for certain about this man.

Περδίκκου: When we last heard of Perdikkas, the king of Macedonia (early in 415, vi. 7. 3 f.), his territory was under Athenian attack. It is never a surprise to find that he has changed sides, but a little surprising that Thucydides does not tell us in this case why or when he did so.

ἐπ' Ἀμφίπολιν: Amphipolis, an Athenian colony at the mouth of the Strymon, was detached from allegiance to Athens by a Spartan force in 424.

Θρᾳξὶ πολλοῖς: This does not mean that the king of the Odrysian Thracians, or any other Thracian potentate, was in formal alliance with Athens; Thracians commonly fought for Athens as mercenaries (cf. 27. 1).

ἐξ Ἱμεραίου: This place never appears in the Athenian tribute lists, and its exact location is unknown.

NOVEMBER–DECEMBER 414

10–15. Nikias' Letter is Read at Athens

The tone of this letter is one of hopelessness, for which we are not fully prepared even by the Syracusan successes described in the previous few chapters or by the description (8. 1) of Nikias' apprehensiveness. Nikias apparently envisages no action of his own by which he might recover the initiative or even arrest the deterioration of his own position; he can only wait for reinforcement, recall, or retreat (14. 3; he does not at this stage envisage disaster). In Greek wars, as in Greek battles, the tide often turns very suddenly. Possibly there was already widespread sickness among the Athenians (cf. 47. 2), but the fundamental cause of their troubles was that by the time that Gylippos had been added to the one side Lamachos had been subtracted from the other. Nikias, left to himself, had too little confidence in the practicability of defeating Syracuse, he had a chronic illness (15. 1), and he was temperamentally inclined to blame anyone but himself (13. 2, 14. 2, 14. 4, 15. 1 f.). Nothing can destroy an army's morale more rapidly than the knowledge that its experienced and trusted commander accepts failure as inevitable.

10. ὁ δὲ γραμματεὺς ὁ τῆς πόλεως: The business of this official, who is called 'secretary to the People' in fourth-century inscriptions, was simply to read documents aloud; the far more important secretary who prepared and recorded business for the Council and the Assembly was called 'secretary to the Council' in the fifth century and 'secretary κατὰ πρυτάνειαν' in the fourth.

11. 1. ἐν ἄλλαις πολλαῖς ἐπιστολαῖς ἴστε: lit., 'you know ... *in* many other reports', i.e. 'you have been informed ...' or 'I have told you ...'. Cf. 'learn now ...' = 'I will now tell you ...'.

2. **ἐφ' οὓς ἐπέμφθημεν:** In the original instructions given to the generals in 415 (vi. 8. 2) the real purpose of the expedition, the defeat of Syracuse, was circumspectly expressed: 'help Segesta against Selinus, assist in the refoundation of Leontinoi, and carry out the other operations required in Sicily in such manner as they (= the generals) judge in the best interests of Athens.' When the three generals first arrived at Rhegion and held a conference, Nikias, who did not want to attack Syracuse at all, proposed (vi. 47) that they should simply sail to Selinus, ἐφ' ὅπερ μάλιστα ἐπέμφθησαν. Now, speaking not to his colleagues in conference but to the Assembly itself, he is compelled to recognize the truth.

3. **οὐδὲ γὰρ ξυμπάσῃ κτλ.:** οὐδέ here rebuts an imagined criticism: 'for it is not as if we were able to use our whole army together.'

4. **οὐδὲ γὰρ τῆς χώρας κτλ.:** The point of οὐδέ is: ' our attempted siege-wall has come to nothing, and we do not have control of the open country *either*.'

12. 2. ὡς ἐγὼ πυνθάνομαι: Not only by inference from their training (§ 5, cf. 7. 4); as we learn later (48. 2), Nikias was in communication with treacherous elements inside Syracuse.

3. **ὅπερ κἀκεῖνοι πυνθάνονται:** The Syracusans too were not wholly dependent on observation and deduction; the rate of desertion described in 13. 2 would have ensured that they were well informed on conditions in the Athenian camp.

διάβροχοι: 'Saturated', and so heavier in the water and slower in manœuvre. Triremes were normally hauled on shore and 'aired' when the situation permitted; cf. § 4.

4. **ἀντιπάλους τῷ πλήθει**: There was no good reason yet for Nikias to say that the Syracusan navy was the equal of the Athenian in *quality*, though he hints at this in 13. 2–14. 1. τῷ τε πλήθει in B may indicate an original τῷ γε πλήθει (conj. Bodin); if that is right, Nikias is drawing attention to the difference between quantity and quality.

καὶ ἔτι πλείους: 'Or even more'; καί normally = English 'or' in such expressions.

5. **καὶ αἱ ἐπιχειρήσεις . . . ἐξουσία**: lit., 'the attacks ⟨are⟩ in their power'—i.e. 'the initiative lies with them'—'and ⟨there is for them⟩ freedom more to dry out their own ⟨ships⟩', i.e. 'they have more opportunity than we to dry out their ships'.

13. 1. **τοῦτο**: Attacking at times and places of their own choice, and drying off ships in turn.

καὶ νῦν: '*Even* now', implying 'it will be worse if we relax our guard'.

2. **τῶν ναυτῶν [τῶν] μὲν κτλ.**: With the MSS. text, θεράποντες are a subdivision of ναυτῶν; there is no grammatical objection to the transition from a participial μέν-clause to a finite δέ-clause (cf. Intr. I. 3. 15*b*). But the historical objection is considerable. The use of slaves as rowers is not attested at Athens before 406/5 (X. *HG* i. 6. 24), and the enfranchisement of the slaves who fought in that year suggests that the measure was exceptional; when the Athenians needed extra crews in 428 they found them by enrolling hoplites and metics (iii. 16. 1), not slaves. Poppo's deletion of the second τῶν is therefore desirable; for the transition from genitive absolute to finite verb cf. 15. 2, τῶν πολεμίων κτλ. The casualties incurred by the sailors and the rate of desertion among the slaves are two different aspects or causes of deterioration in the manning and servicing of ships. We should then punctuate strongly after αὐτομολοῦσι, so that καὶ οἱ ξένοι makes a fresh point; of course foreign sailors would be killed by Syracusan cavalry just as much as Athenian sailors were, but Thucydides is concerned with the special causes of loss in each category.

ἀναγκαστοί: Not 'press-ganged' as individuals, but supplied as contingents by subject-allies.

εὐθύς: 'As soon as they can', 'without more ado'; cf. X. *Hiero* 2. 8, 'for private individuals can go εὐθύς (= without more ado) wherever they like . . . but tyrants go everywhere as if through enemy territory'.

κατὰ τὰς πόλεις: sc. of Sicily.

ἐπ' αὐτομολίας προφάσει: No wholly satisfactory explanation of these words has yet been offered. πρόφασις often means '(true) reason' (or 'motive') for an action, or 'cause' suggested in explanation of an event; but in (ἐπὶ) (. . .) προφάσει it means 'alleged (but subordinate or false) reason', i.e. 'pretext'; cf. vi. 78. 1 τῇ ἐμῇ προφάσει, 'using me as a pretext', iv. 80. 2 ἐπὶ προφάσει, 'on some pretext' (in order to conceal the real intention). Hence, apparently, 'giving desertion as their pretext'; but obviously the foreign sailors did not *pretend* to be deserting to the enemy while actually going for some other reason. It is possible that the phrase may mean no more than ἐπ' αὐτομολίᾳ, and that Thucydides has expressed misleadingly what could have been put better as οἱ μὲν ἐπ' αὐτομολίᾳ ἀπέρχονται, οἱ δ' ἐφ' ᾗτινι ἂν προφάσει ἕκαστοι δύνωνται. Of many emendations, the two most attractive are αὐτονομίας (Passow), 'giving as their justification the fact that they are not our subjects' (sc. and therefore cannot be kept against their will), and αὐτουργίας (Schwartz), '. . . that they have to cultivate their own land' (sc. and therefore cannot be away from home so long).

Ὑκκαρικά: Hykkara, a non-Greek town on the north coast of Sicily, an enemy of Athens' ally Segesta, was captured at the end of 415 (vi. 62. 3 f.) and its inhabitants were enslaved.

ἀκρίβειαν: 'High quality'; cf. vi. 18. 6 τὸ φαῦλον . . . καὶ τὸ πάνυ ἀκριβές, 'the mediocre . . . and the really first-rate'.

14. 1. βραχεῖα ἀκμὴ πληρώματος: 'A crew's period of maximum efficiency is short.' Nikias' sequence of argument is: (i) at first our fleet was highly efficient (ἤκμαζε 12. 3), (ii) but our ships are saturated, (iii) and we have lost many sailors, (iv) therefore our efficiency has deteriorated (this consequence of the loss of men in general is attached to the type of loss last specified, the substitution of Hykkaran slaves for Athenian sailors), (v) and you know that (sc. in any case) (a) a crew is not at its peak of efficiency for very long, and we have been at Syracuse a long time, and (b) few sailors are really skilful (sc. therefore everything has accelerated a process which in any case is hard to avoid). Some editors have translated 'the efficient *element* in a crew is *small*'; but this introduces a high degree of tautology into Nikias' argument, and conflicts with viii. 46. 5 'by keeping on saying that the Phoenician ships were going to arrive . . . he took away the ἀκμή of their fleet, which had been powerful (ἰσχυρά)' and with Plutarch's imitation (*Caes.* 40. 2), 'he said that they should wear down the ἀκμή of the enemy ,which was βραχεῖα'.

ξυνέχοντες τὴν εἰρεσίαν: 'Rowing in time', the one thing upon which the efficient movement of any oared vessel depends.

2. χαλεπαὶ γάρ . . . ἄρξαι: This has little bearing on the difficulties of the situation as Nikias has described them, but it is a theme

prominent in his mind (cf. § 4 infra and 48. 4), and it may have been his habit to suggest that he could have dealt with all difficulties if only his troops had not let him down. Greek troops were by modern standards temperamental and recalcitrant, but the Athenians were not necessarily worse than others (cf. 72. 4).

ἀλλ' ἀνάγκη κτλ.: lit., 'but it is necessary that both what we have and what is expended comes from what we had with us when we came', i.e. 'what we have is what we brought with us, and what is lost is necessarily all lost from that'. Given ἐπιπληρωσόμεθα and the fact (§ 3) that supplies were replenished from Italy, the reference must be to *crews*, despite the neuter; presumably Thucydides has πληρώματα in mind.

3. τὰ τρέφοντα ἡμᾶς χωρία τῆς Ἰταλίας: Save for the mention of ships and shipbuilding timber in 25. 1 f. Thucydides tells us nothing specific about supplies from Italy; vi. 103. 2 is a highly general reference.

4. ἡδίω μὲν ἄν . . . ἐπιστέλλειν: 'I could have sent you a different report, which would have been more welcome'; Nikias does not mean that he *could have had* better news which he refrained from sending, but that he *would have been able* to send a more agreeable but misleading or evasive report. The contrast between telling an audience the disagreeable truth and telling it what it likes to hear is a rhetorical commonplace.

ἦν τι ὑμῖν . . . ἐκβῇ: 'If you find that anything after that' (the welcome but false report) 'turns out different.'

ἀσφαλέστερον: Not 'safer' for himself, but 'conducive to a right decision'; the Greeks were aware of the etymology of ἀσφαλής.

15. 1. ὡς . . . γεγενημένων, οὕτω τὴν γνώμην ἔχετε: lit., 'as . . . having been not open to criticism, thus have your judgement', i.e. 'I can assure you that . . . have not failed you'. Cf. X. *An.* i. 3. 6 ὡς ἐμοῦ οὖν ἰόντος ὅπῃ ἂν καὶ ὑμεῖς, οὕτω τὴν γνώμην ἔχετε = 'I can assure you that I shall go wherever you do'.

ἐφ' ἃ μὲν ἤλθομεν τὸ πρῶτον: They have failed to achieve the *objects for which* they were sent, and have failed to conquer the *enemy against whom* they were sent; therefore (lit.) 'on to which we came' must mean '⟨in respect of⟩ the situation with which we were sent to deal', by contrast with 'but now that all Sicily is uniting . . .'.

μηδὲ τοῖς παροῦσιν ἀνταρκούντων: 'Unable to cope even with the existing difficulties'; cf. vi. 89. 4 τοῖς παροῦσιν ἕπεσθαι = 'fall in with the existing trend'.

2. ὅτι δὲ μέλλετε: 'What you intend to do.'

ὡς τῶν πολεμίων . . . φθήσονται: With σχολαίτερον understand
ποριοῦνται (on the type of μέν/δέ construction, cf. 13. 2 n.), and with
λήσουσιν and φθήσονται understand ποριζόμενοι. Nikias' criticism of
the Athenians, referring especially to their failure to prevent the
assembly of Gylippos' little fleet at Leukas, is unfair, in view of his
own failure to prevent Gylippos' crossing from Rhegion to Messene
(1. 2) or the subsequent arrival of the Corinthian ships (7. 1).

DECEMBER 414–FEBRUARY 413

16–17. Measures to Reinforce the Expedition

16. 1. Μένανδρον καὶ Εὐθύδημον: If the annual election of generals was
held in the fifth century, as it was in the fourth, after Prytany VI (i.e.
in February or March), the appointment of Menandros and Euthydemos cannot have been made at an ordinary election, for it was not
yet the winter solstice (§ 2); but this creates no real difficulty. The
Athenians could give temporary and local military command to any-
body at any time, without deposing any of the ten 'full' generals of
the year. After the arrival of Demosthenes and Eurymedon in Sicily,
there were three 'full' generals there, and the association of Menandros
and Euthydemos with them in command seems to have been a matter
for their discretion. In the night attack on Epipolai Menandros commanded the attacking force with Demosthenes and Eurymedon (43. 2)
but there is no mention of Euthydemos. Neither seems to have been
asked for his opinion in the debate which followed the failure on
Epipolai (47 ff., esp. 49. 3 f.). In the last battle in the harbour, Eurymedon being by then dead, Demosthenes and Menandros and Euthydemos 'went on board the ships as generals' (69. 4).

Euthydemos is likely to be the man of that name who was among the
takers of the oath of peace in 421 (v. 19. 2) and also the 'Euthydemos son
of Eudemos' who was a general in 418/17 (*IG* i² 302); we hear nothing
of him on the retreat from Syracuse or afterwards, and he may have
been killed in the last battle in the harbour. Menandros is probably the
general of 405/4 (X. *HG* ii. 1. 16); it is not known what happened to him
after that.

ἐκ καταλόγου: The board of generals had a single list which contained
the names of all those required, by virtue of their capital and age, to
serve as hoplites; in vi. 43 there is an antithesis between hoplites ἐκ
καταλόγου and hoplites who were θῆτες (i.e. below the hoplite property-
rating and therefore needing to be armed at the state's expense).

2. Δημοσθένη τε . . . καὶ Εὐρυμέδοντα: The choice was a wise one.
Demosthenes, who last held a command (so far as we know) in 418/17,

appears in Thucydides as a quick and energetic general, aggressive, ingenious, with a good tactical eye, and capable of learning from experience (cf. especially iii. 95 ff., iv. 3 ff., 29 f.). He had won the good opinion of Athens' allies in the north-west (cf. 57. 10). On his arrival in Sicily (42. 3 ff.) he acts and argues briskly and forcefully, and his solutions are drastic; but once the situation has become desperate he has little positive contribution to make, and in the final retreat he acquits himself less well than Nikias.

Eurymedon had experience of Sicily, though he was fined on his return thence in 424 (iv. 65. 3) for not accomplishing what Athens had hoped, and he may have been out of favour since then. This last point has some bearing on the question whether Demosthenes and Eurymedon were already generals for 414/13 and were now appointed to Sicily on the assumption that only some flagrant inadequacy on their part could stand in the way of their re-election for 413/12, or pre-elected for 413/12 and given immediate authority to assemble the forces voted; and it tells somewhat in favour of the second alternative. In that case the generals at the end of December 414 comprised (i) nine generals—including Nikias—elected for 414/13, (ii) possibly a tenth, a general-suffect, elected after the death of Lamachos, (iii) Menandros and Euthydemos, given 'local' rank, (iv) Demosthenes and Eurymedon as generals-elect.

καὶ ἑκατόν: These words are in H and are implied by Valla; they are not to be found anywhere else. Probability is in their favour; so is Diod. xiii. 8. 7, who says '140 talents'.

17. 2. εἴκοσι ναῦς: Naupaktos was their destination, and Konon their commander; cf. § 4, 19. 5, 31. 4. It follows from this—and from the fact that when Corinthian ships destined for Syracuse assembled at Leukas in the autumn of 414 (vi. 104. 1) they do not seem to have worried about Athenian interception—that the Athenians were not at this time maintaining a standing force at Naupaktos.

3. παρεσκευάζοντο . . . ἀποστελοῦντες . . . πέμποντες: παρασκευάσθαι is commonly used with ὡς and a future participle; Thucydides sometimes omits the ὡς, as in vi. 54. 4 παρεσκευάζετο προπηλακιῶν αὐτόν.

4. πρὸς τήν . . . φυλακήν: The twenty ships referred to in § 2.

τῶν τριηρῶν: With ἀντίταξιν; lit., 'against their own opposing array of the triremes'.

ὅπως . . . ἀποπειράσωσι . . . καί . . . κωλύοιεν: There is no distinction of 'vividness' or 'remoteness' between the subjunctive and optative; the co-ordination of the two is an instance of Thucydides' tendency to deliberate variation (cf. Intr. I. 3. 16), and occurs also (in reverse order) in vi. 96. 3.

18. Spartan Preparations

18. 1. ὥσπερ τε . . . ἐναγόντων: 'In accordance with their previous decision and at the instigation of the Syracusans and Corinthians.' According to vi. 93. 2, the Spartans 'turned their attention' at the beginning of 414 to the establishment of a fort at Dekeleia. §§ 2 f. explain why they did not establish it at once.

ὅπως δή . . . διακωλυθῇ: The total number of Athenian hoplites sent to Sicily was not large, and the Athenians could afford to send away many more without making the fortified area of Athens, Peiraieus, and the Long Walls vulnerable to a Peloponnesian assault. From that point of view, an invasion of Attica would do no more to curtail Athenian reinforcement of Nikias than the invasions of the Archidamian War did (e.g.) to save Mytilene; δή implies that the author doubts the validity of the reasoning which he is reporting. But the absence of Athenian ships was not unimportant; it meant that the Athenians' ability to inflict reprisals on the Peloponnese for the damage they suffered in Attica would be limited.

καὶ ὁ Ἀλκιβιάδης . . . τὸν πόλεμον: It was Alkibiades who, having fled to Sparta at the end of 415 when threatened with trial and execution for impieties, urged the Spartans to establish a fort at Dekeleia.

2. τὰς σπονδάς: The peace treaty of 421.

σφέτερον . . . γενέσθαι: The Theban attack on Plataiai in 431, the first fighting of the Peloponnesian War, was not initiated by Sparta or by any decision of the Peloponnesian League, but by having Thebes as an ally Sparta shared her guilt.

ἐν ταῖς πρότερον ξυνθήκαις: The Thirty Years Peace of 445.

ἐθέλωσι: sc. any state alleged to have offended against the terms of the peace.

αὐτοὶ οὐχ ὑπήκουον: Sparta did indeed send envoys to Athens at the end of 432, ἐγκλήματα ποιούμενοι (i. 126. 1); but in Thucydides' view this was done not in order to open the way to arbitration, but after the decision to fight had been taken by Sparta and her allies, and it was done in such a way as to provoke refusal and to gain an ostensible moral advantage from that refusal.

εἰκότως δυστυχεῖν τε: The belief that the gods punished the breaking of oaths was one of the oldest and firmest in Greek theology. The parties to an interstate agreement swore oaths that they would keep it; if they broke it, they expected divine punishment. Since Thucydides himself was unconventional in theology, and may well have been an atheist, his matter-of-fact statements about the religious motivation of states must be taken seriously. The Spartans were not the only people to interpret misfortune as a sign of divine displeasure; in 421 the

Athenians restored to Delos the population which they had previously removed, 'reflecting on their own military setbacks, and at the behest of the god at Delphi' (v. 32. 1).

τήν τε περὶ Πύλον ξυμφοράν: Their loss of Pylos in 425 and the capture of the Spartiates on Sphakteria.

3. ταῖς τριάκοντα ναυσίν: This attack on Lakonian territory was made in the summer of 414, in co-operation with Argos (vi. 105).

Ἐπιδαύρου τέ τι: Epidauros Limera, in Lakonia, as vi. 105 shows, not the better-known Epidauros which lay on the east coast of the Argolid.

ἐληστεύοντο: sc. the Spartans, although the subject of ἐδῄωσαν and ἤθελον is the Athenians.

τῶν κατὰ τὰς σπονδὰς ἀμφισβητουμένων: Some of the provisions of the Peace of Nikias— -notably the return of Pylos to the Spartans and of the Thraceward cities to allegiance to Athens—were not carried out.

ἐς δίκας . . . τῶν Λακεδαιμονίων: We are told nothing else about this.

4. σίδηρόν τε: For the clamps and dowels which would hold the masonry of the fort.

NINETEENTH YEAR OF THE WAR

MARCH 413

19–20. Activity in Greece

19. 1–19. 2. *Peloponnesian Invasion of Attica*

19. 2. ἀπέχει δέ . . . καὶ ἀπὸ τῆς Βοιωτιάς: Dekeleia is 18 km. from Athens by the shortest route, so that 150 m. is the value of the stade implied here (cf. 2. 4 n.) On the other hand, from Dekeleia across Parnes to the edge of the Boeotian plain is less, 9–10 km. Thucydides is presumably speaking of the main route via Oropos, not of the isolated traveller, much less of the crow's flight.

ἐπὶ δὲ τῷ πεδίῳ . . . τὸ τεῖχος: The point of ἐπί is a little more than a purely locative 'overlooking'; a punning translation 'with . . . in view' would be appropriate.

19. 3–19. 5. *Peloponnesian Reinforcements Sail for Syracuse*

19. 3. τῶν τε Εἱλώτων: A force composed entirely of Helots, armed as hoplites, had been sent to Brasidas in 424 (iv. 80. 5).

καὶ τῶν νεοδαμωδῶν: This category of the Spartan population appears from v. 34. 1 to have been of much the same status as freed Helots, but not identical with them.

4. τοὺς δέ . . . Ἀρκάδων: Thus there were Arkadians on both sides, as mercenaries; cf. 57. 9.

5. αἱ τοῦ χειμῶνος πληρωθεῖσαι: 17. 4.

20. *Departure of Demosthenes*

20. 1. καὶ Χαρικλέα: It is plausible, though not inevitable, to identify him with the notorious Charikles who later became so powerful a member of the Thirty Tyrants.

κατὰ τὸ ξυμμαχικόν: The alliance in force at this time between Athens and Argos dated from the summer of 417 (v. 82. 5).

2. καὶ πέντε Χίαις: After the suppression of the revolt of Mytilene, Chios and Methymna were the only states in the Athenian Empire left with fleets of their own; cf. 57. 4.

ἐκ καταλόγου: cf. 16. 1 n.

εἴ ποθέν τι εἶχον . . . ξυμπορίσαντες: Despite the neuter gender, the reference can hardly be to anything except specialized categories of troops, e.g. archers and slingers.

MARCH–MAY 413

21–25. The Fall of Plemmyrion

21. 1–21. 4. *Syracusan Decision to Fight at Sea*

21. 3. τοῦ ταῖς ναυσί . . . ἐπιχειρῆσαι: τοῦ μή with the infinitive is not uncommon in a final sense; hence, apparently, 'in order that they should not despair of attacking the Athenians at sea'. But we would expect that τοῦ κτλ. would specify the *content* rather than the *purpose* of ξυνανέπειθε, and this may in fact be the sense; cf. Lys. viii. 17, 'I thought that I was a special friend of yours, τοῦ μηδὲν ἀκοῦσαι κακόν, for precisely the reason that you slandered others to me', i.e. 'of such a kind as not to be slandered by you'.

ἀλλ' ἠπειρώτας . . . γενέσθαι: The second part of this allegation is untrue, since the Athenians had, and used, a fleet of respectable size even before their great naval expansion in the 480's; and the first part is at least questionable, since we have no evidence for any Syracusan naval activity before the fifth century.

χαλεπωτάτους ἂν [αὐτοῖς] φαίνεσθαι: If πρὸς ἄνδρας τολμηρούς is taken with τοὺς ἀντιτολμῶντας, αὐτοῖς with χαλεπωτάτους ἂν φαίνεσθαι is neither ungrammatical nor tautological.

καὶ σφᾶς ἂν . . . ὑποσχεῖν: τὸ αὐτό refers to 'that by which the Athenians frighten their enemies', which is explained as 'attacking with boldness' (LSJ s.v. ὑπέχειν I. 2 is badly astray). θάρσος τοῖς ἐναντίοις ὑποσχεῖν, lit. 'hold daring under the enemy', would mean 'show a bold face to the enemy', 'confront the enemy with boldness'. There is no exact parallel, and ὑπάρχειν, the reading of H, deserves consideration; the word can denote being the aggressor or taking the initiative, e.g. Pl. *Grg.* 456 E ἀμυνομένους, μὴ ὑπάρχοντας, and since it is used in the passive with a neuter pronoun as subject as early as Antiphon v. 58, there is no decisive objection to its use in the active with a neuter pronoun object.

4. καὶ Συρακοσίους . . . βλάψοντας: The subject of εἰδέναι is 'he', ἀντιστῆναι depends on τολμῆσαι, and τὸ τοιοῦτον refers to τῷ τολμῆσαι κτλ.; 'the advantage gained by the Syracusans . . . would be greater than any harm which the Athenians could inflict . . .'.

21. 5–24. Syracusan Capture of Plemmyrion

21. 5. καὶ εἴ του ἄλλου: εἴ τις ἄλλος can be treated syntactically as a pronoun, not as a clause, and declined accordingly.

22. 1. ἀγαγών . . . τὴν πεζήν: Crossing Epipolai from east to west, descending at Euryelos, doubling back south-eastwards, and crossing the river; all this in the dark, and apparently without any interference from the Athenians.

ἐκ τοῦ μεγάλου λιμένος . . . ἐκ τοῦ ἐλάσσονος: cf. 3. 5 n.

[καὶ] περιέπλεον: If καί is adverbial, it is unobjectionable.

23. 1. ἅμα τῇ ἕῳ: The movement of the ships must therefore have begun before it was fully light.

2. ὑπὸ τριήρους μιᾶς καὶ εὖ πλεούσης: (i) 'By one ship, which was a trireme and fast'; or (ii) 'By one fast trireme', cf. the familiar πολλὰ καὶ ἀγαθά; or (iii) 'By one very fast trireme', cf. adverbial καί in καὶ μάλα &c., or (iv) 'By a trireme which was by itself' (sc. and thus favourably placed for pursuit) 'and fast'. None of these solutions is altogether easy, and it is probable that a phrase such as 'separate from the others' or 'ahead of the others' is lost after μιᾶς.

4. πλὴν ὅσον: ὅσον merely reinforces πλήν.

24. 2. καὶ χρήματα πολλά: 'Stores', and in 25. 1 'cargo'; these meanings were concurrent with the meaning 'money' even in the fourth century.

καὶ ἱστία . . . τριήρων: The main sails were, if possible, stored on land when action was expected, and the Athenian triremes at Syracuse had to be ready for action continuously.

καὶ τριήρεις . . . τρεῖς: On the beach below the forts. The Athenians may well have had more ships than crews at this time; cf. 12. 3–14. 1.

3. ἤδη: 'From then onwards.'

25. 1–25. 4. Expedition of Agatharchos

25. 1. οἵπερ . . . φράσουσιν: οἵπερ (rather than οἵτινες) is abnormal in a clause of this type; note that B has ὅπως, and the original hands of all the MSS. have φράσωσιν and ἐποτρύνωσι.

γίγνεσθαι: An unusually clear instance of γίγνεσθαι serving as the passive of ποιεῖν.

χρημάτων: cf. 24. 2 n.

2. ἐν τῇ Καυλωνιάτιδι: Nothing is known of the politics of Kaulonia at this time.

3. τῶν ὁλκάδων: 19. 3 ff.

25. 5–25. 8. Fighting round the Old Docks

25. 5. πρὸ τῶν παλαιῶν νεωσοίκων: Since 'the dockyard' was in the Little Harbour (22. 1), we should expect 'the old docks' to be at the northern end of the Great Harbour, where the Syracusan ships would naturally need more elaborate protection against Athenian attack.

6. ναῦν μυριοφόρον: Technical terms are rarely self-explanatory, and though a μυριοφόρος ship clearly held 10,000 units of some commodity, we do not know what units, or of what. If the unit was a talent, this ship was much bigger than any others of which we happen to hear from classical sources, but our evidence on all these matters is extremely scanty.

ἔκ τε τῶν ἀκάτων . . . τοὺς σταυρούς: If we had no other clue to the meaning of ἄκατοι, we should certainly infer from this passage that they were some part of a big ship; but in Hdt. vii. 186. 1 ~ 191. 1 ἄκατοι = ὁλκάδες, and in 59. 3 infra it appears to mean 'small boat'. Now, 'having brought up a big ship . . . they winched up the stakes from the boats' approaches a non sequitur. Was the big ship solely for the housing of archers to protect the boats? And why winch up stakes from small boats (a peculiarly difficult operation) when a big one is available? These considerations suggested to Breusing that Thucydides wrote ἀκατείων, sc. ἱστῶν, 'foremasts', and HJK actually have ἀκατίων. The practicability of winching up stakes by cables which passed from the winch on deck over a pulley near the top of a foremast satisfied Breusing, who had an intimate acquaintance with sailing ships.

25. 9. Syracusan Envoys

25. 9. Κορινθίων . . . καὶ Λακεδαιμονίων: These words go with πρέσβεις, not with πόλεις, for the envoys went to the west and south of Sicily (32. 1).

ἐπ' αὐτούς: 'Against the Athenians'; cf. iv. 25. 9 βοηθοῦντες ἐπὶ τοὺς Μεσσηνίους.

ὡς καὶ τῶν Ἀθηναίων . . . στρατιᾷ: lit., 'as the Athenians being expected with another force', i.e. 'on the grounds that the arrival of Athenian reinforcements was expected'.

MAY–JUNE 413

26. Demosthenes' Voyage round the Peloponnese

26. 1. τῷ τε Χαρικλεῖ . . . τῶν Ἀθηναίων: 20. 1.

τῶν Ἀργείων: These Argives were to co-operate only in the attack on Lakonia, and would not be taken on to Sicily; cf. § 3.

2. τῆς Ἐπιδαύρου τι τῆς Λιμηρᾶς: cf. 18. 3 n.

ἐς τὰ καταντικρὺ Κυθήρων: Kythera itself was occupied by the Athenians in 424 (iv. 54. 4). Its evacuation was required by the peace treaty, but since Κυθήριοι were present in the Athenian force at Syracuse (57. 6) it had evidently not been evacuated by 413. Demosthenes and Charikles will have landed somewhere in the bay of Boiai; the sanctuary of Apollo which Thucydides mentions has not been identified.

ἰσθμῶδές τι χωρίον: The most conspicuous place of this kind 'opposite Kythera' is a rocky peninsula which projects from the southeast coast of the island of Onugnathos, which was not an island in classical times. The Athenian fort was abandoned in the winter of 413/12 (viii. 4).

ἵνα δὴ οἵ τε Εἵλωτες . . . αὐτομολῶσι: Helots had deserted to Pylos when it was in Athenian hands, and except for the period between the autumn of 421 and the end of 419 Messenians and Helots constituted its garrison. The area of Boiai was a long way from Sparta, but that was an advantage; the fact that Boiai and Pylos were in opposite directions made them more troublesome to the Spartans, and both were accessible by sea to the Athenians.

ὥσπερ ἐκ τῆς Πύλου: The Helots brought back to Pylos by Athens in 419/18 and later reinforced by Athenians had done a lot of damage by raids on Spartan territory.

27–30. The Thracian Mercenaries

27. 1–2. *The Decision on the Mercenaries*

27. 1. τοῦ Διακοῦ γένους: In ii. 96. 2 Thucydides gives the name Dioi to the 'mountain Thracians' who inhabited the Rhodope range and were αὐτόνομοι (i.e. not controlled by the king of the Odrysians) and μαχαιρο-φόροι.

οὖς ἔδει . . . ξυμπλεῖν: 'Who were supposed to sail . . .'

2. τὸ γὰρ ἔχειν . . . ἐφαίνετο: 'For keeping them seemed an extra-vagance in view of the offensive based on Dekeleia.'

27. 3–28. Digression: the Effects of Dekeleia

The framework is:

> 27. 2. The Athenians decided it was too expensive to keep the Thracians.
>
> 27. 3–28. 2. For the occupation of Dekeleia inflicted severe losses on them.
>
> 28. 3. And they were fighting a war on two fronts.
>
> 28. 4. Therefore they were bankrupt.
>
> 29. 1. Therefore they sent the Thracians home.

The date of the dispatch of the Thracians cannot be determined with exactitude, but it can hardly have been later than the beginning of July, and it may have been substantially earlier. The enemy fort at Dekeleia had been built in March (19. 1), so that the Athenians had certainly begun to feel its effects, and may have felt them severely for three months, by the time they decided to send the Thracians away. We naturally expect that 27. 3–28 will describe the situation as it was *in the summer of 413*; but (i) 'first built in this summer by the whole army and subsequently occupied by a succession of garrisons' (27. 3) . . . 'sometimes with the enemy continuously at their door and at other times [with a garrison of varying size] ravaging their territory' (28. 4) seems to look rather further ahead, and (ii) 'they suffered in summer and winter alike' (28. 2) plainly looks beyond the summer of 413. On the other hand, 28. 3, referring to the Athenians' 'two wars', amplifies this reference by specifying Dekeleia and the *sending of reinforcements to Sicily*, which decisively brings us back to the summer of 413. 28. 3 is so linked to 28. 2 (μάλιστα δ' αὐτοὺς ἐπίεζεν) that we cannot say that in 27. 3–28. 2 Thucydides is deliberately and consistently describing the situation as it was when the occupation of Dekeleia had lasted a full year. He *means* to describe it as it was in June/July 413; but since the processes which had by then become established—the continuous relief of the enemy in Dekeleia and the continuous vigilance of the Athenians—lasted for several years thereafter, he uses at certain points language appropriate to a description of that whole period.

27. 3. τὸ μὲν πρῶτον . . . τειχισθεῖσα ὕστερον δέ . . . ἐπῳκεῖτο: The 'co-ordination' of a participial clause with a finite verb by μέν / δέ is extremely rare.

χρημάτων: 'Property', not confined to money; cf. 24. 2.

4. βραχεῖαι: The invasion of 430, which lasted forty days, was the longest.

τὸν ἄλλον χρόνον: 'The rest of the time', i.e. when the enemy was not actually in Attica.

ἐξ ἀνάγκης τῆς ἴσης φρουρᾶς κτλ.: lit., 'from necessity the equal garrison overrunning the country . . .'; but 'the equal garrison' does not mean 'the regular' (or 'normal') 'garrison', and to say that it overran Attica 'from necessity' involves a curious temporary shift from the Athenian to the Peloponnesian standpoint. No wholly satisfactory interpretation or emendation of this passage has yet been offered, but possibly Thucydides wrote τῆς ἐξ ἀνάγκης φρουρᾶς κτλ., with ἐξ ἀνάγκης = ἀναγκαίας, 'minimum', 'bare'.

5. καὶ ἀνδραπόδων ηὐτομολήκεσαν: The specification of a number with the pluperfect tense shows that Thucydides must have a particular date in mind, and this can only be (v. supra), roughly, the date at which the decision was taken to send the Thracians home.

χειροτέχναι: 'Craftsmen', 'specialists'. Many of the slaves listed in the confiscated property of the men condemned for impieties in 415 are designated, e.g., as 'cobbler', 'gold-worker', 'table-maker', &c. There is no justification for supposing that the majority of the 20,000 slaves who deserted were mineworkers from Laureion, though no doubt a high proportion of the mineworkers were included in the 20,000. Although Alkibiades, in urging the Spartans to occupy Dekeleia, attached importance to stopping the Athenians from working the mines at Laureion (vi. 91. 7), we are never told that Agis made the mines a special objective.

28. 1. ἐκ τῆς Εὐβοίας: In 431 the Athenians transferred all their livestock to Euboia (ii. 14. 1), and though much must have been brought back after the Peace of Nikias Euboia remained of supreme importance; its loss in 411 was a very grave blow (viii. 96. 2).

πολυτελής: At least in the fourth century, sea transport was *less* expensive than land transport; but the transport of animals raises special problems, and our knowledge of the fifth-century economy is not detailed enough to justify challenging Thucydides on this point.

2. πρὸς γὰρ τῇ ἐπάλξει: ἔπαλξις, literally, is the parapet on a fortification-wall, but παρ' ἔπαλξιν in ii. 13. 6 means 'on duty in defence of the walls', and πρὸς τῇ ἐπάλξει here must also be general, including both those posted on the walls and the reserves held at various points.

οἱ μὲν ἐφ' ὅπλοις †ποιούμενοι†: This makes no sense, but που (B) does: 'some under arms somewhere', i.e. stationed with their arms in one part or another of the area enclosed by the walls. Possibly Thucydides wrote ποι (having τεταγμένοι or some such word in mind), the inevitable variant που (cf. 73. 1) was conflated with it, giving ποιου, and ποιούμενοι was an attempt to make sense of that.

3. **καὶ ἐς φιλονικίαν καθέστασαν**: To the Greek way of thinking φιλο··· ία is not so much something which one embraces by an act of will, but something to which one falls victim, like love, fear, and grief. The φιλονικία of the Athenians, like the fact itself that they were fighting two wars at once, was something which oppressed (ἐπίεζεν) them.

τὸ γὰρ αὐτούς . . . ἐκ Πελοποννήσου: 'The fact, I mean, that they . . .' This vast complex is appositional in character, stating the nature and content of the Athenians' incredible φιλονικία; γάρ, as not uncommonly, means 'that is', 'namely', or 'I mean'.

καὶ τον παράλογον τοσοῦτον . . . ὅσον . . . ἐνόμιζον . . . ὥστε . . . ἦλθον: παράλογος means 'unexpectedness' or 'surprise' (cf. 55. 1), not 'miscalculation'. τοσοῦτον and ὥστε must be correlative, giving the sense 'they displayed to the Greek world such unexpected resources and boldness . . . that they attacked Sicily . . .', the ὅσον-clause being parenthetic. We cannot make τοσοῦτον and ὅσον correlative without depriving ὥστε of any intelligible meaning; but it would be fair to say that the choice of ὅσον to denote 'in so far as' or 'considering that' is influenced by the presence of τοσοῦτον.

οἱ δὲ τριῶν γ᾽ ἐτῶν οὐδείς: 'And of the rest' (sc. although some thought that they would last three years) 'no one thought that they would last *more* than three years'. τῶν δέ . . . οὐδείς would have been normal syntax, but Thucydides tends to avoid the juxtaposition of genitives with different reference, and τῶν δὲ τριῶν γ᾽ ἐτῶν would be misleading. τριῶν δ᾽ ἐτῶν οὐδείς would be unobjectionable linguistically, but γε is wanted for the sense, and δέ γε in Thucydides is an adversative, so that τριῶν δέ γ᾽ ἐτῶν would, again, be misleading. Altogether it is hard to see how Thucydides could have expressed what he meant except by writing what the MSS. give us.

ἤδη . . . τετρυχωμένοι: This is strikingly at variance with what Thucydides tells us in vi. 26. 2 about Athens' recovery, by 415, from the ravages of the Archidamian War; but here he is looking at Athens from the (erroneous) point of view of the rest of the Greek world, which, according to the words he attributed to Alkibiades in vi. 16. 2, did regard Athens in 416 as 'exhausted by war'.

4. **δι᾽ ἃ καὶ τότε κτλ.**: ἃ looks back to the beginning of § 3; τότε refers to the summer of 413, by contrast with 415, which is the subject of the end of § 3.

καὶ τὴν εἰκοστήν . . . ἐποίησαν: If the procedure adopted in the Archidamian War was still followed, a quadrennial reassessment of tribute was due in the autumn of 414. This would be a natural time at which to impose a 5 per cent. tax in place of tribute, and there is no great difficulty in 'about this time'. The next sentence, however, includes among the Athenians' reasons for the change 'their revenues were dwindling', and this was not in the least true until Dekeleia was occupied (there was, indeed, no reason for *tribute* to dwindle until 412). It must therefore have been in the summer of 413 that the tax was substituted for the tribute.

πλείω . . . προσιέναι: Such data as we have for tribute in the quadrennium 418/17–415/14 suggest that it amounted annually to *c.* 900 talents. It follows that the Athenians estimated that the annual value of the seaborne traffic on which they could hope to collect a 5 per cent. tax exceeded 18,000 talents.

29–30. *The Thracians at Mykalessos*

29. 1. Διειτρέφει: Probably the man of this name who was appointed to a command in the Thracian area in 411 and was active in the oligarchic cause (viii. 64. 2).

2. ἔς τε τὴν Τάναγραν: i.e. into the territory of Tanagra; the city itself lay well inland.

ἐπὶ Μυκαλησσόν: The modern Ritsona, north-west of Tanagra.

ἀπροσδοκήτοις: 'Not expecting', followed here by an accusative and infinitive as if it were a participle.

τοῦ τείχους . . . ᾠκοδομημένου: Boeotia was a federation of states dominated by Thebes, and possibly Thebes did not encourage the other states to fortify themselves; in 423 she even demolished the city-walls of the Thespians, having grounds for suspecting their loyalty.

4. ὁμοῖα . . . φονικώτατόν ἐστιν: τοῦ βαρβαρικοῦ is that part of the human race which does not speak Greek; ὁμοῖα = ὁμοίως, and the superlative is tautologous; hence lit., '. . . is most murderous, on a level with the most ⟨murderous races⟩ of the barbarian world'. One wonders what Thucydides would have thought of the Romans, who, on occasion, extinguished all life in a town (Polybius x. 15. 5).

5. καὶ ξυμφορά . . . καὶ δεινή: lit., 'this, ⟨being⟩ a disaster second to none for the whole city, fell upon ⟨it⟩ ⟨as⟩ unexpected and terrible more than another', i.e. 'this disaster which fell upon the whole city in an exceptionally unexpected and terrible form was as great as any which it ever suffered'. οὐδεμιᾶς ἧσσον makes the primary point that Mykalessos had never suffered a greater disaster, μᾶλλον ἑτέρας κτλ. the secondary point that this disaster was peculiarly horrible.

30. 1. **ἐπὶ τὸν Εὔριπον καὶ τὴν θάλασσαν**: 'To the sea at the Euripos.'

2. **τοὺς πλείστους**: i.e. the majority of the 250 who were killed (§ 3), not the majority of the whole force of 1,300.

προεκθέοντές τε καὶ ξυστρεφόμενοι: This not very illuminating description probably means that the main body, as it moved towards the Euripos, would send out detachments to the flanks to keep the pursuers at bay and would continuously relieve these detachments at high speed.

3. **τῶν βοιωταρχῶν**: The βοιωτάρχαι were the annually elected generals of the Boeotian federation; there were eleven of them, of whom four were Thebans.

ὡς ἐπὶ μεγέθει: lit., 'as in consideration of size', i.e. 'relatively speaking'; other states suffered heavier losses than Mykalessos, but none lost so high a proportion of its population at one tragic and horrible blow. Thucydides makes a very similar remark about the losses suffered by Ambrakia at the battle of Idomene in 426/5 (iii. 113. 6): 'no greater disaster than this fell upon any one Greek city, in a comparably brief period, in the course of this war; and I have not given the number of the dead, because the number reported to have perished, in proportion to the size of the city, is hard to believe.' Possibly he wrote those words before 413; but he stresses the *tragic* character (ὀλοφύρασθαι ἀξίῳ) of the fate of Mykalessos, where every kind of living being was slaughtered, and deals more coolly with the death of the fighting-men of Ambrakia.

οὐδενός . . . ὀλοφύρασθαι ἀξίῳ: The massacre at Mykalessos must have aroused much bitterness among the enemies of Athens, especially when linked to rumours—which existed from time to time (cf. ii. 101. 4, vi. 90. 3)—of Athens' willingness to employ barbarians against Greeks. Parallels are to be found in the feelings aroused by the use of Red Indians by British, French, and Americans in the late eighteenth and early nineteenth centuries. No firm inference on Thucydides' values can be drawn from the fact that he expresses a sympathy for Mykalessos which he denies to Melos; his emotions are rather more in evidence in Book VII than elsewhere, and the Melians had, after all, the opportunity to avert the fate which they had done something to provoke.

JUNE 413

31. Demosthenes and Eurymedon at Naupaktos

31. 1. **ἐκ τῆς Λακωνικῆς**: When what would logically be expressed by ἐν + dat. occurs in a sentence which describes movement in space or sequence in time, ἐν + dat. may be replaced by ἐκ + gen. or ἐς + acc.

ἐν Φειᾷ τῇ 'Ηλείων: Pheia lay on the west side of the root of the promontory which has the modern harbour of Katákolo on its east side. At the beginning of the Peloponnesian War Elis belonged to the Peloponnesian League. After the Peace of Nikias she joined the anti-Spartan alliance of Argos and Mantinea; this alliance was broken up by the Spartan victory at Mantinea in 418, and we have no accurate information on the relations between Elis and Sparta between that time and the outbreak of war between them in 402.

2. ἐς τὴν Ζάκυνθον καὶ Κεφαλληνίαν: These two islands had been Athenian allies since the beginning of the war.

τῶν Μεσσηνίων: The people of Naupaktos were Messenians who had been allowed to leave Messenia, under Athenian protection, at the end of the Helot Revolt against Sparta c. 460.

ἐς Ἀλύζιάν τε καὶ Ἀνακτόριον: Alyzia is the modern Kandyla, and Anaktorion lay at the south-east corner of the bay between Actium and the modern Vonitsa. Anaktorion was originally a Corinthian colony, but was captured by the Athenians and Akarnanians together in 425 and was thereafter occupied by Akarnanians; hence 'which ⟨the Athenians⟩ themselves held'.

3. τότε τοῦ χειμῶνος: 16. 2. Eurymedon had taken the best part of six months to sail from Athens to Syracuse and back to Kerkyra. He can hardly have been sheltering from storms most of that time; presumably he took part in the fighting at Syracuse, or busied himself in diplomatic or logistic activity in Italy, or both, until he judged that Demosthenes was on the way.

4. καὶ Κόνων: This is the first appearance of the famous general in history and his only appearance in Thucydides.

οὔτε καταλύουσι τὸν πόλεμον: This can hardly mean 'so far from going home without a fight' or 'so far from abandoning their hostile attitude', and Madvig was right to delete τὸν πόλεμον; intransitive καταλύειν = 'cease hostilities' (cf. its common meaning 'stay', 'put up', 'end one's journey') in v. 23. 1.

οὐχ ἱκανάς: Sixteen years earlier Phormion, based on Naupaktos, had confidently attacked and defeated 47 Peloponnesian ships with 20 Athenian. Now Konon will not pit 18 against 25; no doubt when the needs of the force in Sicily had been met Konon and other commanders of small detachments were left with inferior ships and crews, while every year of training and experience saw an improvement in the Peloponnesian fleets.

5. καὶ πέντε . . . καταλεγόμενος: Since 427 Kerkyra had been a full ally of Athens.

ξυνῆρχε γάρ: The point lies in ξυν-, not in -ῆρχε; the fleet now had the joint command assigned to it the previous winter.

32–33. 2. Sikeliot Help for Syracuse

32. 1. τότε: 25. 9.

Κεντόριπάς τε καὶ Ἀλικυαίους καὶ ἄλλους: The name of the Kentoripes survives in the modern town Centorbi, some 40 km. north-west of Katane. Halikyai is located by later writers in the west of Sicily, inland from Selinus. If the force set out from Selinus already knowing of the Akragantines' refusal (infra) to allow passage through their territory, it might well strike north-eastwards into the interior; this would encourage the Halikyaioi (we do not know how far eastwards their territory extended) to follow it until an attack could be concerted with the Kentoripes 'and others'.

Ἀκραγαντῖνοι γάρ . . . ὁδόν: Akragas was presumably among 'all the Dorian states except Kamarina' (iii. 86. 2) which supported Syracuse against Leontinoi in 428/7, but it welcomed Phaiax's mission in 422/1 (v. 4. 6). Cf. 33. 2 infra. The reversion to the finite tense ἐνεδίδοσαν after the infinitive πειράσειν shows that this is a comment by Thucydides, not part of Nikias' message.

33. 1. καὶ οἱ Καμαριναῖοι: In the winter of 415/14 Kamarina, allied to both Syracuse and Athens, was still prevaricating; but now news of the capture of Plemmyrion has achieved what persuasive arguments could not.

2. πᾶσα ἡ Σικελία: Thucydides is referring only to the Greek cities, ignoring Sikels, Sikans, and Carthaginians.

οἱ δ' ἄλλοι: δέ is not a connective here, but the text is sound; cf. IG i² 39 (GHI 42). 52 ff. τοὺς δὲ ξένους . . . ὅσοι οἰκοῦντες μὴ τελοῦσιν Ἀθήναζε . . . τοὺς δὲ ἄλλους τελεῖν ἐς Χαλκίδα, 'all the foreigners living in Chalkis, except those who pay taxes to Athens, are to pay taxes to Chalkis'.

οἱ πρότερον περιορώμενοι: In fact, out of eight possible cities, only four (Selinus, Gela, Kamarina, and Himera) fought on the side of Syracuse; Akragas was neutral, Naxos and Katane helped Athens, and Messene, though unfriendly to Athens, is not mentioned in 58. 1–2 among the allies of Syracuse. 'Almost the whole of Sicily except Akragas' is therefore a striking rhetorical exaggeration.

33. 3–6. Demosthenes and Eurymedon Reach Thurioi

33. 3. ἐπ' ἄκραν 'Ιαπυγίαν: The tip of the 'heel' of Italy.

4. ἐς τὰς Χοιράδας νήσους: These must be the small islands lying off the harbour of Taras.

τοῦ Μεσσαπίου ἔθνους: A closer specification of the generic *'Ιαπύγων*.

καὶ τῷ Ἄρτᾳ . . . φιλίαν: The origin of this relationship is unknown; it may be pre-war, or it may be one of the details which Thucydides warns us (iii. 90. 1) he has omitted in his account of the operations in Sicily in 427–424. *παλαιάν* does not imply very long duration; Leontinoi in 427 considered herself an Athenian ally *κατὰ παλαιὰν ξυμμαχίαν* (iii. 86. 3), but the alliance was not in fact of more than twenty years' standing.

ἐς Μεταπόντιον τῆς 'Ιταλίας: *'Ιταλία* is used here in the restricted sense 'Bruttium and Lucania'; Taras is in 'Iapygia', Kyme in 'Opikia'. This accords with common fifth-century usage, though elsewhere Thucydides uses *'Ιταλία* in its later, wider sense.

5. κατὰ τὸ ξυμμαχικόν: The origin of this alliance too is unknown.

τοὺς τῶν Ἀθηναίων ἐναντίους: Thurioi rebuffed Gylippos in 414. This is the first we have heard of a significant anti-Athenian faction.

6. τοὺς αὐτούς . . . νομίζειν: This type of 'full' alliance, according to which A and B promise to help one another if either of them chooses to attack a third state, differs from a defensive alliance (*ἐπιμαχία*), in which A and B promise to help one another only if one of them is attacked by a third state.

34. Naval Battle at Naupaktos

34. 1. οἱ ἐν ταῖς πέντε καὶ εἴκοσι ναυσίν: 17. 4, 19. 5, 31. 4.

κατὰ 'Ερινεόν . . . ἐν τῇ 'Ρυπικῇ: Erineos was the bay which lies below the modern village of Kamáres, 29 km. east of Patras and 9½ km. west of Aigion. Rhypes, already uninhabited by the beginning of the Christian era, lay somewhere in this region.

2. μηνοειδοῦς ὄντος: The coastline runs south-east and east, and a line of ships anchored in it *ἐμφάρξασαι* would have to wheel through a right angle to meet an enemy sailing into the Gulf from Naupaktos. The purpose of the Corinthian ships was to prevent the Athenians from interfering with the departure of troopships from Elis. They could achieve this purpose by lying well to the east of the narrows, for the Athenians would be unwilling (as is shown by their taking their initiative in attack) to search westwards for the troopships so long as the

Corinthians could sail out of the Gulf behind them and attack Naupaktos.

3. τριάκοντα ... Δίφιλος: Since Konon had 18 ships, Demosthenes
had added 10 to these (31. 4 f.), and Konon would have needed one
ship for his journey home, Diphilos must have brought 6 with him.
The natural explanation of this relief is that Konon was one of the
generals of 414/13, Diphilos one of those of 413/12, and that Diphilos
arrived at Naupaktos in the middle of July.

5. κατέδυ μὲν οὐδεμία ἁπλῶς: 'Not one could be described as "sunk" .'
καὶ ἀναρραγεῖσαι ... τὰς ἐπωτίδας ἐχουσῶν: ἐπωτίδες were anchor-
blocks fixed one each side of the bows, the ears (ὦτα), as it were, of
a trireme. παρεξειρεσία was the 'balcony' running along each side of the
ship and housing the θρανῖται, the uppermost and outermost line of
oarsmen. The strengthened anchor-blocks of the Corinthian ships tore
into the παρεξειρεσία on one side of the enemy ship, taking with it
some unfortunate θρανῖται and no doubt much of the attached super-
structure. One such blow would not render a ship totally unnavigable,
but would make it an easy victim for further attacks; yet so long as it
was not rammed on the waterline it would stay afloat.

6. καὶ ὡς αὐτούς ... νικᾶν: 'And to such effect that each side claimed
itself to be victorious.'

7. οἵ τε γὰρ Κορίνθιοι ... ἐνίκων: These attitudes were the product of
overwhelming Athenian naval superiority in the Archidamian War.

8. ὡς νικήσαντες: Greek verbal aspect has not yet been investigated
with sufficient rigour to provide an objective explanation of the difference between ὡς νικήσαντες here and ὡς νικῶντες in § 7.

35. Demosthenes and Eurymedon Reach Rhegion

35. 1. ἐπὶ τῷ Συβάρει ποταμῷ: Thurioi was founded close to the site of
the earlier city Sybaris, which was destroyed in 510. The river Sybaris
was the southern of the two rivers flowing on parallel courses through
the territory.

2. ἐπὶ τῷ Ὑλίᾳ ποταμῷ: This is mentioned nowhere else, and we do
not know the limits of the territory of Kroton.
πλὴν Λοκρῶν: cf. 1. 2 n.
ἐπὶ Πέτραν τῆς Ῥηγίνης: Petra, otherwise unknown, may be another name for 'Leukopetra', a name given in later times to two
different promontories on the 'toe' of Italy: (a) Punta di Pellaro,
which projects westwards towards Sicily, and (b) Capo delle Armi,

which is conspicuously light-coloured and projects southwards. As we
hear no more of Demosthenes and Eurymedon until they arrive at
Syracuse (42. 1), it seems that they crossed to Sicily from 'Petra' and
did not go to Rhegion itself.

36–41. Battles at Syracuse

36. *Syracusan Preparations*

36. 2. ὡς ἐκ τῆς προτέρας . . . σχήσοντες: 'In the manner in which
they saw from the previous naval battle they would gain some advantage.'

καὶ τὰς ἐπωτίδας . . . παχείας: cf. 34. 5 n.

καὶ ἀντηρίδας . . . καὶ ἔξωθεν: Since the axis of each anchor-block
was at right angles to the bows, a head-on collision would tend to force
it backwards and break it off from its base. To prevent that, a heavy
strut was inserted behind it to take the strain of collision. As these
struts are described as being 'about six cubits long *inside and outside*'
they must have extended from the anchor-blocks not only *to* (πρός) the
sides of the ship but also *through* the sides, bearing at the rear on a main
transverse beam.

3. ἢ ἐκ περίπλου: The Athenians normally exploited their superior
speed and training by 'sailing round' their adversaries, choosing a point
from which to ram in the side or stern.

οὐκ ἐν πολλῷ . . . οὖσαν: οὐκ negatives only πολλῷ: 'a battle with
many ships in a restricted space.'

4. οὔτε διέκπλουν: 'Sailing through and out'—and then turning,
more quickly than the enemy, to ram him—was practicable only if
there was enough space between the enemy ships. On the open sea
close array, a protection against διέκπλους, would invite περίπλους; but
in a restricted space this danger was removed.

5. τὸ ἀντίπρῳρον ξυγκροῦσαι: τό, which is in a papyrus text of this
passage, is probably sound; cf. 67. 1 τῆς δοκήσεως . . . τὸ κρατίστους εἶναι
where the content of the δόκησις is expressed by τό with the infinitive
and not by a strictly concordant apposition.

ἐξωθουμένοις: 'When they were forced out of the battle.'

37. 1–38. 1. *First Day*

37. 1. πρὸς τὴν ἑαυτῶν . . . δύναμιν: πρός here = 'to suit', 'in conformity
with'.

2. καθ' ὅσον . . . ἑώρα: Although ὅσον . . . αὐτοῦ is the subject of
ἑώρα, the clause ὅσον . . . ἑώρα as a whole is also treated as a substantive

in the accusative governed by κατά. The possibility of giving the neuter gender this dual role always exists formally, but its exploitation is rare.

3. πέντε καὶ ἑβδομήκοντα ναῦς: Cf. 22. 2 n.

38. 2–**38.** 3. *Second Day*

38. 2. ἐλπίδων: 'Expecting', almost 'fearing'.

πρὸ τοῦ σφετέρου σταυρώματος: Whether this was semicircular, or a pair of converging lines of stakes, or three sides of a rectangle, it must have had several substantial exits, for a single narrow exit into the waters of the harbour would have caused impossibly difficult and dangerous delays in putting to sea against a Syracusan attack, and would have rendered the barrier of merchant ships now described unnecessary. It is even possible that the σταύρωμα was simply a pair of parallel breakwaters, one each side of the beach occupied by the Athenians, but this depends on the interpretation of 41. 2, q.v.

3. ὅσον δύο πλέθρα: Hdt. ii. 149. 3 reckons six πλέθρα to a stade; hence two πλέθρα = between 45 and 65 metres (cf. 2. 4 n.).

κατάφευξις ἀσφαλής: Why this should be so is explained in 41. 2.

39–41. *Third Day*

39. 2. τὴν ἀγορὰν τῶν πωλουμένων: lit., 'the market of things (sc. normally) sold', clearly distinguished from (lit.) 'whatever edibles one has', which would be the private stores of individuals, not normally for sale.

ὅπως αὐτοῖς κτλ.: αὐτοῖς refers to all the people who would then be selling food.

εὐθὺς παρὰ τὰς ναῦς: 'Just by the ships', 'immediately next to the ships'.

40. 5. οἱ ἀπὸ τῶν καταστρωμάτων αὐτοῖς: 'The men on their decks.' The Athenians were soon compelled (62. 2 f., 67. 2) to imitate this feature of Syracusan tactics, peculiarly suited to fighting in a restricted space.

ἔς τε τοὺς ταρσοὺς ὑποπίπτοντες: In fourth-century naval documents ταρρός is a collective noun, 'oars', and in Hellenistic writers 'bank of oars'; so too Hdt. viii. 12. 1, where τοὺς ταρσοὺς τῶν κωπέων ἐτάραξον means 'they threw the banks of oars into confusion', i.e. prevented the oars from moving in ordered unison. It is doubtful whether the Syracusan boats could really be rowed *beneath* the banks of oars of the Athenian triremes, for a trireme was low in the water, but they could certainly have been rowed into contact with the oars nearest the bows or nearest the stern. ὑποπίπτειν here serves (cf. other compounds of πίπτειν) as the passive of ὑποβάλλειν.

καὶ ἐς τὰ πλάγια παραπλέοντες: There is no part of a ship called τὰ πλάγια; the expression means 'on the flank', as in iv. 35. 4.

ἐξ αὐτῶν: sc. τῶν λεπτῶν πλοίων.

41. 2. αἱ κεραῖαι . . . ἐκώλυον: These were spars from each of which a 'dolphin', i.e. a fish-shaped weight of iron, was suspended; when an enemy ship came close, the spar was swung round over it and the iron weight dropped, with the intention that it should fall straight through the bottom of the ship. This odd but effective device is twice referred to in Comedy. In saying (38. 3) that the merchant ships were two plethra apart Thucydides probably does not mean that an expanse of that size was protected by the dolphins of two ships, for that would imply spars of remarkable size and strength, but that the passages (ἔσπλοι) through the line of stakes, each passage being protected by a merchant ship carrying one or more dolphins, were two plethra apart. Each dolphin ship naturally constituted its own protection against ramming.

3. καὶ ἡ ἑτέρα αὐτοῖς ἀνδράσιν ἑάλω: 'And one of them was captured' (presumably in a sinking condition) 'complete with its crew.'

JULY 413
42. 1–5. Arrival of Demosthenes and Eurymedon

42. 1. τρεῖς καὶ ἑβδομήκοντα μάλιστα: Demosthenes started with 65 (20. 2), ordered 15 from Kerkyra (31. 5), and gave 10 to Konon (ibid.); Eurymedon sailed to Sicily with 10 (16. 2), and when he returned to meet Demosthenes at Kerkyra must have left 9 of these 10 in Sicily. On the voyage along the Italian coast they collected 2 from Metapontion. If μάλιστα (which B omits) is right, it means not quite 'about' but 'I calculate (sc. assuming the correctness of all the individual data)'.

ξὺν ταῖς ξενικαῖς: ξύν here = 'including', not 'plus'.

καὶ τῶν ξυμμάχων: cf. 17. 1, 26. 1, 26. 3, 31. 2, and 31. 5.

ἀκοντιστάς τε βαρβάρους: cf. 33. 4 f.

2. κατάπληξις . . . οὐκ ὀλίγη: The control of entrance to the harbour, which the capture of Plemmyrion helped the Syracusans to achieve (36. 6), did not extend to the exclusion of Demosthenes' powerful fleet, which, according to Plu. Nic. 21. 1, sailed in with impressive flamboyance.

εἰ πέρας μηδὲν ἔσται κτλ.: εἰ = '⟨as they wondered⟩ whether.' For πέρας . . . τοῦ ἀπαλλαγῆναι cf. D. xl. 40 τί ἂν ἦν πέρας ἡμῖν τοῦ διαλυθῆναι;

ἴσον καὶ παραπλήσιον: 'as large, *or* approximately as large, as . . .';
cf. i. 22. 4, τῶν μελλόντων ποτὲ αὖθις . . . τοιούτων καὶ παραπλησίων
ἔσεσθαι, '. . . in the same, or similar, form'.

ῥώμη: Psychological rather than material; cf. 18. 2.

3. ἰδών . . . ἐκπλήξει: The formal resemblance of this sentence to the
description of the generals' motives in vi. 64. 1—γιγνώσκοντες . . .
(τοὺς γὰρ ἂν ψιλούς . . .), τοιόνδε τι οὖν . . . μηχανῶνται—is less important
than its formal difference; there, the whole parenthesis is expressed in
the accusative and infinitive of reported thought (cf. 51. 1 infra),
whereas here it is expressed in finite tenses and includes (ἦν οὐδ' ἂν
μετέπεμψαν κτλ.) a statement about what might have happened in
certain circumstances. We must therefore regard the parenthesis as
expressing Thucydides' own judgement, not merely his report of
Demosthenes' judgement, though the two may largely have coincided.
ii. 13 provides the clearest example of parenthetic γάρ-clauses 'glossing'
a report of another's speech (note especially ii. 13. 7, which by its nature
cannot be part of what Perikles told the Athenians in 431 : 'for that was
the number which at first guarded the walls whenever the enemy in-
vaded Attica'); and ii. 94. 1, iii. 113. 6, viii. 87. 4, 96. 4, are examples of
Thucydides' hypothetical judgements on the past. 6. 1 supra is intermediate in character—νομίζοντες . . . (ἤδη γάρ . . .), ἀντεπῆσαν οὖν κτλ.—
since the first part of its parenthesis is a statement of objective fact,
while the second part (εἰ προέλθοι, ταὐτὸν ἤδη ἐποίει κτλ.) is a judgement
in which Thucydides necessarily concurs with those whose thought he
is reporting.

Thucydides, then, blames Nikias primarily for spending the winter at
Katane and not 'laying siege to Syracuse at once', and secondarily, by
implication, for allowing Gylippos to reach Sicily. If we had lost Book
VI and knew only that the Athenian expedition arrived in Sicily during
the summer of 415, we should infer from this passage that there was
no attack on Syracuse until the spring of 414; but that would be wrong,
for they landed in the Great Harbour, won a battle by the Helorine
road, and then sailed away, late in 415 (vi. 64–71). As it is, two interpretations of the passage are open to us :

(i) Thucydides is condemning the failure of Nikias—and of Lamachos,
who was not killed until the summer of 414—to press the advantage
they gained by their surprise landing and victory by the Helorine road
in the autumn of 415. This interpretation makes the clearest contrast
with 'spent the winter at Katane'. It necessitates reference of ἀφικόμενος to the landing in the harbour, not to the Athenians' arrival in
Sicily.

(ii) He is condemning the adoption by the three generals of Alkibiades' plan instead of Lamachos' at the conference held when they

first arrived in the West (vi. 49). This interpretation accords well with
ἀφικόμενος . . . φοβερός and with the representation of Demosthenes'
insistence on the importance of seizing the initiative while the enemy's
morale is still affected by his arrival, for Lamachos' original plan laid
great emphasis on the moral advantage to be gained by speed and
aggressive action, whereas Alkibiades' plan was for negotiations with
potential allies. Again, if Thucydides has the Athenians' first arrival in
Sicily in mind, ὑπερώφθη accords well with his description (vi. 63. 2) of
how the Syracusans' courage revived *before* the landing in the harbour.
But it would mean that 'spent the winter in Katane' is a compressed
and misleading way of saying 'established a summer base at Katane
with the intention of returning there for the winter'.

Neither interpretation is in tune with vi. 71, where we are given the
impression that the Athenians would indeed have established themselves at Syracuse after their victory if only the enemy cavalry had
not proved so formidable ; there, Thucydides makes no comment at all
on the generals' decision to withdraw. Neither interpretation, again,
absolves Thucydides from a charge of rhetorical distortion (both are
unjust to Nikias, in so far as they ignore the responsibility of his
colleagues, but this injustice is determined by the context, where the
issue is essentially between Demosthenes and Nikias). The distortion
is much less gross in interpretation (i). To say that the Syracusans
'would have thought that they were a match for Nikias, and by the
time they discovered that they were not they would have been walled
off' is fair, since Syracusan morale was broken not (vi. 72 f., 75) by
their defeat at the Helorine road but by the Athenian victories and
siege-walls in 414 (vi. 103. 3, cf. Plu. *Nic.* 17. 1 ff.), and they were saved
from capitulation by the arrival of Gongylos in the nick of time (2. 1),
just as they were saved from circumvallation by Gylippos (2. 4).

The tone of the whole passage suggests that Thucydides believed
that Lamachos was right in his initial plan, and, therefore, that Alkibiades was wrong. Yet this conclusion has to be reconciled with ii. 65.
11, where the failure of the expedition is (a little obliquely) attributed
to the exile of Alkibiades. Reconciliation may be achieved by the
hypothesis that Thucydides changed his mind, vii. 42. 3 representing
his opinion at the time he wrote Book VII, ii. 65. 11 his opinion after
the end of the war, under the influence of the activities of Alkibiades in
411–407, so highly praised in vi. 15. 3 f. (a passage which on this hypothesis would be a later insertion into the narrative of Book VI).
A fundamental change of opinion, however, is not a necessary hypothesis ; it is rather a matter of two different strands of opinion. It was
quite possible for Thucydides to believe simultaneously that (*a*) Lamachos put forward the best plan at the start of the campaign, (*b*) even
though the wrong plan—Alkibiades' plan—was adopted, victory was

still possible, as his own narrative of the events of 414 makes plain, (c) if Alkibiades had been present at the victory by the Helorine road, he would have persuaded his colleagues to press on with the siege at once and not be deterred by the Syracusan cavalry, and (d) even if he had failed to do that, he would at least have accelerated operations after the death of Lamachos and would have taken effective steps to prevent the arrival of Gylippos in Sicily. It would be correct, however, to speak at least of a change of emphasis; considerations (a) and (b) seem to have been prominent in Thucydides' mind at the time of writing vii. 42. 3, while (c) and (d) were uppermost at the time of writing vi. 15. 3 f.

οὐχ οἷόν τε εἶναι διατρίβειν οὐδὲ παθεῖν κτλ.: 'Not possible to waste time and ⟨thereby⟩ to incur the difficulties which Nikias had incurred' (cf. 61. 2), rather than 'not possible to waste time *without incurring* (sc. as a consequence of wasting time) . . .'.

ἀφικόμενος γάρ . . . φοβερός, ὡς . . . ὑπερώφθη κτλ.: Not 'for when Nikias arrived he first inspired fear', sc. ἦν, for that would require ὡς δέ to follow, and there is no δέ. φοβερός goes closely with ἀφικόμενος, τὸ πρῶτον being pleonastic, as in vi. 46. 2 πρῶτον ἤρξαντο; hence lit., 'for Nikias, having arrived formidable at first, when he did not press . . . was despised', i.e. 'for when Nikias, whose first arrival inspired fear, did not at once . . .'.

ἔτι: οὐκέτι often means 'not, after all' or 'not thereafter', and the sense here is lit., 'so that not even if they had sent for it would it have helped them thereafter similarly', i.e. 'so that even if they had sent for it it would not have helped them thereafter as in fact it did'.

μάλιστα: This word is, strictly speaking, tautologous, but the intensification is progressive: 'at that moment, on the first day, more than at any other time, most formidable.'

τῇ παρούσῃ τοῦ στρατεύματος ἐκπλήξει: 'The consternation caused (sc. in Syracuse) at this moment by his force.'

4. τοῦ ἐν αὐταῖς στρατοπέδου: 'The force stationed on it', of which we hear more in 43. 4.

5. καὶ οἱ ξυντομωτάτην ἡγεῖτο διαπολέμησιν: lit., 'and he thought ⟨it⟩ most concise completion of the war for him', i.e. 'and he thought it was his quickest way of finishing the campaign'. οἱ is absent from ACEFM, but it makes sense, and it is hard to imagine that a pronoun little enough used in classical prose and never in Hellenistic Greek should be an interpolation in B. For Thucydides' use of it cf. 49. 3.

Throughout this sentence Thucydides speaks as if Demosthenes had come not to act as a colleague of Nikias but to supersede him in supreme command; this was not so, but it is characteristic of the Greek

historians to speak of a member of a collegiate office who is at any given
time morally dominant as if he were also constitutionally superior.

ἀπάξειν: sc. from Sicily.

42. 6–45. The Night Attack on Epipolai

42. 6. τήν τε γῆν ... ἔτεμον: West and south-west of the lower half of
the Athenian fortifications.

ἀπὸ τοῦ Ὀλυμπιείου: cf. 37. 2 f.

43. 1. μηχαναῖς ... ἀποπειρᾶσαι κτλ.: These attacks must have been
based on the Circle and made against the southern face of the counterwall. Had the Athenians been able to deploy forces against the northern
face of the counterwall by day, there would have been no need for the
night attack which Thucydides now goes on to describe. The μηχαναί
are battering-rams, as used by the Peloponnesians against Plataiai in
429 (ii. 77. 4).

καὶ τοὺς ἄλλους ξυνάρχοντας: Menandros, Euthydemos, and Eurymedon; cf. 16. 1 n.

τὴν ἐπιχείρησιν τῶν Ἐπιπολῶν: cf. 4. 1 n. on the limitation of the
term 'Epipolai' to the more westerly parts of the plateau which lies
above Syracuse.

2. τοξευμάτων: Elsewhere in Thucydides, 'arrows' (e.g. iv. 34. 1), but
here it covers also the archers who use them, just as 'the guns' or 'the
tanks' in English covers the men who man them. Cf. Hdt. v. 112. 2
οὔτε ἵππου (= 'cavalry') ὑπαρχούσης οὔτε τοξευμάτων.

πρὸς τὰς Ἐπιπολάς: Going north-westwards from the lower Athenian
fortifications.

3. κατὰ τὸν Εὐρύηλον: cf. 2. 3 n.

4. τὰ στρατόπεδα: The προτειχίσματα in which these forces were
stationed cannot have lain west of the end of the counterwall, for, as
we see in § 5, the Athenians made contact with the counterwall *before*
they could be met by the enemy coming from the προτειχίσματα. They
must therefore have projected from the southern face of the counterwall, where, given the existence of the Circle, the Syracusans naturally
had most reason to fear attack. They cannot have been *separated* from
the wall; for if they had been, the Syracusans would have had to come
round the western end of the wall in order to make contact with the
Athenians, and would have taken the leading Athenian units in the
rear; but it is clear from the narrative that this did not happen.
Therefore the troops coming out of the προτειχίσματα emerged on the
northern side of the wall; cf. the map.

τοῖς ἑξακοσίοις: This body of 600 picked men was constituted in 414 (vi. 96. 3); it suffered very heavily in its first encounter with the Athenians (vi. 97. 4).

5. αὐτοὶ μέν: The force with Demosthenes, which now presses on eastwards, north of the counterwall, while the following contingent (ἄλλοι δέ) begins to demolish the counterwall.

ὅπως τῇ παρούσῃ ὁρμῇ ... γένωνται: If the text is sound, βραδεῖς is constructed with a genitive on the analogy of ὕστερος, ὑστερεῖν, and ἐλλιπής: 'so that they might not be slow, with the impetus of the moment, in the accomplishment of the purpose for which they had come.' περαίνεσθαι is always passive (though there is a middle διαπεραίνεσθαι). It is possible that ὅπως and μὴ βραδεῖς γένωνται are interpolated, and that Thucydides used the infinitive of purpose.

ἀπὸ τῆς πρώτης: cf. ἀπὸ πρώτης = 'to begin with', 'at the start', in i. 77. 3; hence 'they began *straight away* to take possession of the counterwall ... and pull off its battlements', instead of attending to the more important matter of defeating the enemy's troops.

6. τοῦ τολμήματος: The Athenians'.

7. ἐν ἀταξίᾳ: So far, all has gone well—too well; the Athenians lose formation as some press on faster than others, and the advantage now lies with the first solid enemy formation that encounters them.

οἱ Βοιωτοί: The 300 hoplites mentioned in 19. 3.

44. 1. ἦν οὐδὲ πυθέσθαι ... ξυνηνέχθη: ἐπυθόμην τὴν ταραχὴν ὅτῳ τρόπῳ ξυνηνέχθη, with 'anticipatory' accusative, would be straightforward Greek; the relative ἥν is an accusative of this kind, but the 'anticipation' is subtly varied by a shift from 'confusion' to 'the various events' (ἕκαστα) which were all part of the confusion.

οὐδ' ἀφ' ἑτέρων: = ἀπ' οὐδετέρων. Thucydides tells us in v. 26. 5 that because of his exile from Athens he spent time 'on both sides'. So many nationalities fought at Syracuse—some of them from temporary and uncertain loyalties—that Thucydides' words here do not require us to believe either that he himself had been to Sicily before writing Book VII or that he had to wait until the end of his exile before he could get any information from the Athenian side.

ἐν μὲν γὰρ ἡμέρᾳ ... οἶδεν: lit., 'for ⟨in a battle⟩ by day ⟨one knows⟩ more clearly ⟨what happened⟩, but nevertheless not even these ⟨do⟩ those who were present ⟨know⟩ completely, except each man knows with difficulty what happened in his own part of the field'. We expect ἴσασιν at the end of the sentence, taking πλήν ... μόλις as a parenthesis and *understanding* οἶδεν; but the verb is accommodated to the nearer ἕκαστος when logically it should agree with the further οἱ παραγενόμενοι. Cf. vi. 65. 2 ὅσοι Σικελῶν αὐτοῖς ἢ ἄλλος τις προσεληλύθει.

Thucydides complains in his Introduction (i. 22. 3) of the uncertain memory and partiality of eyewitnesses, but very seldom refers in his narrative to any difficulty in discovering the facts; v. 68. 2 has something in common with the present passage.

ἐν δὲ νυκτομαχίᾳ, ἣ κτλ.: i.e. 'and in a night battle—and this one . . .'.

ἔν γε τῷδε τῷ πολέμῳ: From 431 to the time of writing; night battles were not common, and the point that this was the only one in the Sicilian campaign would not have been worth making.

2. ἑώρων δέ . . . ἀπιστεῖσθαι: lit., 'and they saw one another in the way in which it is to be expected in moonlight that one should see beforehand' (i.e. before coming to close quarters) 'the sight of the body but that the recognition of one's own should be doubted', i.e. '. . . as naturally happens in moonlight; one can see the form of a man in time, but cannot be sure that it is a friend'.

ἐν στενοχωρίᾳ: The area between the counterwall and the northern edge of the plateau; hardly a 'restricted space', one would have thought, even for much larger forces, but the wall was a real barrier to free movement on one side, and the Athenians' fear of being forced off the northern edge of the plateau would naturally restrict their movement on the other side far more in the dark than would have been justified in daylight.

3. ἀήσσητοι: '(sc. so far) unbeaten', not (as the word sometimes means) 'invincible'.

τὰ πρόσθεν: 'Their forward troops.'

4. σημῆναι: 'Give an order', as commonly (cf. 50. 3).

τοῦ ξυνθήματος: 'The password'; passwords were commonly used for recognition in battle even in daylight (e.g. X. *An.* i. 8. 16).

5. τὸ δ' ἐκείνων . . . διεφθείροντο: lit. 'but the Syracusan password they (Ath.) did not get to know in the same way, because of the fact that they (Syr.), as they were winning and not scattered, were less unknown'—i.e. the failure of one body of Syracusans to recognize another was less frequent—'so that if they (Ath.), in superior strength, encountered a body of the enemy, they (Syr.) escaped them (Ath.) inasmuch as they (Syr.) knew their (Ath.) password, but if they (Ath.) themselves did not answer'—i.e. when challenged for the Syracusan password by Syracusans—'they (Ath.) were killed'.

6. **ὁ παιανισμός**: The singing of the paian as a prayer before a battle or as a hymn of thanks after a victory was a universal Greek custom; but in Thucydides the paian as a warcry in battle or as a signal to attack occurs only in connexion with the Dorian peoples or Boeotians, never Athenians or Ionians.

καὶ ὅσον Δωρικόν . . . ἦν: Including Cretans, Rhodians, Messenians from Naupaktos, and Megarian exiles (57. 6–9).

παρεῖχε: The singular verb implies that 'whenever the Argives . . .' is subject.

8. **κατά τε τῶν κρημνῶν**: There are no towering cliffs at the edge of the plateau, but many places where a man in the dark could break his legs or even his neck.

[οἱ] πολλοί: If οἱ is sound, the reference must be to 'the majority' of those who became casualties, not to the majority of the whole Athenian force.

ῥίπτοντες ἑαυτούς: Not in suicidal despair, but in the hope of landing on their feet.

καὶ ὅσοι ἦσαν: καί is 'appositional': 'the majority, those who belonged to the original force', contrasted with 'those who came later'.

45. 2. **ἔτι πλείω ἢ κατὰ τοὺς νεκρούς**: 'even more than in accordance with the corpses' = 'quite out of proportion to the number of dead'.

ψιλοὶ [ἄνευ τῶν ἀσπίδων]: Since ψιλός in 78. 3 = 'without hoplite armour', it naturally means here 'having discarded their arms', and ἄνευ τῶν ἀσπίδων is almost certainly an inadequate explanatory interpolation.

JULY–AUGUST 413

46. Syracusan Activity

46. **Ἀκράγαντα στασιάζοντα**: On the polities of Akragas cf. 32. 1 n.

Σικανόν: Elected general in the autumn of 415 (vi. 73. 1), and deposed the following summer after the Syracusan setbacks (103. 4), he is now back in favour; cf. 70. 1.

47–49. Conference of the Athenian Generals

47. 1. **ἀρρωστίαν**: κατὰ πάντα and the details which follow show that ἀρρωστία here has the general sense 'weakness' or 'impotence' (cf. iii. 15. 2 ἀρρωστία τοῦ στρατεύειν), not (as LSJ) 'loss of morale'.

2. **νόσῳ τε γὰρ ἐπιέζοντο . . . τά τε ἄλλα ὅτι κτλ.**: 'For they were oppressed by sickness . . . and because everything else . . .' κατ'

ἀμφότερα = 'for two reasons', which are then given, the first in a participial clause (τῆς τε ὥρας . . . οὔσης κτλ.) and the second in an independent finite clause (καὶ τὸ χωρίον . . . ἦν).

The Athenians may have fallen victim, like other armies after them, to the malaria of the coastal regions of Sicily; and, like armies in all ages, they knew that marshy ground was unhealthy without knowing why. But it is uncertain how far Sicily was malarial at that period of history, and there will have been other diseases; fly-borne intestinal infections must have flourished in the conditions in which the Athenians were compelled to live.

3. καὶ μὴ διατρίβειν: The recurrence of this word (42. 3, 43. 1) conveys the urgency with which Demosthenes strove to make Nikias see the situation as it was; cf. the repetition of αἰσχρόν in the summary of Phrynichos' arguments in viii. 27. 2 f.

ἕως ἔτι . . . κρατεῖν: lit., 'while it was still possible for them to be conveyed across the sea' (i.e. before bad weather made a return voyage risky) 'and, of their force, they had the upper hand at least with the ships which had come as reinforcements'. As it is still only August (cf. 50. 4 n.) it is remarkable that Demosthenes should be thinking of the onset of winter storms, but the words leave no doubt of this; he speaks of crossing the sea, not simply of getting away from Syracuse, and the position of τοῦ στρατεύματος points to an emphatic distinction between the two elements on which the issue turned, nature and arms, both at the moment in their favour. Demosthenes had formed a strong impression of Nikias' capacity for delay, and he may well have thought that unless a decision to withdraw were taken at once he might not persuade Nikias to consider it again until the winter was at hand.

4. τοὺς ἐν τῇ χώρᾳ σφῶν ἐπιτειχίζοντας: The fact that Demosthenes could use this argument is a strategic vindication of the Spartan occupation of Dekeleia.

εἰκός: Here 'reasonable' or 'rational'.

48. 1. ἐγίγνωσκεν: 'Argued.' γνώμη is the term used for the opinion which one delivers in an assembly or conference (e.g. vi. 47).

ψηφιζομένους μετὰ πολλῶν: How large a body Nikias had in mind is not clear; he may possibly have contemplated putting the issue to the vote of the whole Athenian component of his forces, but he does not seem to envisage that in § 4, and even if only the taxiarchs (as in 60. 2) and trierarchs were brought into the discussion enough men would be involved to make it certain that the decision would become generally known.

λαθεῖν γὰρ ἄν . . . πολλῷ ἧσσον: As γάρ commonly = 'for thus', 'for then they would have much less chance of doing this', i.e. withdrawing, 'when they wanted to, without the Syracusans' knowledge' is a more probable translation than 'for if they did this', i.e. voted for withdrawal after discussion, 'they would have much less chance of escaping the Syracusans' notice', i.e. in withdrawing.

2. τὸ δέ τι: lit., 'and this, a certain thing', i.e. 'and, for another thing . . .'.

ἀφ' ὧν . . . ᾐσθάνετο αὐτῶν: lit., 'from the perception which he had of them' (αὐτῶν refers to τὰ τῶν πολεμίων, 'the enemy's situation') 'to a greater extent than the others', i.e. 'as he judged from his knowledge of it, which was greater than his colleagues' '.

θαλασσοκρατούντων: The reference is to the Athenians, who are the subject of ἐκτρυχώσειν; the accusative would have created ambiguity, and evidently Thucydides felt that a genitive absolute was more elegant than a nominative.

καὶ (ἦν γάρ τι . . .) ἐπεκηρυκεύετο κτλ.: The identity, strength, and motives of this 'fifth column' are unknown to us; cf. 49. 1 n. Probably some of the wealthy citizens of Leontinoi who in 422 had become citizens of Syracuse and had not broken away among the earlier malcontents (v. 4. 3 f.) were now hankering after an independent Leontinoi; when the Athenians first arrived in Sicily they issued a proclamation calling on men of Leontinoi in Syracuse to come over to their side (vi. 50. 4), and Diod. xiii. 18. 5 says that the Athenians believed that the seeming-friendly message delivered to them after the final battle in the harbour came from Leontinians. Whoever they were, these men, in order to retain the help of a powerful ally, would not have hesitated to deceive Nikias, and themselves too, by an exaggerated picture of Syracusan difficulties—the conduct of émigrés in our day provides abundant parallels—but Thucydides does not deny (49. 1) that Syracuse was short of money.

οὐκ εἴα ἀπανίστασθαι: οὐκ ἐᾶν commonly means not 'forbid' but 'ask . . . not to . . .' or 'urge . . . not to . . .', even sometimes 'disapprove of . . .'.

3. σφῶν ταῦτα . . . ἀπελθεῖν: lit., 'will not accept this of them, so as to go away when they themselves', i.e. the assembly at Athens, 'had not voted (sc. for their going away)', i.e. '. . . would not approve such conduct on their part, departure from Sicily without a vote of the Assembly'. Nikias and his colleagues had been dispatched αὐτοκράτορες (vi. 8. 2), i.e. empowered to end the campaign when they judged that its purposes had been fulfilled or had become impossible to fulfil, but this would not save them from punishment if the Assembly disapproved of the manner in which they had exercised their judgement.

οὐ τοὺς αὐτούς . . . γνώσεσθαι: lit., 'for not the same men will vote about them' (i.e. the Athenian forces in Sicily; αὐτῶν must be wrong, for σφῶν αὐτῶν could only refer to those who are the subject of ψηφιεῖσθαι) 'and will understand the situation by seeing it, as they themselves' (the forces in Sicily) 'do, and not having heard ⟨about it⟩ through the criticism made by others', i.e. 'for those who would pass a verdict on them would not be men who would depend for their knowledge of the situation on their own eyes—as they themselves did—rather than on the criticisms of others'.

ἀλλ' ἐξ ὧν ἄν τις . . . πείσεσθαι: lit., 'but from what one could, speaking well, vilify, from this they (the Athenian assembly) would believe', i.e. 'they would be convinced by whatever vilification a plausible speaker could produce'.

4. τἀναντία βοήσεσθαι: Nikias is afraid that if they return to Athens not only will the majority in the Assembly be judging them in ignorance of what the situation really was at Syracuse but even some of those who were there and do know will fall in with the prevailing mood and blame the generals for their failure.

ὑπὸ χρημάτων καταπροδόντες: The three generals who had returned from Sicily in 424 after the Peace of Gela were punished on a charge that they were bribed to withdraw (iv. 65. 3); accusations of this kind were made very freely in a Greek state.

τὰς Ἀθηναίων φύσεις: cf. 14. 4 n.

τοῦτο παθεῖν ἰδίᾳ: Death under sentence from a jury would be death δημοσίᾳ, the decision being taken by the state; ἰδίᾳ therefore means 'on his own initiative', 'at a time, and in a manner, of his own choosing'. Nikias' pride and consequent moral cowardice in the face of personal disgrace lead him to put forward as discreditable a proposition as any general in history. Rather than risk execution, he will throw away the fleet and thousands of other people's lives and put his country in mortal peril. We might compare Phaidra's false accusation against Hippolytos in the interests of her own reputation; we might even wonder whether a perverse spite (like Phaidra's) underlay Nikias's later obstinacy (50. 4).

5. ὅμως: 'In spite of everything'; cf. 1. 2 n.

δισχίλια . . . τάλαντα: We have no other evidence for the revenue and expenditure of Syracuse in peace or war at this period.

τῷ μὴ διδόναι τροφήν: τροφή, 'sustenance', is commonly used of the pay on which a soldier or sailor supports himself. Nikias' point is that if Syracuse cannot pay the forces of her allies they will go home.

τὰ πράγματα: 'Their strength', 'their forces'.

ἐπικουρικὰ μᾶλλον ἢ δι' ἀνάγκης: Whereas ἐπικουρία is 'help', ἐπικουρικός normally implies 'mercenary'; δι' ἀνάγκης, lit. 'in circumstances of compulsion' = 'under compulsion', is used in place of ἀναγκαστά for linguistic variety (note -κά . . . τὰ -ρα -τα).

6. τρίβειν: 'Wear ⟨them, i.e. Syracuse⟩ down'; cf. 49. 2 (v. n.) and viii. 46. 4 τρίβειν οὖν ἐκέλευε πρῶτον ἀμφοτέρους. There is no certain example of intransitive τρίβειν = διατρίβειν.

χρήμασιν, ὧν πολὺ κρείσσους εἰσί: ὧν B: ᾧ f: ᾧ [sic] JK: ὡς cett. ᾧ is supported by 62. 3 παχύτητας, ὥπερ δὴ κτλ., and in this context corruption of ᾧ to ὧν or ὡς is much more likely than the reverse process. The expression χρημάτων κρείσσων = 'incorruptible' (ii. 60. 5), which is inappropriate here.

49. 1. πολύ: This is Linwood's conjecture for που (B: om. cett.), and since Plutarch (Nic. 20. 5) speaks of οὐκ ὀλίγοι, he probably read πολύ, surprising though it may seem; cf. 48. 2 n.

ταῖς γοῦν ναυσὶ μᾶλλον ἢ πρότερον ἐθάρσησε κρατήσειν: The MSS. are confused here; B has θαρρῶν (om. cett.), for which μᾶλλον is Herwerden's conjecture; then ἐθάρσησε B, θαρσήσει cett., and at the end κρατηθείς codd. (κρατήσειν Herwerden). I suppose that θαρρῶν (note -ρρ-, contrary to Thucydides' practice) is an intrusive gloss designed to 'correct' the construction αἰσθόμενος . . . καὶ ἅμα . . . ἐθάρσησε into a 'regular' co-ordination of two participles, and that Thucydides in fact wrote ταῖς γοῦν ναυσὶν ἐθάρσησε, πρότερον κρατηθείς, 'he felt confidence at any rate in the fleet, the arm in which he had previously lost superiority'. Cf. 55. 2 ταῖς ναυσὶν ἐκρατήθησαν = 'they lost superiority at sea', ii. 79. 5 θαρσήσαντες τοῖς προσγεγενημένοις = 'regaining confidence through this accession of strength', and vi. 16. 2 μείζω ἡμῶν τὴν πόλιν ἐνόμισαν . . . πρότερον ἐλπίζοντες αὐτὴν καταπεπολεμῆσθαι, iii. 81. 2 λαβόντες τούς τε Μεσσηνίους ἐς τὴν πόλιν ἤγαγον, πρότερον ἔξω ὄντας.

2. τρίβειν αὐτοῦ: The MSS. have τρίβειν αὐτούς, which is right, = 'wear Syracuse down'; cf. 48. 6 n.

Θάψον: The little low-lying peninsula projecting from the coast between Syracuse and the site of Megara.

πρὸς τῶν πολεμίων: cf. 36. 3.

3. καὶ ὁ Εὐρυμέδων . . . ξυνηγόρευεν: Whether this gave Demosthenes' proposal a majority we cannot say, in view of the uncertainty (cf. 16. 1 n.) about the constitutional position of Menandros and Euthydemos; nor, in any case, do we know what they thought.

4. πλέον εἰδώς: 'With special knowledge' not shared by the others.

AUGUST 413

50. 1–2. Reinforcements for Syracuse

50. 1. ὁ δὲ Γύλιππος καὶ ὁ Σικανός . . . παρῆσαν: cf. 46.

[ἐς] φιλία ἐξεπεπτώκει: ἐς, deleted by Bauer, is impossible, since (a) ἡ τοῖς Συρακοσίοις στάσις is not Greek for 'the pro-Syracusan faction', and (*b*) ἐς φίλια (neut. plur.) would be an unexampled expression for 'into friendly territory'. Hence: 'the faction which was friendly to Syracuse had been expelled'. On the situation at Akragas cf. 46.

τοὺς ... τοῦ ἦρος ... ἀποσταλέντας: cf. 19. 3 f.

2. Κυρηναίων: Kyrene, as a colony of Thera (and thus ultimately of Sparta) could reasonably be expected to help Peloponnesians.

Εὐεσπερίταις: Euesperides is the later Berenike, the modern Benghazi.

Νέαν πόλιν: The modern Nabeul, on the east coast of C. Bon in Tunisia. The distance from there to Selinus is 230 km., so that the average speed implied by Thucydides' datum is rather less than 6·5 km.p.h. It is interesting that the Peloponnesians preferred this circuitous route, which brought them eventually to the wrong end of Sicily, to a direct voyage from Euesperides to Syracuse; possibly the direct route was little used and the distance exaggerated, but more probably they were uncertain about the naval situation at Syracuse and intended in any case to land elsewhere.

50. 3 f. Athenian Decision to Withdraw
Eclipse of the Moon

50. 3. οὐδὲ ὁ Νικίας ... ψηφίζεσθαι: 'Not even Nikias now opposed ⟨the decision⟩ as he had done before, except to the extent of saying that they ought not to vote on it openly.' Cf. 48. 1 n.

προεῖπον ... σημήνῃ: lit., 'told everyone in advance, as secretly as possible, a sailing out from their station and to prepare ⟨now⟩ ⟨to sail out⟩ when the order ⟨to sail out⟩ was given'; ἔκπλουν and παρασκευάσασθαι are co-ordinated objects of προεῖπον, and obviously the generals did not want the men to delay getting ready until some future order to get ready should be given, but to get ready at once so that a future order to depart could be carried out without delay.

4. ἡ σελήνη ἐκλείπει: 27 August 413.

πασσέληνος: Thucydides may have known that a lunar eclipse can occur only when the moon is full—cf. his empirical statement about solar eclipses in ii. 28—or γάρ may make only the simple point that the visible event which we call a lunar eclipse was able to happen on this occasion because there was a substantial amount of moon to be eclipsed.

ἐπισχεῖν ἐκέλευον: Later writers have tended to blame Nikias and so to exonerate 'the majority' of the Athenians who demanded delay. Thucydides' own criticism of Nikias is not that he was more superstitious than the men whom he commanded, but that an educated man in a responsible position should have been much *less* superstitious.

Perhaps he thought that Demosthenes, left to himself, would have persuaded the men to disregard the omen.

θειασμῷ: Utterance which claims to reveal through a human medium the intentions of the gods (LSJ is wrong about this word), including the production of oracles, the interpretation of omens and dreams, and 'inspiration'.

οἱ μάντεις: Seers were regarded as indispensable members of Greek expeditions.

τρὶς ἐννέα: The phraseology is oracular; cf. v. 26. 4, where Thucydides recalls that some people said, from the very beginning of the Peloponnesian War, that 'it was destined to last thrice nine years'.

ὅπως ἂν πρότερον κινηθείη: '(Decide) . . . on how any earlier move could be made'; πρότερον is superfluous, given πρίν . . . μεῖναι.

SEPTEMBER 413

51–54. Syracusan Victory in the Harbour

51. 2. πρὸς τὰ τείχη: This attack was made against the eastern face of the upper Athenian fortifications (ἄνω, 54).

κατά τινας πύλας: πύλαι here, as commonly, is used of a single gate.

ἵππους . . . ἀπολλύασι: They abandoned their horses in order to escape into the fortifications on foot.

52. 1. ἓξ καὶ ὀγδοήκοντα: Before the arrival of their reinforcements the Athenians had put 75 ships to sea (37. 3), of which 'one or two' were sunk on the first day's fighting (38. 1), and 'seven sunk and many damaged' on the second day (41. 4). Thereupon Demosthenes and Eurymedon arrived with 73 (42. 1); but the majority of these ships were carrying troops, and, apart from the technical problem of re-converting troop-carriers in a hurry, casualties, sickness, and desertion must have made it impossible to man every ship.

2. ἐν τῷ κοίλῳ . . . τοῦ λιμένος: At the beginning of the action the Athenian fleet must have faced east or north-east, the Syracusan fleet west or south-west. Therefore the land which Eurymedon approached in trying, from his station on the Athenian right wing, to encircle the Syracusan left, must have been Ortygia. When the Syracusans defeated the Athenian centre, pushing it back westwards and south-westwards, Eurymedon found himself at the northern end of the harbour with the bulk of the Syracusan fleet between him and his base.

53. 1. ἔξω τῶν σταυρωμάτων . . . καταφερομένας: South of their base, between it and the river-mouth. Gylippos has therefore approached from Plemmyrion or the Olympieion.

ἐπὶ τὴν χηλήν: The narrow spit of land which lay north of the river-mouth and between the sea and the lake (Lysimeleia).

2. οἱ Τυρσηνοί: On the Etruscans in the Athenian force cf. 57. 11 n.

ἐς τὴν λίμνην: The Etruscans, whose purpose was to protect the crews of the ships which had been forced ashore, naturally pressed on southwards to occupy the whole of the spit, and Gylippos' men had to disperse and escape across the southern part of the 'lake'.

3. καὶ τοὺς ἄνδρας πάντας ἀπέκτειναν: In similar circumstances earlier in the summer (41. 4) the Syracusans took some prisoners; now their temper is harsher.

4. [τὴν ναῦν]: These words are superfluous, since without them we have a quite normal construction—'a merchant ship, having filled . . . they sent . . .'—and are probably interpolated.

σβεστήρια κωλύματα: 'Preventive measures to extinguish the fire', or, more exactly, 'measures which prevented ⟨disaster⟩ by extinguishing ⟨the fire⟩'; we have no idea what these were.

παύσαντες . . . τὴν ὁλκάδα: lit., 'having stopped the flame and the *not* approaching near of the merchant ship', i.e. 'having put an end to the flames and to the approach of the vessel'. The negative is used here as it is with words meaning 'prevent'.

55–56. The Morale of Both Sides

55. 1. λαμπρᾶς: 'Decisive.'

καὶ τοῦ ναυτικοῦ: The night battle on Epipolai had been the λαμπρὰ νίκη on land.

2. δημοκρατουμέναις: Aristotle *Pol.* 1304^{a}27 says that *after* the defeat of the Athenians the Syracusan people changed from πολιτεία to δημοκρατία; it appears from other passages that he means by πολιτεία a constitution more democratic than oligarchic but restricting the rights and powers of the poorest citizens. Similarly, Diod. xiii. 34. 6 dates to 412 the introduction of certain democratic measures at Syracuse, notably appointment to office by lot. But there is no reason to question the clear implication of Thucydides' words that Syracuse in 415–413 was in essentials a democracy and to be classified constitutionally with Athens herself rather than with the Peloponnesian states. Indeed, both Aristotle *Pol.* 1316^{a}33 and Diod. xi. 68. 6 speak of the democracy at Syracuse as enduring from the end of the Deinomenid tyranny (466) down to the tyranny of Dionysios (405).

μεγέθη ἐχούσαις: lit. 'having bignesses', i.e. 'with all resources on a large scale'.

οὐ δυνάμενοι . . . κρείσσονος: 'Not being able to bring to bear upon them' (or 'use as a weapon against them') '. . . either through (ἐκ) a change in political structure . . . or through greatly superior forces . . .' clearly says something about the consequences of the similarity between Syracuse and the Athenians; the Athenians could neither overcome Syracuse by strength (because she was a strong city herself) or gain the help of a revolutionary democratic party within the city (for a democracy was in power already). The interpretation of τὸ διάφορον is difficult.

(i) If it refers to political difference only, lit., 'to bring to bear upon them something from a change of constitution, ⟨I mean⟩ the ⟨political⟩ difference ⟨between them⟩, by which they were accustomed to bring ⟨an enemy⟩ over', the separation of αὐτοῖς from ἐπενεγκεῖν is remarkable, for it is thrust into the middle of a parenthesis which amplifies τι.

(ii) If, on the other hand, τὸ διάφορον refers to difference of all kinds, political and military, the position of αὐτοῖς is less abnormal (cf. ὑμῖν in 64. 1), τι will have to be an internal accusative with the verbal noun μεταβολῆς, and προσῆγοντο will cover the inducement of surrender by any means, including the threat of force: lit., 'to bring to bear upon them the difference ⟨between them⟩, by which they were accustomed to induce ⟨an enemy⟩ to surrender, either through a ⟨promised⟩ change, in some respect, of constitution, or through much greater forces'.

No one will pretend that either is easy Greek; (ii) seems to me less difficult. It is possible that τὸ διάφορον is in origin an intrusive gloss on τι.

Thucydides represents Nikias in the debate before the expedition (vi. 20. 2) as warning the Athenians that they were going to attack an enemy who did not seek political liberation.

ὃ οὐκ ἂν ᾤοντο: 'Which they did not think would happen.'

56. 2. κωλύσουσι: sc. σωθῆναι.

ἐλευθεροῦσθαι . . . ἀπολύεσθαι: The association of these words with futures (φανεῖσθαι, ἔσεσθαι, θαυμασθήσεσθαι) shows that they are prophetic and do not imply that the Syracusans believed that the Athenian Empire was already dissolving.

οὐ γὰρ ἔτι . . . ἐνεγκεῖν: This belief, at any rate, was wrong.

αὐτῶν: 'The situation' described in the preceding lines.

3. τὴν σφετέραν πόλιν ἐμπαρασχόντες προκινδυνεῦσαι: lit., 'and among these (ἐμ-) having offered their own city for running a risk beforehand', i.e. confronting a danger which, if the Athenians had beaten Syracuse, would afterwards have come upon the rest of the Greek world.

4. τοῦ ξύμπαντος λόγου: λόγος commonly means 'account' or 'reckoning', and (in some inscriptions of Epidauros) 'total'; cf. English 'count' = 'counted total'.

57–59. 1. Catalogue of Allies

These chapters are a specimen of a genre which extends in European literature from Book II of the Iliad, via Book VII of Herodotus, to the Order of Battle printed as an appendix to a modern war history. Thucydides' purpose, however, is not to provide us with *numbers* of men and horses and ships; indeed, he gives us none in these chapters, and though some are to be found elsewhere in Books VI and VII we never learn, for example, how many troops, or of what categories, were provided by Zakynthos or the Aitolians. His purpose is quite different: to comment on the international relationships which led, for example, Chios or Metapontion to participate in the fighting.

In the course of the catalogue he makes certain statements which have a bearing on the date of its composition. These are:

(i) 57. 2: 'The Aiginetans, who at that time (τότε) possessed Aigina.' Aigina was occupied by Athenians from 431 (ii. 27. 1) to 405 (X. *HG* ii. 2. 9). τότε might therefore imply either a contrast with the period before 431 or a contrast with the period after 405. It is unlikely that Thucydides, writing a κτῆμα ἐς αἰεί between those two dates, would assume either that Athens would win the war but voluntarily give up Aigina or that Athens would lose the war and be compelled to give it up. If, therefore, he wrote these words before 405, he would more naturally have said οἱ νῦν Αἴγιναν ἔχουσιν.

(ii) 57. 8: 'Those who are now (νῦν) called Messenians, from Naupaktos and from Pylos, which was at that time (τότε) held by Athens.' The Messenians were expelled from Naupaktos after the end of the war, but probably not before 401/400 (Diod. xiv. 17. 4 ff., 34. 1 f.), and Μεσσήνιοι as a state thereupon ceased to exist. Pylos was lost by the Athenians in 409 (X. *HG* i. 2. 18, Diod. xiii. 64. 5 ff.). If, however, Thucydides wrote these words before 409 he could reasonably assume that however the war ended it would not leave Athens in permanent control of Pylos.

(iii) 58. 1: 'The Himeraeans from the north coast of Sicily, ἐν ᾧ καὶ μόνοι Ἕλληνες οἰκοῦσιν.' Himera was totally destroyed in 409 (Diod. xiii. 62); but a people calling themselves 'Ἱμεραῖοι, and independent of Carthaginian rule, existed in 397–6 in the region of the site of the city (Diod. xiv. 47. 6, 56. 2).

Thus if we are to think of the whole of the Catalogue as composed at one time, 57. 2 suggests 405 as the upper terminus, and the reference to the Messenians in 57. 8 indicates 401 as the lower terminus. The references to Pylos and Himera are reconcilable with these termini.

57. 1. ἐπὶ Συρακούσας: If the correct analysis of the sentence is 'having come to Sicily and to decide the fate of Sicily . . . fought at Syracuse', ἐπί with the accusative is an unusual way of saying 'at', and Bauer's emendation ἐπὶ Συρακούσαις is plausible. Yet it is unnatural to associate ἐπὶ Σικελίαν with ἐλθόντες—the words from τοῖς μέν to ξυνδιασώσοντες naturally isolate themselves as parenthetic—and that leaves, lit.: 'fought a war to Sicily and about Sicily, to Syracuse', i.e. 'came to Sicily to fight at Syracuse for the fate of Sicily'. This analysis raises a fresh stylistic objection, the accumulation of two ἐπί-phrases with the same verb, ἐπολέμησαν; the awkwardness is, however, diminished by (i) the absorption of the first phrase into a larger complex, ἐπί . . . Σικελίας, and (ii) the intervention of τοῖς μέν . . . ξυνδιασώσοντες.

κατὰ δίκην: i.e. in the prosecution of the redress of a grievance.

ὡς ἑκάστοις . . . ἔσχεν: Since impersonal ἔχειν does not occur elsewhere in Thucydides, read ἕκαστοι (B) and ἔσχον (JK), and cf. i. 22. 3 ὡς . . . τις εὐνοίας ἢ μνήμης ἔχοι. Hence, lit., 'according as each nation had of chance . . .', i.e. 'in accordance with the situation in which each nation found itself at the time, either in respect of its own interest or under compulsion'.

57. 2–57. 11. *Allies of Athens*

The fundamental criterion of classification is geographical: Athenian allies from Greece and the Aegean are listed (§§ 2–10) before those from the West (§ 11). The further criteria may be represented as follows:

    (A) (§ 2) Athenian colonies.
    (B) (§§ 4–6) Subject-allies.
        (i) (§ 4) Ionians, plus Karystos.
        (ii) (§ 5) Aeolians.
        (iii) (§ 6) Dorians.
    (C) (§§ 7–8) Formally independent, but in fact dependent in varying degrees.
    (D) (§§ 9–10) Essentially independent; this category includes mercenaries.

Thucydides obviously attaches importance to racial divisions; not only is difference of race the basis for the sub-classification of (B), but race is mentioned in (A), (C) and (D). As we would expect from his introductory section, the extent to which a nation's participation was determined by 'interest' or 'necessity' is mentioned in each case, and attention is drawn to the cases in which this made members of the same race fight against each other. No explicit comment is made on participation κατὰ δίκην, but εἰκότως in § 5 indicates that the fighting of Plataians against other Boeotians came into this category.

57. 2. αὐτοῖς: With τῇ αὐτῇ.

Λήμνιοι καὶ Ἴμβριοι: Athens gained possession of Lemnos and Imbros at the beginning of the fifth century.

Αἰγινῆται: cf. supra.

Ἑστιαιῆς: The territory of Hestiaia was confiscated by Athens in 445, after the suppression of the Euboian revolt.

ἄποικοι ὄντες: Athenian ἄποικοι were citizens of the ἀποικίαι which they constituted, not of Athens; κληροῦχοι owned pieces of land confiscated by Athens from other states, but their rights and obligations as Athenian citizens were not impaired.

3. οἱ μὲν ὑπήκοοι . . . ξυνεστράτευον: 'Subjects' are listed in §§ 3–6, 'independent allies' in §§ 7–8.

4. αὐτόνομοι: In § 3 a firm distinction was drawn between 'subject' and 'independent'; now Thucydides rather confusingly distinguishes, within the category 'subject', (i) 'subject and compelled to pay tribute', (ii) Chios, 'not compelled to pay tribute, but independent, providing ships', and (iii) Methymna in § 5, lit., 'subject with ships and not with tribute'. Clearly Chios had a degree of 'independence' not shared by other 'subjects', not even by Methymna, which was the only state in the Empire apart from Chios to possess a fleet of her own. Presumably Chios was exempted from some of the measures which Athens took to increase her political, juridical, and economic control over her allies, but we do not know from which ones. Since Athens ruled her empire to a large extent by meeting individual difficulties as they arose singly, 'independence' was a matter of degree, and sometimes, no doubt, of opinion and feeling.

καὶ τὸ πλεῖστον . . . ἠκολούθουν: Thucydides is making three points: (i) the states listed in this section constituted the greater part of the Athenian force, τὸ πλεῖστον οὗτοι ἠκολούθουν; (ii) they were all, except Karystos, Ionian, Ἴωνες ὄντες πάντες; (iii) therefore, although subjects, they belong to the familiar category 'Ionians against Dorians'. The manner in which this third point is made is obscured by something which is either a textual corruption or incoherent expression. ἀνάγκῃ must qualify ἠκολούθουν, since ὑπήκοοι ὄντες καὶ ἀνάγκῃ 'being subjects and under compulsion' is not Greek; one cannot say ἀνάγκῃ εἰμί, 'I am under compulsion'. So then must ὑπήκοοι ὄντες qualify ἠκολούθουν. But although Ἴωνες ὄντες, ὑπήκοοι δ' ὄντες καὶ ἀνάγκῃ ἠκολούθουν, 'they followed as Ionians, but as subjects and under compulsion', is correct Greek, Ἴωνες ὄντες, ὑπήκοοι δ' ὄντες καὶ ἀνάγκῃ ὅμως Ἴωνες ἠκολούθουν is not correct Greek for 'since they were Ionians, although they followed as subjects and under compulsion they nevertheless followed as Ionians'. δέ after ὑπήκοοι is suspect, and must be either attributed to a confusion in Thucydides' thought, 'Ionians, but subjects' superimposing itself on 'although subjects, they nevertheless followed as Ionians', or transposed to follow ὅμως, giving: 'these nations, who were all Ionian . . . constituted the greater part of the force which came with the Athenians; they came as subjects, but none the less as Ionians against Dorians'. It is to be noted that the mutilated text of Π[18], although it probably had δ' after ὑπήκοοι, also had at least one and probably two letters between ὅμως and Ἴωνες.

Δρύοπες: Hdt. viii. 46. 4 classifies both Styra and Kythnos as 'Dryopes', but expresses no opinion on Karystos. Thucydides evidently accepted an alternative tradition which made Styra Ionian.

5. **κατὰ τὸ ἔχθος:** Enmity between Thebes and Plataiai went back to the sixth century.

6. **Κυθήριοι:** cf. 26. 2 n.

7. **Κεφάλληνες μὲν καὶ Ζακύνθιοι:** cf. 31. 2 n.

ἀνάγκῃ μὲν ἐκ τοῦ εὐπρεποῦς: Kerkyra was an ally of Athens, and was required to help her under the terms of this alliance. Such help would have been—one might have thought—κατὰ δίκην; but since in § 1 Thucydides makes a clear distinction between κατὰ δίκην and ἀνάγκῃ, and here says that Kerkyra professed to be fighting ἀνάγκῃ, we have to interpret κατὰ δίκην as referring only to the prosecution of grievances, excluding the fulfilment of alliances, and we have to accept the classification of Kerkyra with much less powerful island states such as Kephallenia and Zakynthos. We may compare vi. 44. 3, 46. 2, where, in describing the unfriendly reception given by Rhegion to the Athenians in 415, Thucydides does not think the existence of a longstanding formal alliance between Rhegion and Athens worth mentioning, but speaks only of the *sentiment* of Rhegion.

κατὰ ἔχθος τὸ Κορινθίων: This too was a traditional enmity of very long standing.

8. **καὶ οἱ Μεσσήνιοι . . . ἐχομένης:** cf. 31. 2 n. and 26. 2 n.

Μεγαρέων φυγάδες: The pro-Athenians in Megara had taken refuge with the Athenians in 424; 120 of them served in the Athenian expedition as light-armed troops (vi. 43).

9. **οὐ τῆς ξυμμαχίας ἕνεκα:** cf. 20. 1.

Μαντινῆς δέ . . . μισθοφόροι: Mantinea, like Argos, was pro-Athenian in sentiment, and the importance of this sentiment is emphasized in vi. 61. 5; but here Mantineans are classified unambiguously as mercenaries.

ἐπὶ τοὺς αἰεί . . . ἀποδεικνυμένους: 'Against those who were at any given time indicated to them as the enemy . . .'

Κρῆτες δέ: The Cretan cities as such were indifferent to the Peloponnesian War.

καὶ Αἰτωλοί: The Aitolians' last appearance in Thucydides' narrative was as enemies of Athens (iii. 94. 3 ff.). Demosthenes must have recruited these Aitolians when he was at Kerkyra (31. 2).

10. Δημοσθένους . . . εὐνοίᾳ: A result of Demosthenes' successful campaign in 426/5, which brought the Akarnanians some spectacular gains (iii. 94 ff., 100 ff., 105 ff.).

11. ἐν τοιαύταις . . . κατειλημμένοι: cf. 33. 5 f. στασιωτικὸς καιρός is a stage or moment in a process of internal conflict, and the point of τοιαύταις is 'of such a kind as to lead to their fighting on the Athenian side'. Hence: 'as was inevitably imposed upon them by the state of their internal conflicts at that time.'

καὶ Σικελῶν τὸ πλέον: According to vi. 88. 4, the Sikels of the inland districts came over to the Athenians in the winter of 415/14, and many more, who had up to that time been under Syracusan control, in the summer of 414 (vi. 103. 2).

Τυρσηνῶν τέ τινες: The Etruscans took the initiative in 415/14 in offering help to Athens; enmity between them and Syracuse went back to the early fifth century.

καὶ Ἰάπυγες: cf. 33. 4.

58. Allies of Syracuse

The fundamental criterion is again geographical: from Sicily, or from overseas. The category 'from Sicily' is classified thus:
(A) Greeks.
    (i) South coast.
    (ii) North coast.
(B) Sikels.

Just as Thucydides commented on race and political compulsion throughout the list of Athenian allies, so here he comments that all the states in (A) were Dorian and independent.

58. 1. μετ' αὐτούς: This is said from the point of view of a man travelling along the coast westwards, not from that of a man reading a map.

2. ἐν ᾧ . . . οἰκοῦσιν: cf. supra.

3. Δωριῆς τε: This is contradicted by vi. 5. 1, where we are told that Himera was founded by Zankle (i.e. Messene), which was Ionian, that exiles from Syracuse later joined it, and that though its dialect was

mixed Ionian and Dorian its laws and customs were Chalkidian (i e. Ionian; Zankle, mother-city of Himera, owed its origin to Chalkis).

καὶ [οἱ] αὐτόνομοι: [οἱ] is impossible, as it would imply that these Greek allies of Syracuse constituted all the independent cities of Sicily; and they did not.

ξυνεμάχουν: The plural verb may be justified by the intervention of Δωριῆς τε κτλ.

Σικελοί: cf. 57. 11 n. μόνοι is to be taken with βαρβάρων, 'alone among the foreign peoples', not with ὅσοι κτλ.

ἡγεμόνα Σπαρτιάτην: Ekkritos (19. 3) commanded the force described in νεοδαμώδεις δὲ κτλ., but the reader more naturally thinks of Gylippos.

νεοδαμώδεις δέ: cf. 19. 3 n.

δύναται δέ . . . εἶναι: Although the inference drawn in the apparatus criticus of the Oxford Text, 'ut videtur, non legit Schol.', is unjustified, it is probable that these words are an interpolation, since (a), given the complexity of structure of the Spartan state, they offer a vague and inadequate explanation, (b) they are a characteristic scholion in form, and (c) Thucydides has already used the word νεοδαμώδεις in this book (19. 3) without explaining it. This last objection is, of course, of limited validity, for Thucydides may have written this chapter before he wrote ch. 19.

καὶ Λευκάδιοι καὶ Ἀμπρακιῶται: cf. 7. 1. Leukas and Ambrakia, like Syracuse, were colonies of Corinth; hence τὸ ξυγγενές.

ἀναγκαστοί: A consequence, rather allusively expressed, of the Spartans' intervention to restore control of Sikyon in 417 (v. 81. 2). The 'compulsion' was perhaps exercised by Corinth, not directly by Sparta; cf. 19. 4.

4. **κατὰ πάντα:** 'In all arms', amplified by καὶ γὰρ ὁπλῖται κτλ.

59. 2–74. The Great Battle in the Harbour

59. 2–59. 3. *The Syracusans Close the Harbour Mouth*

59. 3. **ὀκτὼ σταδίων μάλιστα:** The distance from the rocks at the southern tip of Ortygia to the little island off the tip of Plemmyrion is 1·04 km., and to the western projection of Plemmyrion 1·24 km. On the term 'stade' cf. 2. 4 n. It should be noted that Syracusan sources would naturally magnify the width of the mouth, to emphasize the difficulty of blocking it, and Athenian sources would minimize it, to emphasize the difficulty of breaking out.

60. *Athenian Plans for a Break-out*

60. 2. **καὶ οἱ ταξίαρχοι:** These men corresponded roughly to the battalion commanders of a modern army. Their invitation to conferences seems to have lain within the discretion of the generals.

προπέμψαντες γάρ: Before the eclipse (50. 3 f.).

τὰ μὲν τείχη τὰ ἄνω: The fortifications on the plateau, and, as the following words suggest, part, at least, of the 'double wall' between the plateau and the shore.

καὶ δυναταὶ καὶ ἀπλούστεραι: lit., 'both capable and more unfitted for sailing', i.e. 'sound and unsound alike'. Cf. ii. 35. 1 εὖ τε καὶ χεῖρον, 'well or ill'.

3. **ἡλικίας μετέχων**: Since all the soldiers and sailors would naturally have been 'of military age', these words imply that fit slaves too were now pressed into service.

4. **δέκα μάλιστα καὶ ἑκατόν**: This number must include many which were not judged fit for use in the previous sea-battle, in which the Athenians put 86 to sea and lost at least 18 (50. 1, 53. 3).

ἐξ ἀναγκαίου τε ... διανοίας: Either (a) 'as their circumstances dictated' (cf. ἐξ ἴσου, &c.) 'and in accordance with a plan', then either (i) 'which reflected that stress' (cf. τοιαύταις in 57. 11) or (ii) 'of the kind described' (i.e. involving the use of archers, &c.)—in these interpretations we have almost a 'zeugma' with ἐξ—or (b) 'in accordance with a plan which was forced upon them by circumstances and was of the kind described', making ἀναγκαίου agree with διανοίας; for feminine ἀναγκαῖος cf. i. 2. 2. In either case the point is that in the circumstances they were compelled to fill their decks with archers and javelin-men; (a) (ii) is perhaps the least peculiar way of saying that. ὅσα (for ὡς) in B and the presence of καὶ ὡς after ἦν in Π[18] reveal some uncertainties in the textual tradition, but do not solve any problems.

61–64. *Speech of Nikias*

61. 2. τὴν ἐλπίδα ... ἔχουσιν: lit., 'have the expectation of the fear like the setback', i.e. 'the expectation which their fear' (arising from their previous defeats) 'engenders does not rise above their misfortunes'. Nikias cannot pretend that the Athenian situation is not a ξυμφορά; he can only try to encourage optimism.

3. **καὶ τὸ τῆς τύχης ... τοῦ πλήθους**: lit., 'and, expecting that the contribution (τό) of fortune may stand with us, and with the intention of fighting back ...'. τὸ τῆς τύχης is the contribution of fortune to the situation (cf. 62. 2 τὸ τῆς ἐπιστήμης), here to a slight extent personified; cf. 68. 1.

62. 1. ἐπὶ τῇ τοῦ λιμένος στενότητι: ἐπί here almost = 'given'.
ἔσεσθαι: With τὸν μέλλοντα.

2. ναυμαχίαν μέν . . . ἐν πελάγει: 'If we were fighting a (sc. real) ser-battle, on open water.'

3. καὶ πρὸς τὰς τῶν ἐπωτίδων αὐτοῖς παχύτητας: Thucydides dis-likes the juxtaposition of genitives with different references; hence αὐτοῖς here = 'their'.

ᾧπερ δή: i.e. the thickening of their anchor-blocks.

4. ἐᾶν: sc. ἀνακρούεσθαι.

63. 1. πρότερον . . . ἤ . . . ἀπαράξητε: Except for this passage and one in Antiphon, πρότερον ἤ with the subjunctive, equivalent to πρὶν ἄν with the subjunctive, is purely Ionic.

2. τῶν ἄνωθεν: 'Those on deck.'

3. τοῖς δὲ ναύταις: καὶ ταῦτα κτλ. in § 2 show that the tactical advice and encouragement of 62–63. 1 have been primarily directed to the sailors, including the trierarchs and officers, and the last part of 63. 1 makes this doubly clear. Now Nikias returns to the ναῦται in the narrow sense, the oarsmen, to give them moral encouragement rather than tactical instructions.

ἐκείνην τε τὴν ἡδονήν: Nikias treats the sailors, without restriction or qualification, as non-Athenians, culturally and linguistically Atti-cized (there may well be exaggeration here), but not as subjects of Athens, as ἔς τε τὸ φοβερὸν τοῖς ὑπηκόοις and κοινωνοὶ μόνοι . . . τῆς ἀρχῆς show. Again in 64. 1 f. the Athenian contribution is treated as ships and soldiers, not as sailors. Either, then, these men came from subject states, and the ὑπήκοοι in whom they inspired fear were their own fellow citizens, or—and this is the easier interpretation—they were metics and foreigners from states not included in the empire. This casts an interesting light on the statement attributed to a Corinthian speaker in i. 121. 3, 'the power of Athens is bought (ὠνητή), not native', and is in accord with the implication of 'our *pilots* are Athenian citizens' (i. 143. 1), viz. 'our oarsmen are not'. Note also the absence of sailors (except petty officers) from the categories of loss listed in viii. 1. 2.

καὶ τῆς ἀρχῆς . . . μετείχετε: 'Your share in our empire has been no less'—either sc. 'than our own' or sc. 'than your share in our culture'—'so far as benefits are concerned' (i.e. but you have not shared so much in the responsibility, expense, and danger), 'in inspiring our subjects with respect and, far more important, in immunity from wrong'. It is hard to see any decisive grounds for choice between the two possible interpretations of οὐκ ἔλασσον. πολὺ πλέον *looks* as if it belongs with μετείχετε, 'you had a much larger share', and it may be an intrusive variant on οὐκ ἔλασσον.

4. ἤκμαζε: cf. 12. 3, 14. 1.

καὶ μετ' ἀσθενείας ... ῥώμης: The complex antithesis, half concealed by careful phonetic and syntactical variety, is characteristic; ἀσθενείας ~ ῥώμης, ξυμφορῶν ~ εὐτυχούσης, ἡ ὑμετέρα ~ ἑτέρας.

64. 1. τούς τε Ἀθηναίους ὑμῶν: It looks at first sight as if the reference were only to the Athenians among the sailors; but since the Athenian hoplites have so far been given no encouragement of the kind offered in 63. 3–64, 'the Athenians among you' is probably meant to include soldiers.

ὑπομιμνήσκω: Two different constructions are co-ordinated: (i) ὅτι κτλ., and (ii) the participles πλευσομένους ... ἐσομένους.

οὔτε ὁπλιτῶν ἡλικίαν: sc. τοῖσδε ὁμοίαν.

εἴ τε ξυμβήσεταί τι ... ὑμῖν: This euphemism for defeat is more elaborate and artificial than the common ἐάν τι πάθω, 'if anything happens to me'.

οἴᾳ γνώμῃ ἐπήλθετε: Since their position is admittedly desperate, Nikias' point is not that it would be shameful for so proud an enterprise to be defeated, but that they can expect no mercy from an enemy whose independence they proposed to destroy. Cf. 68. 2 n.

65. Syracusan Preparations

65. 2. καὶ τῆς νεὼς ἄνω τὸ πολύ: 'And over much of the upper parts of each (τῆς) ship.'

ὅπως ἂν ἀπολισθάνοι: The distinction intended between this and an ordinary final clause (which would be ὅπως ἀπολισθάνοι or ὅπως ἂν ἀπολισθάνῃ) is not clear; perhaps 'so that ... might be likely to slip off', or, giving a conditional sense to the participle ἐπιβαλλομένη, 'so that if cast on ... it would slip off'.

3. παρεκελεύσαντο ... τοιάδε: Thucydides does not indicate whether we are to think of this speech as made by a single spokesman whom he does not name or as compounded of several speeches made by several people. The sentiment and standpoint are Syracusan throughout, and we cannot at any rate regard the speech as the utterance of Gylippos.

66–68. Syracusan Speech

66. 1. οὐδὲ γὰρ ἄν: 'For otherwise you would not ...'

2. ἐκ τοῦ εἰκότος: 'You have every reason to think ...'; a translation involving 'probability' would strike a false note.

3. τό γ' ὑπόλοιπον αὐτῶν τῆς δόξης: lit., 'the remaining element of their opinion', i.e. 'their opinion ⟨of themselves⟩ thereafter'.

ἀσθενέστερον . . . τὸ πρῶτον: The comparative is followed both by the genitive ἑαυτοῦ and by ἢ κτλ., i.e. weaker than ⟨it would have been⟩ if they had not thought ⟨that they were superior⟩ to start with' is superimposed on 'weaker than it was'.

καὶ τῷ παρ' ἐλπίδα . . . ἐνδιδόασιν: lit., 'and being defeated by that ⟨which is⟩ contrary to the expectation of their boast' (or, sacrificing the balance between the two halves of the sentence but giving more point to τῷ, 'falling short of their boast through that ⟨which happens⟩ contrary to expectation'), 'they also give in contrary to the strength of their power', i.e. 'when their pride is cast down by unexpected events they collapse more quickly than the strength of which they are capable warrants'.

67. 1. τὸ κρατίστους . . . ἐνικήσαμεν. These words give the content of the δόκησις; for the construction cf. 36. 5 n.

2. χερσαῖοι ὡς εἰπεῖν: 'Land animals, so to speak'; χερσαῖος is not normally used of human beings.

οἳ οὐδ' ὅπως καθεζομένους . . . εὑρήσουσι: lit., 'who will not even find how placing themselves it is right that they should discharge the missile', i.e. 'who will not even be able to discover what position to adopt for the discharge of their missiles', or possibly '. . . to discover how, from a sitting position. . .'. Landlubbers are unsteady on a moving ship, and (which is more important) a man needs room for movement if he is to throw a javelin effectively.

3. εἰ τις κτλ: '⟨—I say this⟩ just in case anyone among you—.'

4. τὸ δ' ἀληθέστατον . . . πεπύσθαι: What has preceded is speculation and prediction; now the speaker refers to an existing fact. 'I will tell you the one thing which is quite certain, in the light of what we are confident we have discovered without doubt.' Cf. vi. 17. 6, 'the position in Sicily, ἐξ ὧν ἐγὼ ἀκοῇ αἰσθάνομαι, will be as I have described'.

ἐς ἀπόνοιαν . . . ἵν' ἢ κτλ: 'They are reduced to the desperate expedient—trusting to fortune, not to their arms—of taking a supreme risk in the only way they can, in order . . .'

68. 1. καὶ τύχην . . . πολεμιωτάτων: lit., 'a fortune of most inimical men now that it has handed itself over'. The personification of τύχη here is a phenomenon of language, not of theology; cf. Lys. xii. 80, 'do not be less active in your own cause than τῆς τύχης, ἣ τούτους παρέδωκε τῇ πόλει'.

οἳ ἂν . . . τὸ θυμούμενον: 'If men . . .' or 'that men should . . .'; the whole clause is the subject of νομιμώτατον εἶναι.

ἅμα δέ . . . ἥδιστον εἶναι: 'And secondly, that to punish enemies . . .', and then either (a) 'which will be possible for us, is actually, as the saying goes, the greatest of delights', or (b) 'will be possible for us, and is . . .'. A participial construction after νομίζειν is everywhere rare, and unexampled in Thucydides; this fact favours (a), in which ἐκγενησόμενον ἡμῖν is parenthetic and καί adverbial. Yet τὸ λεγόμενόν που is also parenthetic, and two parentheses in one short clause are stylistically objectionable; this consideration favours (b), in which ἐκγενησόμενον is co-ordinated with ἥδιστον εἶναι by καί (and the whole complex co-ordinated with νομιμώτατον εἶναι) in order to achieve variety.

Greek poetry and tradition agree that revenge is νομιμώτατον, i.e. fully sanctioned by custom and accepted morality, but they seldom say outright that it is also ἥδιστον. Nevertheless, Thucydides appears to be referring to an actual proverb or proverbial verse, of the type κάλλιστον τὸ δικαιότατον κτλ.

2. **ἀνδράσι μὲν ἄν . . . ἐπίκλησιν**: He means that, as happened at Melos, the men would have been killed, the women and children enslaved, and the site of the city would have passed into alien hands; the αἰσχίστη ἐπίκλησις is probably ἀνάστατος. Nothing that Thucydides himself says of the Athenian plans suggests that they actually intended the massacre and enslavement of the population of Syracuse; Diod. xiii. 2. 6 calls this a *secret* decision of the Athenian generals and the Council, which is tantamount to saying that there was no evidence that such a decision was taken by anyone. The Syracusan generals would naturally inflame their men by representing Athenian intentions in the worst light.

3. **πραξάντων**: sc. *both* sides.
παραδοῦναι: sc. the Syracusans.

69. 1–2. *Final Exhortations of Nikias*

69. 1. ᾐσθάνοντο: sc. πληροῦντας.

2. **πάσχουσιν**: sc. 'generals'.
σφίσιν . . . αὐτοῖς: 'The generals . . . to the men.'
πατρόθεν τε . . . καὶ φυλήν: lit., 'naming ⟨them⟩ from their fathers and themselves by name and ⟨each one's⟩ tribe'. To praise or exhort a man by addressing him as 'son of . . .' was normal. Nikias reminded each trierarch of his tribe, not of his deme, because the eponymous hero of each tribe was a paradigm of valour, whereas few demes (the Acharnians are a notable exception) were felt to have martial traditions of their own. Cf. Demosthenes' use, in his *Epitaphios* (lx. 27 ff.), of legends about the eponymous heroes of the tribes.
ἀξιῶν . . . μὴ προδιδόναι τινά: lit., 'demanding that one to whom there already existed something of distinction should not betray his

own part', i.e. 'demanding that no one who had distinguished himself before should fail to do his best'.

ὧν ... οἱ πρόγονοι: ὧν is masculine, and the relative clause is the subject of ἀφανίζειν.

καὶ τῆς ἐν αὐτῇ ... ἐξουσίας: An appeal on the eve of battle to the liberal organization of society represents a great advance on a simple appeal to ἐλευθερία, which in Greek eyes was consistent with the tyranny of law and custom. Athenian society was remarkably liberal by Greek standards; cf. the words attributed to Perikles in a famous passage of the Funeral Speech, ii. 37.

καὶ ὑπὲρ ἁπάντων ... προφερόμενα: The structure of the sentence as a whole is:

$$\begin{cases} πατρίδος \ τε \ ὑπομιμνῄσκων \\ ἄλλα \ τε \ λέγων \mid ὅσα \ ἄνθρωποι \begin{cases} οὐ \mid φυλαξάμενοι \mid εἴποιεν \ ἄν \\ ἀλλὰ \ ἐπιβοῶνται \end{cases} \end{cases}$$

καί before ὑπὲρ ἁπάντων cannot be co-ordinated with ἄλλα τε, making παραπλήσια a second object of λέγων, for the superimposition of the antithesis οὐ ... εἴποιεν ἄν / ἀλλὰ ... ἐπιβοῶνται upon this co-ordination would be impossible, and ὑπὲρ ἁπάντων παραπλήσια 'things in similar form for all occasions' must refer to general practice, not to Nikias on this one occasion. καί = 'including especially', as in 62. 3. Hence: 'and saying all the other things which men would not say if they ... (including ...) but do invoke ...'

ἀρχαιολογεῖν (absurdly translated by LSJ, apparently with reference to this passage, as 'discuss antiquities') means 'say what has always been said'. The kind of thing Thucydides has in mind is exemplified by A. *Pe.* 403 f. 'free your children and wives and the shrines of the gods and the graves of your ancestors!'

69. 3–71. *The Battle*

69. 3. ἢ καὶ ἀναγκαῖα: 'A bare minimum.'

4. πρὸς τὸ ζεῦγμα: The barrier described in 59. 3. Nothing is said there of a gap left in it, but clearly one was needed for the Syracusans' own transference of ships between the Great and the Lesser Harbour.

70. 1. καὶ πρότερον: 52. 1.

2. οἱ ἄλλοι Ἀθηναῖοι: οἱ ἄλλοι does not appear to be contrasted, either retrospectively or prospectively, with any other portion of the Athenian force. If it is correct (B omits it), it can hardly mean 'one of the several detachments', for whereas οἱ ἕτεροι can mean 'one of the two detachments' no comparable use of οἱ ἄλλοι is attested. Ἀθηναῖοι cannot be an intrusive gloss on οἱ ἄλλοι, for Thucydides does not say 'the others' =

'the opposing side' in any of his numerous descriptions of battles. It is possible that if πανταχόθεν . . . ἐπιφερομένων was regarded by Thucydides as a statement not of what the Syracusans did but of what the Athenians experienced—and the use of σφίσι rather than αὐτοῖς gives some support to this interpretation—οἱ ἄλλοι does in fact make a prospective contrast with all the rest of the Athenian ships, upon which the enemy fell; but it must be admitted that this is a recherché explanation.

4. διακόσιαι: About 76 Syracusan ships (§ 1) and 110 Athenian (60. 4). αἱ μὲν ἐμβολαί . . . αἱ δὲ προσβολαί: 'Ramming attacks . . . collisions.'

ὡς τύχοι: 'Whenever . . .' is the natural translation; the choice of ὡς is perhaps determined by the fact that ships collided in different ways.

5. ἐπιβαίνειν: ἐπιβάται were not so named from 'boarding' enemy ships—for boarding tactics were most abnormal in classical times—but because they went on board ship.

6. τὰ μέν . . . ἐμβεβλῆσθαι: 'That on one quarter they had rammed an enemy, while on another they had themselves been rammed.' The choice of the perfect aspect, not the aorist, shows that Thucydides is speaking of the condition in which a ship found itself after such an event.

7. ἀφ' ἑκατέρων τοῖς κελευσταῖς: 'On both sides by the coxwains'. κατά τε τὴν τέχνην . . . ἐγίγνετο: lit., 'in accordance with their skill and to deal with the zeal for victory of the moment'; the exercise of their duty required them to give technical orders, but they also shouted encouragement in response to the emotional demands of the situation.

τοῖς μὲν Ἀθηναίοις: At first glance it might be thought that these words were in apposition to τοῖς κελευσταῖς; but ἐπιβοῶντες—the transition to the nominative is characteristic (cf. Intr. I. 3. 18)—refers to the coxwains, while τοῖς μὲν Ἀθηναίοις and τοῖς δὲ Συρακοσίοις are the sailors to whom they shouted.

βιάζεσθαί τε . . . ἀντιλαβέσθαι: These infinitives represent imperatives of direct speech, unlike the infinitive in καλὸν εἶναι. ἀντιλαβέσθαι is 'absolute' here, as περί shows (ctr. ii. 61. 4 τοῦ κοινοῦ τῆς σωτηρίας ἀντιλαμβάνεσθαι); cf. Pl. Grg. 506 A ἐάν . . . μὴ τὰ ὄντα δοκῶ ὁμολογεῖν ἐμαυτῷ, χρὴ ἀντιλαμβάνεσθαι καὶ ἐλέγχειν.

νῦν . . . ἀντιλαβέσθαι: The correct punctuation is a comma after ποτε and none after αὖθις: 'now again, if ever ⟨before⟩'; cf. εἴπερ ποτε in 64. 2.

71. 1. ὁ αὐτόθεν . . . οἱ ἐπελθόντες: 'The Siceliot . . . the invaders.'

2. **οὐδενὶ ἐοικώς**: 'Indescribable'; cf. our expression 'like nothing on earth'.

3. **ἀνεθάρσησάν τε ἄν**: ἄν with the aorist in a frequentative sense is rarer than with the imperfect.

διὰ τὸ ἀκρίτως ξυνεχὲς τῆς ἁμίλλης: cf. Intr. I. 3. 8.

αἰεὶ γάρ . . . ἀπώλλυντο: 'For all the time they were either just on the point of escaping or just on the point of destruction.'

4. **νικῶντες κρατούμενοι**: This splendid and lucid incoherence does justice to the subject: 'wails, yells—winning, losing—.' Contrast the frigid correctness of X. *Cyr.* vii. 1. 40, 'he saw the plain full of horses, men, chariots', φευγόντων διωκόντων, κρατούντων κρατουμένων.

5. **λαμπρῶς**: Not quite 'decisively', as in 55. 1, but 'manifestly victorious' or 'in manifest triumph', in contrast to the uncertainty which had prevailed before (3 f.).

6. **μετέωροι**: 'On the water.'

οὐκέτι διαφόρως: By contrast with the situation described in §§ 3 f.

72–74. *Aftermath of the Battle*

72. 2. **νεκρῶν μὲν πέρι ἢ ναυαγίων**: For the recovery of wrecks under truce cf. ii. 92. 4: 'they recovered the dead and the wrecks on their own shore, and gave the enemy his (τὰ ἐκείνων) under truce.' In the immediate aftermath of a battle it would be mainly from the wrecks that the dead would be collected; the bodies of drowned men would not yet have risen to the surface.

3. **ἦσαν γάρ . . . ἢ πεντήκοντα**: It follows that the Athenians had lost fifty ships, the Syracusans 30.

4. **καὶ ξυγχωροῦντος Νικίου**: Now, at least, Nikias is not in a dilatory or obstructive mood, but the initiative lies with Demosthenes.

οὐκ ἤθελον ἐσβαίνειν: The tragedy of this refusal lay in the fact that Demosthenes' plan might well have worked, to judge from what we are told in 73. 2.

73. 1. **τοῖς ἐν τέλει οὖσιν**: The meaning of this expression in any given context depends on the state concerned and on the level of authority required for the issue concerned. Thus 'οἱ ἐν τέλει declared war on Sparta', said of Athens, would refer to the Assembly, whereas 'οἱ ἐν τέλει fined the butcher for giving short weight' would refer to a minor magistracy. In the present case the reference is clearly to the Syracusan and allied generals, τοῖς ἄρχουσι in § 3.

λέγων ταῦτα ἃ καὶ αὐτῷ ἐδόκει: The object of λέγων is a summary reference to the content of Hermokrates' thought, set out in δεινὸν εἶναι . . . ποιεῖσθαι above; and the parenthesis is put just where his reasons for saying οὐ χρεών . . . περιιδεῖν would be given if they had not already been given in an earlier part of the sentence. ταῦτα means 'this which I have just described' (cf. the first clause of § 2), and, combined with ἃ . . . ἐδόκει, 'these thoughts of his which I have just described' (in Thucydides ταῦτα ἃ is not simply synonymous with ἃ). The position of καί, which in B, C, H, and Oxyrhynchus Papyrus 1376 immediately follows ἃ—in other MSS. it precedes or comes in both places—is important. To say (e.g.) ἔλεγε ἃ καὶ ἐδόκει αὐτῷ, 'he said what he also thought', is not the most logical way of expressing 'what he thought, he also said' (we should expect, on the lines of viii. 1. 4, ἃ ἐδόκει αὐτῷ, ταῦτα καὶ ἔλεγε), but it is a way often used in Greek. If, therefore, we could here treat καί as modifying ἐδόκει, despite the intervening αὐτῷ (and this is not impossible, though the parallels adduced are open to alternative explanations), the meaning would be '*speaking* these thoughts of his'. But καὶ αὐτός, common in Thucydides, regularly means 'he, too', 'he, in turn', or 'he, for his part'; cf. οἱ δέ . . . καὶ αὐτοί in § 2. The best interpretation is therefore, lit., 'saying these things, what seemed to him himself', i.e. 'speaking these thoughts of *his*'. καί looks forward, as it were, to the fact that the Syracusans are going to agree with him.

2. τοὺς δὲ ἀνθρώπους κτλ.: 'But (sc. they said that) the men . . .', τοὺς ἀνθρώπους (i.e. 'the rank and file', cf. 50. 3) being the subject of δοκεῖν; but in the following sentence the generals are to be understood as the subject of ἐλπίζειν, αὐτούς referring to the men.

ταύτην τὴν ἡμέραν: 'That day' rather than '*on* that day'; the day as a whole is regarded as a festival day of Herakles.

οὐ δοκεῖν ἄν . . . ὑπακοῦσαι: It is interesting to observe that the Syracusan army in victory, even with a Spartan commander, was as recalcitrant as the Athenian army in defeat.

σφῶν: The genitive with ὑπακούειν is common, but with πείθεσθαι very rare; this is the only example in Attic prose.

3. τάδε: Amplified by πέμπει κτλ.

τῶν ἔνδοθεν: The gender is doubtful: 'certain men, among those in the city, who brought Nikias news' or 'certain men who brought Nikias news of events in the city'?

74. 1. νομίσαντες . . . εἶναι: They might have had some doubts, recollecting the trick they had played on the Syracusans two years earlier (vi. 64. 2 ff.); but there were, after all, pro-Athenian elements in

Syracuse (49. 1), and in any case the Athenians may have thought it would be easier to fight through a well-established blocking force in daylight than through a hastily organized one in the dark.

καὶ ἐπειδή . . . ὥρμησαν: Let us call the day of the battle 'Day 1', the following day 'Day 2', and the day of their departure (75. 1) 'Day 3'. The decision here described (ἔδοξεν) was taken either during the night of Day 1 or on the morning of Day 2. (a) If it was taken during the night of Day 1, καὶ ὡς must mean 'in spite of their original intention', περιμεῖναι 'wait *during*', and τὴν ἐπιοῦσαν ἡμέραν Day 2. On this interpretation καὶ ὡς is somewhat vague (but cf. ὅμως in 77. 3) and the aorist aspect of περιμεῖναι surprising. (b) If the decision was taken on Day 2, καὶ ὡς means 'in spite of their intention to depart that morning', οὐκ εὐθὺς ὥρμησαν 'they did not succeed in getting away promptly' (why, Thucydides leaves to our imagination), περιμεῖναι 'wait *for*' (cf. vi. 56. 2 al.), and τὴν ἐπιοῦσαν ἡμέραν Day 3. If we are content not to be told just why they could not get away promptly on the morning of Day 2, we can be satisfied with the second interpretation. If we are not content, and so fall back on the first interpretation, we can remove one of its difficulties by Stahl's καὶ ὡς for καὶ ἐπειδὴ καὶ ὡς.

αὐτά: 'Simply.'

2. ὥσπερ διενοήθησαν: 60. 2.

ὡς ἑκάστην ποι ἐκπεπτωκυῖαν: = ὅποι ἑκάστη ἐκπεπτωκυῖα εἴη.

75–77. The Athenian Retreat

75. *Departure from the Camp*

75. 1. τρίτῃ ἡμέρᾳ: With ordinal numerals the count is inclusive; hence '*two* days later'.

2. δεινὸν οὖν ἦν . . . τῶν πραγμάτων: καθ' ἕν, like καθ' ἕκαστ- (cf. 8. 1), may function as subject or object of a verb; it gave rise in later Greek to a new pronoun, καθείς.

3. ἀτάφων ὄντων: This indicates low morale; and cf. the Ambrakian herald at Olpai (iii. 113. 5), who 'aghast at the magnitude of the disaster . . . did not ask again for the return of the bodies'.

πολύ . . . ἀθλιώτεροι: 'More distressing' (sc. in sight and sound) 'than the dead to the living, and less fortunate than those who had perished'; λυπηρός describes them from the point of view of the living, ἄθλιος from their own point of view, while τεθνεῶτες denotes dead men as objects, ἀπολωλότες as beings whose capacity for action or suffering was ended.

4. οὐκ ἄνευ ὀλίγων . . . ὑπολειπόμενοι: ὀλίγων, 'few' (not, as in English 'a few' = 'some') strikes a false note in this scene. οὐκ ἄνευ in classical

prose is not a synonym for μετά, and were it so here οὐκ ἄνευ ὀλίγων would mean 'without many' (cf. 79. 1 οὐκ ἐπ' ὀλίγων ἀσπίδων = 'many shields deep') ; it implies inevitability or indispensability.• The point is that the sick and wounded did not lightly accept their fate, and hearing their lamentations was the price which the able-bodied had to pay for leaving them behind. Therefore οὐκ ἄνευ ὀλίγων must be emended, preferably (and most simply) to οὐκ ἄνευ πολλῶν ; Valla has *non sine multis*. οὐκ ἄνευ οὐκ ὀλίγων would give the right sense, but would be very bad Greek.

κατήφειά τέ τις: This word is used by no extant author between Homer and Thucydides, though the adjective κατηφής occurs in tragedy and in Hippokrates.

5. **μυριάδες γάρ . . . ἐπορεύοντο**: The figure of 40,000 men 'lost in Sicily' recurs in Isoc. viii. 86 (where, however, the figure given for the triremes lost is higher than can be reconciled with Thucydides). Thucydides may have arrived at 40,000 from the data which he has given in vi. 43, vii. 16. 2, and 42. 1, on the assumption that forty ships in the original expedition and the same number in the reinforcement were troop-transports. Unless he has simply disregarded casualties (which would be surprising), he has included slaves in the 40,000 on the assumption that the number of slaves left was roughly equal to the number of soldiers and sailors killed, missing, or left behind.

παρὰ τὸ εἰωθός: This is our clearest evidence for the extent to which a hoplite force in the field used slaves.

ἀπηυτομολήκεσαν γάρ . . . παραχρῆμα: lit., 'for they had deserted some time before and the majority of them at once', i.e. 'for some had deserted long before, and the greatest number did so now'.

6. **καὶ μὴ ἡ ἄλλη . . . ἐδοξάζετο**: If the text is right, the meaning is, lit., 'and the rest of their suffering and the equal sharing of their evils, although it had nevertheless—"in company", as they say (τό)— a certain lightening, not even so was regarded as easy in their present situation', and ἡ ἄλλη . . . τῶν κακ ῶν is treated as a single concept, 'the impartial distribution of the misery of their degradation in every other way'. But the dative τῇ ἰσομοιρίᾳ would be easier (and B has the dative of the noun, though the nominative ἡ): 'their degradation in every other respect, even though by reason of the impartial distribution of misery it contained—"in company . . .", as they say—in spite of everything, an element of relief, even so did not at the present moment seem to them lightened.'

καὶ ἀπὸ οἴας . . . ἀφῖκτο: sc. 'as they reflected . . .'. ἀφῖκτο, if correct, can only be impersonal ; but Thucydides almost certainly wrote ἀφίκατο (= ἀφιγμένοι ἦσαν), cf. 4. 6.

7. [τῷ]: This is impossible, and its interpolation was perhaps occasioned by οἷς, for which ('. . . to a Greek army; for to this army . . .') cf. 44. 1.

76. Nikias' Exhortations

76. ὡς ἐκ τῶν ὑπαρχόντων: 'As best he could in the circumstances.'

βοῇ τε χρώμενος The two reasons why Nikias raised his voice are (i) his προθυμία and (ii) his desire to be heard. τε therefore belongs with ὑπὸ προθυμίας, not with βοῇ χρώμενος, and should be moved.

ἔτι μᾶλλον: This means 'even more', never 'more and more'. As there is no point of reference for any comparison except 60. 5, which is now impossibly remote, emendation is required; either (i) αἰεί τι μᾶλλον (Weidgen), or (ii) ⟨ἤ⟩ before καθ' οὕς, giving the sense, lit., 'even more than in proportion to those on whose front he was', i.e. 'even more than was required by (sc. the numbers of) those before whom he stood'. For the 'double' sense of κατά cf. vi. 31. 6 στρατιᾶς πρὸς οὓς ἐπῇσαν ὑπερβολῇ, where πρός has to mean both 'in comparison with' and 'against'; and for ἔτι μᾶλλον ἢ κατά cf. 45. 2.

77. Speech of Nikias

77. 1. The absence of (e.g.) ἔλεξε τοιάδε (cf. 60. 5) is noteworthy, but to suppose these words lost by accident and tack them on would yield a stylistically graceless sentence.

μηδὲ καταμέμφεσθαι . . . αὐτούς: μηδέ co-ordinating the positive ἔχειν with the negatived καταμέμφεσθαι is highly abnormal in Attic prose; καὶ μή would be normal. μέμφεσθαι and its compounds do not always mean 'blame' in the sense of attributing moral responsibility; the sense here is not 'blame yourselves *for* your reverses' but 'judge yourselves inadequate *because of* your reverses'.

παρὰ τὴν ἀξίαν: lit., 'contrary to your worth'; the point is that a strong, well-equipped, well-trained force ought not to have failed.

2. κἀγώ τοι . . . αἰωροῦμαι: The sequence of thought here is unusually obscure. The point of § 1 and § 3 is: 'we are good enough to win', and § 2 must be so interpreted that it is relevant to that point. In saying that he is, lit., 'neither superior in strength nor inferior in luck' to others, Nikias means that whereas in respect of strength fault can be found with him and victory is not his ἀξία, in respect of good luck— which he treats as a lasting attribute—he *does* 'deserve' to win.

καίτοι πολλὰ μέν . . . καὶ ἀνεπίφθονα: cf. 86. 5 n.

3. ὅμως: 'In spite of our present condition.'

οὐ κατ' ἀξίαν δή: The point of δή is that disaster has led the Athenians to question their own ἀξία, as § 1 indicates, and Nikias is saying that for him the question of ἀξία does not arise. Hence: 'so far as "desert" is concerned, our reverses do not alarm me', implying 'we are still good enough to win through'.

ἱκανὰ γάρ . . . τετιμωρήμεθα: Nikias joins together two ideas: one is that they have surely been adequately punished for any respect in which they may have incurred divine anger (recollection of heroic legend must have made him wonder in his heart whether one can judge what a god will think adequate); the other is that complete success in itself provokes divine resentment, so that the anger of the gods may now be re-directed against the Syracusans.

4. καὶ ἀνθρώπεια δράσαντες: The traditional antithesis δρᾶσαι/παθεῖν suggests crime and punishment, and the argument requires ἀνθρώπεια to mean 'acts such as men, prone to error, commit'. Cf. X. Cyr. vi. 1. 37 συγγνώμων τῶν ἀνθρωπίνων ἁματημάτων. Nikias implies: 'we have certainly done nothing worse than men in general do' (the Athenian speakers in the Melian Dialogue [v. 105. 1] defend their demands on Melos as ἀνθρώπειος), 'and therefore our fate, like that of other armies which have been punished in the past, is likely to be bearable.'

τά τε ἀπὸ τοῦ θεοῦ: When a Greek speaks of ὁ θεός in a context where there is no reference to the recognizable functions of some particular god, he may mean Zeus, or he may mean 'whatever god is concerned with this'.

οἴκτου γάρ: In E. El. 1329 f. one of the Dioskuroi, justifying his exclamation of distress at the plight of Orestes, asserts that the gods are capable of pitying mortal suffering; but in general the Greek gods do not feel pity, although mortals sometimes appeal to them for it.

δέξαιτο: 'Stand in your way' or 'stand up to you'; in this military sense, δέχεσθαι is the opposite of φεύγειν.

6. σπουδὴ δέ . . . τῆς ὁδοῦ: These words are a promise by the generals, not an order (which would not be grammatically impossible) to the troops.

οὗτοι γὰρ ἡμῶν . . . βέβαιοί εἰσιν: The Athenians were to have no opportunity of discovering how long the friendship of the Sikels would survive defeat.

7. ἀνδράσιν ἀγαθοῖς γίγνεσθαι: 'To be good men' = 'to be good soldiers', i.e. to fight well and endure; this is a normal Greek expression.

ὧν ἐπιθυμεῖτέ που ἐπιδεῖν: i.e. your homes.

ἄνδρες γὰρ πόλις: This famous sentiment was not invented by Thucydides; it is at least as old as Alkaios.

78–85. March and Destruction of the Athenians

78. 1–4. *Day 1; across the Anapos; 40 stades*

78. 1. **καὶ ὁ Δημοσθένης**: sc. ἐπῄει.

2. **ἐν πλαισίῳ**: The formation called πλαίσιον was a hollow rectangle; it was commonly used on the move, and had a 'mouth' and a 'tail' (X. *An.* iii. 4. 42 f. &c.), which suggests resemblance to a snake rather than to a square. In the present case it is not clear whether there was only one πλαίσιον, Nikias commanding the 'mouth' and Demosthenes the 'tail', or two separate πλαίσια, Nikias commanding one and Demosthenes the other. If there was only one, we may wonder who commanded the hoplites on each flank; X. *An.* iii. 2. 36 f. thinks of a πλαίσιον as needing *four* commanders. If there were two, we may wonder *why* there should be two; and later, when Demosthenes' force becomes separated from Nikias', the word ἀπεσπάσθη (80. 4) and the remark 'the Syracusan cavalry encircled them more easily δίχα δὴ ὄντας' (81. 2) suggest that the two forces had hitherto constituted a single formation. Possibly, however, the very large numbers involved made it desirable to organize two separate πλαίσια, even if the intention was that the two forces should keep as close together as possible.

ἐν πλαισίῳ is the reading of B; the other MSS. have ἐν διπλασίῳ, which is not Greek, but prompted Heitland's ingenious conjecture ἐν διπλαισίῳ (cf. διστάδιον &c.).

ἡγούμενον κτλ.: We would expect genitive absolutes; but an appositional construction is used since τὸ Νικίου and τὸ Δημοσθένους are the components of τὸ δέ, which refers to τὸ στράτευμα.

3. **καὶ ἐπειδή [τε] κτλ.**: τε is unlikely, since two statements of events which stand in a strict temporal succession ('when they arrived . . . they found . . .' + 'having defeated them . . . they moved . . ') are not normally co-ordinated by τε/καί.

ἐπὶ τῇ διαβάσει . . . ποταμοῦ: Due west of their camp, where the river runs NW.–SE.

οἱ ψιλοί: In 'partitive apposition' to 'the Syracusans'; '. . . and—the light-armed troops—shooting into them'.

78. 4–5. *Day 2; across a plain to the Akraion Lepas; 20 stades*

78. 4. **ἐς χωρίον ἄπεδόν τι**: In the region of the modern Floridia, 10 km. west of Syracuse.

5. **Ἀκραῖον λέπας**: The valley which the Syracusans blocked has traditionally been identified with the Cava di Culatrello, of which the

entrance lies 2·3 km. west of Floridia; it is a deep-sided gorge which suits the description given here, but not a place in which the Syracusan cavalry could easily have attacked the Athenians from the flanks (§ 6). A route further south, through the area now called Contrada Raiana, suits Thucydides' description of the Syracusan tactics better but his description of the ground less well. Both routes would have led the Athenians to Akrai. Certain identification is precluded by Thucydides' characteristic imprecision in his account of the fighting; the cavalry may have attacked the Athenians only as they approached and entered the valley, not after they were in it.

78. 6. *Day 3; no progress*

78. 6. ἐς τὸ αὐτὸ στρατόπεδον: In the plain (§ 4).

79. 1–5. *Day 4; no progress*

79. 1. οὐκ ἐπ' ὀλίγων ἀσπίδων: 'Many shields deep'; the order negative-preposition-adjective is normal.

2. διικνοῦντο: 'Reached their targets.'

3. ἐπὶ τῷ σφετέρῳ ὀλέθρῳ: As indicating divine displeasure.

5. πρὸς τὸ πεδίον μᾶλλον: Near enough the entrance to the valley to avoid the danger of being walled off from the rear during the night.

79. 5–6. *Day 5; attempt to bypass the valley; 5–6 stades*

79. 5. προυχώρουν: Plainly not up the valley again, for after an advance of 5–6 stades they paused in the plain (§ 6). Moreover, the fighting on this day is described in quite different terms from the fighting in the valley; among other things, the Syracusans attack them πανταχῇ . . . κύκλῳ. The Athenians must therefore have been moving south in an attempt to bypass the valley that led to the Akraion Lepas.

κατὰ βραχύ: lit., 'a small bit at a time', almost 'on a narrow front' or 'at a single point'.

80. 1–4. *Night of Day 5; south-eastwards to the coast; Nikias and Demosthenes separated*

80. 1. πυρὰ καύσαντας ὡς πλεῖστα: To make the enemy think that they were still in their camp.

2. ἦν δέ . . . αὕτη: Before the last battle in the harbour the Athenians intention was to go to Katane if their ships could break out, but otherwise to take whatever route would most quickly lead to friendly territory, 'Greek or foreign' (60. 2). Nikias in 77. 4 ff. says nothing of

Katane, but reveals that notice of the retreat had been sent to Sikel tribes; and 80. 5 shows that the intended rendezvous with the Sikels was on the upper Kakyparis, i.e. in the area of Akrai. It is therefore unlikely that Thucydides means here 'their destination was *no longer* Katane, but the south-west coast', and if he did mean that it is surprising that he did not say it plainly; οὐκέτι would have removed any doubts. His point is: 'their destination was not Katane, *as one might expect from their turning back towards the coast*, but . . .'. ἡ ξύμπασα ὁδός is the overall journey, as distinct from any particular stage of it.

τὸ πρὸς Καμάριναν καὶ Γέλαν: They cannot have expected a friendly reception from the Greek cities, which had fought (except Akragas) on the side of Syracuse, but they hoped to reach in safety an area into which the Syracusans would not be interested in maintaining pursuit.

3. οἷον φιλεῖ ... ἐγγίγνεσθαι: = οἷον φιλεῖ ἐγγίγνεσθαι (φόβοι γὰρ καὶ δείματα φιλοῦσιν ἐγγίγνεσθαι).

4. ὥσπερ ἡγεῖτο: = οὕτω γὰρ ἡγεῖτο.

80. 5–82. 3. *Day 6; Nikias reaches the Erineos; Demosthenes surrenders*

80. 5. ὅμως: Given the previous sentence, the point of 'nevertheless' must be that Demosthenes too reached the coast, although the gap between the two forces soon widened to 50 stades (81. 3).

Ἐλωρινήν: Heloron lay near the coast *c.* 25 km. south of Syracuse.
Κακυπάρει: The Cassibili, which rises near Akrai.

6. **φυλακήν τινα:** A product of the activity described in 74. 2.
Ἐρινεόν: A watercourse called Cava Mammaledi—dry since a great earthquake in the seventeenth century—just south of Avola, 9 km. south of the Cassibili. In older maps this watercourse is called 'Miranda', a name which now belongs only to a spring at Avola.
ἡγεμόνες: 'Guides', not 'commanders'.

81. 1. ἑκόντα ἀφεῖναι: It would be interesting to know their interpretation of Gylippos' motives. Possibly they thought that as a Spartan he was content with decisive victory—his training and military instincts would have dissuaded him from fighting an unnecessary battle—while they were in the mood for spectacular revenge provided it did not cost them too much (cf. 81. 5, 84. 4 f.). More probably the 'pan-Siceliot' sentiment encouraged by Hermokrates manifested itself, in a moment of disappointment, in a suspicion that there might exist a similar bond of sentiment between their Spartan general and their enemy. Nikias, too, was regarded as having close relations with Sparta (cf. 85. 1, 86. 3). Gylippos' unwillingness, later, to allow the captured Athenian generals to be executed (86. 2) must have strengthened their suspicions.

3. **ἑκόντας εἶναι**: = ἑκόντας γε, 'if they could *help* it, anyway'; cf. τὸ νῦν εἶναι = 'at present, at least'.

4. **οὐ προυχώρει . . . ξυνετάσσετο**: lit., 'he did not advance rather than drew up his ranks for battle', i.e. '. . . *but rather* drew up . . .'.

5. **φειδώ τέ τις . . . προαναλωθῆναί τῳ**: lit., 'a certain sparingness came into being for a man (τῳ), not to be expended beforehand in furtherance of a success already clear', i.e. 'everyone felt a certain reluctance to lose his life unnecessarily when success was already assured'; προ- implies 'before it was necessary' and carries the further implication that it would *not* be necessary.

καὶ ὥς: lit., 'even so', i.e. 'in any case'.

82. 1. κήρυγμα . . . πρῶτον μὲν κτλ.: lit., 'a proclamation . . . first of all, of the Islanders if anyone wishes . . .', i.e. 'a proclamation . . . first, to invite any Islanders who wished . . .'. On the term 'Islanders' cf. 5. 4 n.

πόλεις οὐ πολλαί: The poor response furnishes an interesting comment on Nikias' speech, 63. 3 f.

2. **μὴ ἀποθανεῖν μηδένα . . . διαίτης**: The Syracusans did not keep their word; cf. 86. 2, 87. 1 f.

3. **ἑξακισχίλιοι**: Since the total number which began the retreat six days before was 40,000 (75. 5), there were few slaves among them (ibid.), Demosthenes had rather more than half the total force with him (80. 4), and 'not many' contingents of islanders took advantage of the Syracusan offer, Demosthenes' force must have suffered casualties on a prodigious scale.

83. *Day 7; Nikias south of the Erineos*

83. 2. ἀπήγγειλε πάλιν: 'Brought word back.'
ἐπικηρυκεύεται: sc. Nikias.

3. **καὶ τούτους**: καί glances back at 82. 1.

4. **ἐπαιάνισαν**: cf. 44. 6 n.

84–85. *Day 8; the massacre at the Assinaros; surrender of Nikias*

84. 2. Ἀσσίναρον: The Fiumara di Noto (called 'Falconara' in some older maps), which flows past Noto and into the sea 11 km. south of the Cassibili.

ῥᾷόν τι σφίσιν ἔσεσθαι: Exhausted men in retreat often feed on the illusory hope that if they can, as it were, get into the next square on the board the rules of the game will allow them a rest from enemy attack.

85. 1. **ἑαυτῷ μὲν χρήσασθαι . . . ὅτι βούλονται**: 'To do what they liked with himself', i.e. to kill him, if they wished.

2. **ἀπεκρύψαντο**: sc. the Syracusan soldiers; the point of 'hiding away' an Athenian captive was to make money for oneself, and not for the public treasury, by selling him.

4. **ἐν τῷ [Σικελικῷ] πολέμῳ τούτῳ**: *ΣΜ*, drawing attention to 87. 5, conjectures *Ἑλληνικῷ*; the conjecture is wrong, since *Ἑλληνικῷ* would be a pointless addition to τῷ πολέμῳ τούτῳ, but the suspicion is right. Thucydides means by 'this war', here as elsewhere, the Peloponnesian War as a whole; demonstratives often attract glosses, and *Σικελικῷ* was in origin a foolish gloss on τούτῳ.

τούτοις δ' ἦν ἀναχώρησις ἐς Κατάνην: Among them was the speaker of [Lys.] xx, who claims to have taken part in raids carried out by Katane against Syracusan territory.

86–87. The Fate of the Prisoners

86. 2. **ἐς τὰς λιθοτομίας**: The great quarries east of the theatre.

Νικίαν δέ . . . ἀπέσφαξαν: This event provided material for historical controversy and rhetorical invention in later times. Philistos followed Thucydides, but Timaios, magnifying the virtues of the Syracusans, represented Hermokrates as trying to give the Athenian generals the opportunity to escape by suicide the disgrace of execution. The story in Plu. *Nic.* 28. 3 that Hermokrates advocated mercy probably comes from Timaios. The execution of Demosthenes, a grim compliment to his quality (cf. the Athenians' execution of Aristeus [ii. 67. 4]), was a flagrant violation of the promise given to him (82. 2).

3. **ἐν τῇ νήσῳ**: Sphakteria.

σπονδάς . . . ποιήσασθαι: Nikias was the protagonist of peace in 421.

ἀφεθῆναι: τούς . . . τῶν Λακεδαιμονίων is the subject.

4. **ἐκεκοινολόγηντο**: cf. 48. 3, 73. 3.

ὅτι πλούσιος ἦν: There is evidence from fourth-century sources independent of Thucydides for Nikias' great wealth.

νεώτερόν τι: 'Trouble'; cf. 87. 1 n.

5. **διὰ τὴν πᾶσαν . . . ἐπιτήδευσιν**: 'Because of his way of life, which he conducted wholly in accordance with high standards.' πᾶσαν agrees with ἐπιτήδευσιν, not with ἀρετήν, for the Greeks do not speak of 'every virtue' or of 'the virtues'. νενομισμένην also agrees with ἐπιτήδευσιν;

cf. E. fr. 87. 3 τοὺς νομίζοντας τέχνην, 'those who practise a craft', and A. *Ch.* 1003 ἀργυροστερῆ βίον νομίζων, 'living a robber's life'. Although it would be grammatically possible for νενομισμένην to agree with ἀρετήν (cf. v. 105. 1 for the coupling of abstract nouns in -σις with phrases with ἐς), if Thucydides had meant to draw a distinction between 'traditional' or 'conventional' virtue and some more original concept of virtue, he could have done so easily and unambiguously by writing ἀρετὴν τὴν νενομισμένην.

There is no reason to think that Thucydides would have wanted to deny the name of ἀρετή to a sustained effort to be just and honest and conscientious in fulfilling one's obligations; cf. v. 105. 4, 'at home the Spartans ἀρετῇ χρῶνται more than anyone, but in their dealings with others . . . they treat what is agreeable to themselves as honourable and what is in their interest as just'. We may think, after reading his history of the Sicilian Expedition, that he is lenient towards Nikias, or that his (and Nikias') standards of ἀρετή were defective; but that is a different question. The expression of the view that Nikias did not *deserve* to be executed does not in itself imply that Thucydides believed in a system of divine rewards and punishments for virtue and vice, but is a natural reaction with which anyone of moderate sensitivity may concur.

87. 1. ἐπιγιγνόμεναι: i.e. succeeding, on each occasion, a hot day.

τοὐναντίον . . . ἐνεωτέριζον: νεώτερος and νεωτερίζειν have unpleasant associations, especially in politics, implying violence and execution.

τῇ μεταβολῇ: The effects of sudden changes in temperature, humidity, diet, or habits were taken very seriously by ancient medical theory.

2. πάντα τε ποιούντων: The point is: including excretion.

ἐπὶ ὀκτὼ μῆνας: Since many were sold after seventy days (§ 3), this figure refers to the Athenians and others who remained. Presumably at the end of eight months these too were sold.

κοτύλην . . . σίτου: A liquid κοτύλη was 0·27 litres, a dry κοτύλη 270-275 cc. Under the terms of the truce at Pylos (iv. 16. 1) the Spartans had been allowed to supply even the slaves on Sphakteria with 4 κοτύλαι of flour per man per day.

4. οὐκ ἐλάσσους ἑπτακισχιλίων: Since 6,000 were captured with Demosthenes (82. 3) it follows that only 1,000 of Nikias' contingent (originally about 20,000 [75. 5 ~ 80. 4]) came into the custody of the Syracusan state.

5. [Ἑλληνικόν]: Since all ἔργα of any significance in 'this war' were Greek, Ἑλληνικόν is a pointless addition and is rightly deleted; cf. 85. 4 n.

6. **τὸ λεγόμενον**: This apologizes for the unusual word πανωλεθρίᾳ, which Herodotos (ii. 120. 5) uses of the destruction of Troy.

No one who has completed Book VII should omit to read viii. 1, which is the real end of the story, describing the resolution with which the Athenians faced the news of the disaster and the prospect of the years to come.

INDEXES

(All references are to pages of the Introduction and Commentary)

I. TEXT

II. GREEK WORDS

III. LANGUAGE AND STYLE

IV. PEOPLE AND PLACES

V. GENERAL